Dynamic Programming for Economists

From Basic Growth Models to Computational Methods

Dynamic programming is a powerful technique for modeling problems requiring sequential decisions in macroeconomics and finance. The drawback is that its analytic foundations are mathematically demanding, making existing textbooks often too technical for beginners. Moreover, dynamic models most often cannot be solved analytically and, therefore, require the use of numerical methods, whose implementation details can be discouraging.

This book is a primer on dynamic programming and related numerical techniques. To assist the reader, the discussion focuses on a specific example: a simple optimal growth model. Once the reader has mastered the most important concepts, these can be easily applied to business cycle models, New Keynesian frameworks, dynamic CAPM, and many other issues.

The deterministic growth model is used to introduce dynamic programming in an intuitive way. Technicalities are reduced to a minimum, though not avoided, to provide a solid foundation for the applications (and to stimulate the interested reader toward further readings). After a discussion of cases where a closed-form solution exists, the most commonly used numerical techniques are introduced. The book considers the value function iteration method, detailing the steps needed to build the pertinent numerical routines using Matlab. The policy function iteration method and the endogenous grid approach are also discussed since—while similar in spirit to value function iteration—they offer ways to save computing time for some applications. Then, collocation methods are used to obtain a 'global' solution. Again, the reader is guided step-by-step in building the numerical routines. Finally, the book introduces the perturbation method, emphasizing its nature as an approximation of the 'true' solution.

Moving in small steps, and with the aim of keeping the presentation as readable as possible, the book then focuses on stochastic versions of the growth model. The numerical techniques introduced for the deterministic version are used to deal with (persistent) productivity shocks. In addition, the book presents a method—the parameterized expectation approach—that only mildly suffers from the "curse of dimensionality".

Gianluca Femminis is a Full Professor of Economics in the Department of Economics and Finance at the Catholic University of Milan, Italy. He obtained his Ph.D. at the University of Warwick. His current research focuses on general equilibrium models with dispersed information. He has published in journals such as the *Review of Economic Studies, Journal of Economic Theory, Journal of Economic Dynamics and Control, European Journal of Political Economy,* and *Journal of Economic Behavior and Organization.* He has served as an Associate Editor of the *Journal of Economic Dynamics and Control* since 2012. He previously directed the Ph.D. Program in Economics and Finance at the Catholic University of Milan.

Gianluca Femminis

Dynamic Programming for Economists

From Basic Growth Models to Computational Methods

ROUTLEDGE
Routledge
Taylor & Francis Group
LONDON AND NEW YORK

IUSTITIAM COLIMUS
G. Giappichelli Editore

First published 2027
by Routledge
4 Park Square, Milton Park, Abingdon, Oxon OX14 4RN

and by Routledge
605 Third Avenue, New York, NY 10158

Routledge is an imprint of the Taylor & Francis Group, an informa business

and by G. Giappichelli Editore
Via Po 21, Torino – Italia

British Library Cataloguing-in-Publication Data
A catalogue record for this book is available from the British Library

Library of Congress Cataloging-in-Publication Data
A catalogue record for this book has been requested

ISBN: 978-1-041-30342-8 (hbk-Routledge)
ISBN: 978-1-041-30339-8 (pbk-Routledge)
ISBN: 978-1-003-77405-1 (ebk-Routledge)
ISBN: 979-12-211-1876-6 (hbk-Giappichelli)

DOI: 10.4324/9781003774051

Typeset in Minion Pro
by G. Giappichelli Editore, Turin, Italy

The title has been subjected to a peer review process prior to publication.

To Paola

She is fantastic: she married me before I started my Ph.D., and not only did she put up with me, but we are still in love.

Contents

List of figures

Preface

As a "boomer," I unfortunately just missed the opportunity to attend computational methods courses during my Ph.D. at the University of Warwick. Consequently, in the second half of the nineties, as a young researcher, I felt increasingly sidelined by the rapid development of new numerical techniques. While existing books on dynamic programming and numerical methods were thorough and excellent, they were not particularly user-friendly (at least for me). In particular, I found it difficult to translate theoretical concepts into practical implementation.

This led me to "teach myself" some applied dynamic programming. In the meantime, I came across *The ABCs of RBCs*, a remarkable book by George McCandless, who had compiled his notes because they seemed to him "a chronicle of learning what is required to be able to use RBC (Real Business Cycle) and New Keynesian models." I then figured that a book in a similar vein, focused on dynamic programming for economists, would be a valuable resource. Teaching Master's and Ph.D. students has reinforced this belief over the years.

In the age of Artificial Intelligence, this stance might seem unduly stubborn. At the time of writing, even a general-purpose AI can quickly solve most of the problems analyzed in this book (I have tried). In my view, however, not only researchers but also practitioners need a deep understanding of these issues to maximize the benefits of interacting with an AI and, occasionally, to avoid significant misunderstandings.

This introductory primer on dynamic programming presents formal concepts through applications to a simple deterministic growth model. Technicalities are kept to a minimum, but not avoided, to provide a solid understanding of the applications (and to direct interested readers to more advanced resources). Moving in small steps, with the aim of keeping the presentation as readable as possible, the book then focuses on the stochastic versions of the growth model. The key concepts can be easily adapted to Real Business Cycle models, New Keynesian models, dynamic Capital Asset Pricing Models, and many other applications in Macroeconomics and Finance.

Organization of the book

1. Utility maximization in a dynamic deterministic setting
This chapter introduces dynamic optimization by analyzing one of the simples and most intuitive problems: the optimal consumption behavior of an agent. This intertemporal problem is solved using the Lagrangian approach to separate the economic logic from the technicalities of dynamic programming. First, the optimal determination of consumption is considered in the simplest possible framework, where a single agent knows the duration of her finite lifetime. Once the finite-lifetime consumption-saving problem is well understood, the agent's horizon is extended to infinity.

2. The Dynamic Programming formulation
The dynamic programming approach is introduced to address the consumption-saving infinite-horizon model. I provide an intuitive introduction to Bellman equations, building on the previous understanding of the solution. It is emphasized that we are now dealing with a functional problem—i.e., a problem whose solution is a function. A more formal section, which can be skipped on a first reading, discusses the existence and uniqueness of the solution and then shows how the envelope theorem can be used to characterize it.

3. Guess and verify
When the solution to a dynamic programming problem exists, it may be conjectured, similar to how solutions for difference and differential equations are found. This chapter presents examples (and exercises) where this

approach is feasible; understanding them will help students familiarize themselves with the workings of the value function.

4. A "paper and pencil" introduction to function iteration
This chapter illustrates several alternative techniques used to approximate the solution of a Bellman problem through function iteration, when a closed-form solution does not exist. First, it introduces the value function iteration method, thoroughly discussing the steps needed to build the related numerical routines. Then, the policy function iteration method and the endogenous grid approach are discussed; while similar in spirit to value function iteration, they offer ways to save computing time for many applications.

The routines are detailed in the appendix to this chapter, where we also present a few proposals for extensions. Since the routines for these latter exercises are not included, AI can be fruitfully employed at this stage.

5. Collocation and perturbation with paper and pencil
This chapter first discusses how to obtain a solution using the "collocation" method, which typically reduces the computation time. The collocation method is introduced as a way to interpolate a function. We then show how it can be used to approximate the solution of a simple differential equation. The final step is the solution of a Bellman problem using the very convenient Chebyshev polynomials, which allow for efficient solutions to a large class of dynamic problems. Next, the chapter discusses the "perturbation" method, which essentially amounts to obtaining a solution around the steady state. The approach is introduced to approximate the solution of a simple quadratic equation and is then gradually extended, yielding a second-order approximation for the solution of the consumption-growth problem.

The routines are detailed in the appendix, where we also present a few proposals for extensions.

6. A Lagrangian approach to stochastic growth
The infinite-horizon consumption-growth model is extended to consider the possibility of random disturbances affecting technology. Once again, the idea is to help readers understand the problem and its solution before introducing the recursive formulation.

7. Stochastic growth: Bellman formulation and closed-form solutions.
This chapter briefly illustrates how to apply the dynamic programming approach to a simple stochastic growth model, including some closed-form examples.

8. Solving the stochastic growth model: a brief tour of the techniques.
The final chapter extends the value function iteration method to the case of stochastic productivity, dealing first with a time-independent process and then discussing the case of autoregressive shocks. The collocation and perturbation methods are then extended to handle autoregressive productivity shocks. Finally, the parameterized expectation approach is presented in some detail.

An appendix to this chapter details the routines and presents a few proposals for extensions.

The book is complemented by a number of exercises, with their solutions provided in the Appendix. The routines used in the book can be downloaded at `www.routledge.com/9781041303398`.

How to Use the Book

The book requires some familiarity with linear difference equations, with standard tools in constrained optimization (such as the Lagrangian method), and with random variables. A very basic knowledge of programming in MATLAB (or one of the available alternatives) is also needed. The more technical material is organized into sections marked with a superscript star. This starred material can be skipped during the first reading, and hopefully revisited later.

Third-Year Bachelor Level The first chapter can be used as a technical introduction to growth theory; the course can then move to dynamic programming, skipping the more technical parts of Chapter 2. After discussing one of the examples in Chapter 3 and some exercises, students with some knowledge of MATLAB coding can be exposed to value function iteration in Chapter 4. (One-semester course, titles: "Introduction to Growth Theory;" "Introduction to Dynamic Programming").

Master Level Possibly skipping Chapter 1 but adding Chapters 4 and 5, one obtains a one-semester course aimed at students with basic coding knowledge. (Course labels: "Macroeconomics I: Dynamic Programming;" "Applied Dynamic Programming;" "Dynamic Macroeconomics I").

Ph.D. Level Leaving aside Chapters 1 and 6, one obtains a one-semester course. (Course labels: "Dynamic Macroeconomics I," "Macroeconomics for Research"); alternatively, the book can be used as a prerequisite for more advanced courses, or within a broader course in computational economics.

Acknowledgments
First, I would like to acknowledge my intellectual debt to those who taught me dynamic macroeconomics, specifically (and in chronological order): Andrea Beltratti, Marcus Miller, Neil Rankin, Philippe Weil, Paolo Pesenti, Argia Sbordone and Mike Woodford.

Then, special thanks go to my colleagues (and friends) at the Department of Economics and Finance of the Catholic University. The working atmosphere at the Department has been nice and lively over the years, greatly benefiting me both professionally and personally.

Last but not least, I wish to thank those who read the book, or part of it, and provided advice and suggestions: Anna Florio, Ben Heijdra, Riccardo M. Masolo, Emiliano Santoro and especially Marco Cozzi, Michele Piffer and Daniele Siena.

Part of the book was written during a summer stay at the Department of Economics, Oxford University, whose hospitality is gratefully acknowledged.

1
Utility maximization in a dynamic deterministic setting

ABSTRACT This chapter first considers the optimal determination of consumption in the simplest possible dynamic framework: one in which a single agent with a known, finite lifespan derives a consumption flow from a production function using capital as the sole input (Section 1.1). Once this problem is well understood, it will be easy to consider its infinite-horizon counterpart (Section 1.2).

1.1 The finite lifetime consumption-growth problem

The analysis of agents' consumption behavior is one of the ingredients that can be found in almost every growth model. Indeed, consumption, through savings, determines capital accumulation, which, in turn, is one of the "engines of growth." To isolate the economic logic from some technical difficulties involved in the use of dynamic programming, this section solves the intertemporal problem for a single agent with a finite lifetime using the Lagrangian approach.

In our setting, time is "discrete," i.e. it is divided into periods of fixed length (a year or a quarter), and our agent is allowed to decide her consumption level only once per period. The consumption goods she enjoys are produced–using capital–by means of a "neoclassical" production function.[1] We are looking for the agent's optimal behavior. The solution prescribes the

DOI: 10.4324/9781003774051-1

amount of consumption to be enjoyed in each period to maximize her overall utility. Consumption choices must account for the fact that resources are limited; in fact, consumption will be expressed as a function of the resources available in each period, i.e. of the capital saved up to that moment.

Intuitively, when the lifetime of an agent is finite, the optimal relationship between consumption and capital will be affected by her age–more precisely, by the amount of time our agent has left to live.

1.1.1 *The ingredients of our setup*

Our consumer optimizes from time 0 onwards; her preferences are summarized by the following intertemporal utility function:

$$W_0 = \sum_{t=0}^{T} \beta^t U(c_t), \tag{1.1}$$

where $\beta \in (0,1)$ is the subjective discount factor (a parameter), c_t is consumption at time t, and the length of our consumer's lifetime (in periods) is $T+1$. As for the single-period utility function, $U(c_t)$, we accept the standard "neoclassical" assumptions, requiring that, in every period:

(i) $U'(c_t) > 0$, and

(ii) $U''(c_t) < 0$.

(In plain English, the marginal utility is positive but decreasing.) Moreover, we assume that:

(iii) $\lim_{c_t \to 0} U'(c_t) = \infty$.

In our one-good economy, it is commonly assumed that output, y_t, can either be consumed or invested, meaning that $y_t = c_t + i_t$, where i_t is investment, gross of depreciation. (Note that we are abstracting from the presence of government expenditure.) Output is obtained through a production function whose sole argument is capital (k_t):[2]

$$y_t = f(k_t). \tag{1.2}$$

Like any well-behaved neoclassical production function, (1.2) satisfies some conditions. When capital depreciates at a constant rate $\delta \in [0,1]$, these are:

(a) $f'(k_t) > 0$,

(b) $f''(k_t) < 0$,

(the marginal productivity of capital is positive, but decreasing),

(c) $f(0) = 0$,

(this means that capital is essential for production),

(d) $f'(0) > \delta + 1/\beta - 1$,

(e) $\lim_{k_t \to \infty} f'(k_t) = 0$.

As will become clear later, hypothesis (d) implies that capital–at least at its lowest level–is productive enough to provide an incentive for saving, while assumption (e) rules out the possibility that capital accumulation goes on forever.[3]

The agent's initial capital stock, k_0, is given. The capital stock for period 1, k_1, is determined by the investment decision (i_0) via the law of motion: $k_1 = i_0 + (1-\delta)k_0$. Substituting investment using the output identity, $y_0 = c_0 + i_0$, and the production function (Eq. 1.2), we can express the capital stock in period 1 as:

$$k_1 = f(k_0) + (1-\delta)k_0 - c_0.$$

Hence, in general, we have that:

$$k_{t+1} = f(k_t) + (1-\delta)k_t - c_t, \tag{1.3}$$

for $t = 0, 1, ..., T$. In addition to the dynamic constraints stated above, we require:

$$k_{T+1} \geq 0. \tag{1.4}$$

Eq. (1.4) imposes that our consumer finishes her life with a non-negative stock of wealth. This condition must obviously be fulfilled by an agent who lives "in isolation" (a negative level of capital stock makes no sense in this case). If our agent were to live in an economy where financial markets are operational, so that borrowing and lending are allowed, a condition like (1.4) would rule out the possibility of dying in debt (a strong assumption when lifetime is uncertain, but a rather natural one when the agent's horizon is known).

To summarize, we wish to solve the problem:

$$\max_{\{c_t\}_{t=0}^{T}} W_0 = \max_{\{c_t\}_{t=0}^{T}} \sum_{t=0}^{T} \beta^t U(c_t),$$

under the $T+1$ constraints of the (1.3)-type (law of motion for capital), under the constraint (1.4) (non-negativity of final-period capital), and given k_0. Note that the solution of the problem requires the determination of $T+1$ consumption levels $(c_0, c_1, ..., c_T)$, and of $T+1$ values for the capital stock $(k_1, k_2, ..., k_{T+1})$.

We can approach the consumer's intertemporal problem by forming a Lagrangian:

$$\begin{aligned}
\mathcal{L}_0 &= U(c_0) + \beta U(c_1) + \beta^2 U(c_2) + ... + \beta^T U(c_T) + \\
&\quad -\lambda_0[k_1 - f(k_0) - (1-\delta)k_0 + c_0] + \\
&\quad -\beta\lambda_1[k_2 - f(k_1) - (1-\delta)k_1 + c_1] + \\
&\quad -... + \\
&\quad -\beta^{T-1}\lambda_{T-1}[k_T - f(k_{T-1}) - (1-\delta)k_{T-1} + c_{T-1}] + \\
&\quad -\beta^T \lambda_T[k_{T+1} - f(k_T) - (1-\delta)k_T + c_T] + \\
&\quad +\beta^T \mu k_{T+1},
\end{aligned} \tag{1.5}$$

in which λ_t, for $t = 0, 1, ..., T$, and μ are the Lagrange multipliers.[4] Note that λ_t, which pertains to the period t constraint, is multiplied by β^t.

1.1.2 Toward the solution: the first-order conditions

To solve the problem, we differentiate (1.5) with respect to c_t, k_{t+1}, λ_t (for $t = 0, 1, ..., T$), and with respect to μ. The conditions we imposed on the utility and production functions guarantee that the first-order conditions pin down a global maximum; indeed, one can show that the problem is concave.[5]

Naturally, we cannot differentiate (1.5) with respect to k_0: this amount of capital represents the initial state of the system. In contrast, consumption can be chosen in any period, and therefore it is usually referred to as a "control" (or "decision") variable.

By taking the derivatives of (1.5) with respect to the $T+1$ consumption levels, we obtain the first order conditions:

$$\begin{aligned} U'(c_0) &= \lambda_0 \\ U'(c_1) &= \lambda_1 \\ \dots &= \dots \\ U'(c_t) &= \lambda_t \\ \dots &= \dots \\ U'(c_T) &= \lambda_T. \end{aligned} \tag{1.6}$$

Each Lagrange multiplier λ_t captures the consumer's marginal utility of period t consumption. Had we not multiplied λ_t by β^t, the multipliers would have expressed the marginal utilities from the perspective of period 0.

By differentiating with respect to the $T+1$ capital levels (from k_1 to k_{T+1}), our agent obtains:

$$\begin{aligned} \lambda_0 &= \beta\lambda_1[f'(k_1)+1-\delta] \\ \beta\lambda_1 &= \beta^2\lambda_2[f'(k_2)+1-\delta] \\ \dots &= \dots \\ \beta^t\lambda_t &= \beta^{t+1}\lambda_{t+1}[f'(k_{t+1})+1-\delta] \\ \dots &= \dots \\ \beta^{T-1}\lambda_{T-1} &= \beta^T\lambda_T[f'(k_T)+1-\delta] \\ \beta^T\mu &= \beta^T\lambda_T. \end{aligned} \tag{1.7}$$

Differentiating (1.5) with respect to the Lagrange multipliers λ_t, for $t = 0, 1, 2, ..., T$ yields the set of constraints like (1.3). Moreover, the differentiation of (1.5) with respect to μ yields the constraint (1.4). Since (1.4) is an inequality constraint, one must consider the "complementary slackness" condition:

$$\beta^T\mu k_{T+1} = 0 \text{ and } \mu \geq 0, \tag{1.8}$$

which will be discussed below. For future reference, bear in mind that the complementary slackness condition (1.8) can be reformulated, by means of the last conditions in (1.7) and (1.6), as:

$$\beta^T U'(c_T)k_{T+1} = 0. \tag{1.9}$$

1.1.3 The Euler equation

Consider now any first order condition belonging to group (1.7), but for the last one: we immediately note that those equations can be manipulated using the appropriate first order conditions of group (1.6). The typical result is:

$$U'(c_t) = \beta U'(c_{t+1})[f'(k_{t+1}) + 1 - \delta]. \tag{1.10}$$

This condition is known as the Euler equation, which is of remarkable importance not only in most growth models but also in consumption theory (and–in stochastic models–to evaluate risky consumption paths).

The Euler equation (1.10) tells us that the optimal consumption path must be such that–in every period–the marginal utility of consumption is equal to the following period's marginal utility, discounted by β and multiplied by the marginal productivity of capital net of depreciation (plus 1). To gain some intuition about the economic meaning of Eq. (1.10), consider that it can be interpreted as prescribing the equality between the marginal rate of substitution between period t and period $t+1$ consumptions (i.e. $U'(c_t)/(\beta U'(c_{t+1}))$), and the marginal rate of transformation, $f'(k_{t+1}) + 1 - \delta$.[6]

To improve our understanding of this point, consider a given initial level for capital, k''_t, and a feasible stock of capital for period $t+2$, k''_{t+2}.[7] Given k''_t, pick a consumption level for period t and one for period $t+1$, say c''_t and c''_{t+1}, that do not satisfy the Euler equation. Note that we have required these two levels to be feasible. In other words, given the initial level k''_t, c''_t and c''_{t+1} must be such that k''_{t+2} fulfills the constraints $k''_{t+2} = f(k''_{t+1}) + (1-\delta)k''_{t+1} - c''_{t+1}$ and $k''_{t+1} = f(k''_t) + (1-\delta)k''_t - c''_t$.

In deciding whether the choice to consume c''_t in period t and c''_{t+1} in period $t+1$ is appropriate, our consumer must consider what would happen to her overall utility if–for given k''_t and k''_{t+2}–she decided to increase time t consumption by a small amount ξ at the expense of period $t+1$ consumption. At time t, her utility would increase by (approximately) $U'(c''_t)\xi$.[8] Furthermore, because her savings would decrease by ξ, her next period resources would also decrease by ξ. To keep k''_{t+2} unchanged, period $t+1$ consumption must be reduced by $[f'(k''_{t+1}) + 1 - \delta]\xi$. This reduction is equal to ξ (the decrease in k_{t+1}) multiplied by the productivity of the marginal savings, that is of the marginal amount of capital the consumer has decided not to save. Accordingly, the reduction in period $t+1$ utility would be given by $U'(c''_{t+1})[f'(k''_{t+1}) + 1 - \delta]\xi$. From the perspective of time t, this variation in utility must be discounted; hence, its period t value is $\beta U'(c''_{t+1})[f'(k''_{t+1})+1-\delta]\xi$.

If $U'(c''_t)\xi > \beta U'(c''_{t+1})[f'(k''_{t+1})+1-\delta]\xi$, it is convenient to increase period t consumption: the utility gain in that period is larger than the utility loss suffered at time $t+1$ once discounted back to period t. Likewise, if $U'(c''_t)\xi < \beta U'(c''_{t+1})[f'(k''_{t+1})+1-\delta]\xi$, it is convenient to decrease period t consumption: the utility loss in that period is smaller than the discounted utility gain. From this reasoning, we can convince ourselves that Eq. (1.10) must hold true when the consumption sequence is optimally chosen. Note further that Eq. (1.10)–relating the consumption level in period t to the one in period $t+1$–applies for $t = 0, 1, ..., T-1$. (It is pointless to plan a positive consumption for the period coming after ... one's death!). Hence, the Euler equation provides us with T conditions that we exploit when we solve analytically our maximization problem.

1.1.4 The solution

We now determine the $T+1$ consumption levels (i.e., $c_0, c_1, ..., c_T$) and the $T+1$ capital stocks (i.e., $k_1,\ k_2,\ ...,\ k_{T+1}$).

The Euler equation (1.10) provides us with T relations in addition to the $T+1$ constraints like (1.3). To close the model we need a further equation, which is provided by the complementary slackness condition (1.8). This condition tells us that, if the consumer uses up her entire capital stock in the final period, so that $k_{T+1} = 0$, then μ is positive. Alternatively, if $\mu = 0$, the final capital stock is positive. Condition (1.7) guarantees that μ must actually be positive, since it is equal to λ_T, and λ_T is the marginal utility of consumption at time T, which cannot be zero. Hence, the final period capital must be zero, which is very sensible in economic terms: since our agent does not consume anything in period $T+1$, it is pointless for her to keep any capital; she can always improve her overall utility by eating up these resources. We can therefore be sure that $k_{T+1} = 0$, a condition that "closes" the model in accordance with the complementary slackness condition (1.8).

The system composed of T equations like (1.10), of $T+1$ equations like (1.3), and by $k_{T+1} = 0$ can–in principle–be solved for the $T+1$ consumption levels and for the $T+1$ capital levels.

As an example, consider an agent with a log-utility function, who discounts the future, lives for three periods (labeled 0, 1, and 2, so that $T = 2$), and is endowed with the technology $y_t = Ak_t^\alpha$, with $\alpha \in (0,1)$; $A > 0$ captures the productivity of the available technology.[9] An important simplifying assumption that we adopt is that capital fully depreciates within one period (so that $\delta = 1$). Our agent inherits an amount of capital $k_0 > 0$ from the past. With these qualifications, the pertinent version of the Lagrangian (1.5) is

$$\begin{aligned}\mathcal{L}_0 \quad = \quad & \ln c_0 + \beta \ln c_1 + \beta^2 \ln c_2 + \\ & -\lambda_0[k_1 - Ak_0^\alpha + c_0] + \\ & -\beta\lambda_1[k_2 - Ak_1^\alpha + c_1] + \\ & -\beta^2\lambda_2[k_3 - Ak_2^\alpha + c_2] + \\ & +\beta^2\mu k_3.\end{aligned}$$

The first order conditions allow us to quickly obtain two Euler equations, which are:

$$c_1 = \beta\alpha Ak_1^{\alpha-1}c_0, \tag{1.11}$$

and

$$c_2 = \beta\alpha Ak_2^{\alpha-1}c_1. \tag{1.12}$$

Three further equations are provided by the "budget constraints":

$$k_1 = Ak_0^\alpha - c_0, \tag{1.13}$$

$$k_2 = Ak_1^\alpha - c_1, \tag{1.14}$$

and

$$k_3 = Ak_2^\alpha - c_2. \tag{1.15}$$

Since our agent wants to deplete her stock of capital by period 3, the system is completed by $k_3 = 0$. Accordingly, from Eq. (1.15) we obtain the consumption function for period 2:

$$c_2^* = Ak_2^\alpha, \tag{1.16}$$

which, together with (1.12) allows us to get:

$$c_2^* = Ak_2^\alpha = \beta\alpha Ak_2^{\alpha-1}c_1.$$

In turn, this equation gives: $k_2 = \beta\alpha c_1$, a relation that, combined with (1.14), allows us to obtain the consumption function for period 1:

$$c_1^* = \frac{1}{1+\alpha\beta}Ak_1^\alpha. \tag{1.17}$$

Taking advantage of the latter equation into (1.11) gives

$$c_0 = \frac{1}{\alpha\beta\,(1+\alpha\beta)}k_1,$$

and finally, by exploiting (1.13), we obtain:

$$c_0^* = \frac{1}{1+\alpha\beta+(\alpha\beta)^2}Ak_0^\alpha. \tag{1.18}$$

Our solution relates the control variable, c_0, to the same period state variable, k_0. Eqs (1.16-1.18) together with the budget constraints, allow us to obtain, for any given k_0, the complete sequence of consumption and capital levels, which is the solution for our problem. Let us assume $\alpha = 0.3$, $\beta = 0.97$, and $A \approx 3.436426$;[10] we also arbitrarily choose $k_0 = 0.5$. The solution is presented in Table 1.

TABLE 1

period #	k_t	c_t
0	0.5	2.028992
1	0.762254	2.453639
2	0.714009	3.106119
3	0	–

Note from Table 1 that the combination of the initial condition for the capital stock, productivity, and discounting implies that our agent decides to accumulate some capital during period 0, while she depletes it in periods 1 and 2.

More importantly, note–from Eqs. (1.16-1.18)–that the consumption function is not time invariant. The propensity to consume out of (gross) income, $c_t/y_t\,(\equiv c_t/Ak_t^\alpha)$ increases from $1/(1+\alpha\beta+(\alpha\beta)^2)$ in period 0 to $1/\left(1+\alpha\beta\right)$ in period 1, and of course to 1 in period 2. This should not be surprising: the willingness to accumulate capital inevitably depends on the agent's residual lifetime: the closer to her "death" she is, the weaker the incentive to save. With the production and the utility functions proposed in the example, one can show (refer to Exercise 1) that the consumption function for an agent living $T+1$ periods is

$$c_t^* = \frac{1}{\sum_{i=0}^{T-t}(\alpha\beta)^i}Ak_t^\alpha,\ t=0,1,...,T. \tag{1.19}$$

Our example may be misleading, as it could suggest that finding an analytical solution to our problem is easy. In fact, we can only obtain a solution for the c_t and k_t variables in terms of the known elements (k_0 and the parameters) in a few special cases. To verify this, consider Exercise 2: although it involves only a minor change–specifically an incomplete depreciation of the capital stock–it is not possible to find a closed-form solution. However, reassuringly, we can still show that the solution exists and is unique.

As we will see, this analytical difficulty motivates the use of numerical techniques, and, at least in part, the decision to resort to the dynamic programming approach.

Exercise 1 *Consider an agent characterized by a log-utility function, and facing the dynamic constraint* $k_{t+1} = Ak_t^{\alpha} - c_t$, *with* $\alpha \in (0,1)$, $A \in (0,\infty)$. *Her subjective discount rate is positive and constant, so that* $\beta \in (0,1)$. *Assuming that she lives for* $T+1$ *periods (from* 0 *to* T*), prove that her optimal plan (from the perspective of period 0) is given by Eq. (1.19).*

Exercise 2 *Consider an agent characterized by a log-utility function, and facing the dynamic constraint* $k_{t+1} = Ak_t^{\alpha} + (1-\delta)\,k_t - c_t$, *with* $\alpha, \delta \in (0,1)$, $A \in (0,\infty)$. *Her subjective discount rate is positive and constant, so that* $\beta \in (0,1)$. *Assuming that she lives for* 3 *periods, prove that the optimal solution is unique.*

1.2 The infinite-horizon consumption-growth problem

Let us now imagine that our agent lives forever. At first glance, this might seem crazy.[11] However, we can view our agent as a person who cares about her offspring. In this case, she might believe that her sons and daughters will, in turn, be concerned about their offsprings' welfare and so on. Therefore, she should optimize over the entire future. If you wish, you can think of our agent not as a person, but as a dynasty. An alternative interpretation is that the optimizing agent is actually a social planner who aims to maximize a social welfare function whose arguments are the discounted utilities of all the agents alive now and at any possible future date. This alternative interpretation allows for the determination of the optimal saving rate for society. In fact, the British economist Frank P. Ramsey originally framed the question in these terms, and the model presented here is essentially his.

Assuming that our agent optimizes from time 0 onwards, her preferences are now given by the following intertemporal utility function:

$$W_0 = \sum_{t=0}^{\infty} \beta^t U(c_t), \tag{1.20}$$

an expression which is analogous to (1.1), but for the fact that now the agent's horizon extends up to infinity.

Our problem is now to

$$\max_{\{c_t\}_{t=0}^{\infty}} W_0 = \max_{\{c_t\}_{t=0}^{\infty}} \sum_{t=0}^{\infty} \beta^t U(c_t);$$

but note that, while the constraints are given by equations such as (1.3), the fact that the consumer's planning horizon is infinite implies that we cannot impose a "terminal constraint" like (1.4). Hence our model will be "closed" in a different way which we will discuss shortly.

The consumer's problem is addressed using the following "present-value" Lagrangian:

$$\begin{aligned} \mathcal{L}_0 \quad = \quad & U(c_0) + \beta U(c_1) + ... + \beta^t U(c_t) + ... + \\ & -\lambda_0[k_1 - f(k_0) - (1-\delta)k_0 + c_0] + \\ & - ... + \\ & -\beta^t \lambda_t[k_{t+1} - f(k_t) - (1-\delta)k_t + c_t] + \\ & - ... \end{aligned} \tag{1.21}$$

Problem (1.21) differs from (1.5) in that it involves an infinite number of discounted utility terms, and an infinite number of dynamic constraints. Additionally–as already remarked–an explicit constraint concerning the final level for the state variable is missing.

Indeed, in our infinite-horizon model, the role of the final condition is played by the so-called transversality condition (henceforth tvc), which–in this setup–is:

$$\lim_{T \to \infty} \beta^T U'(c_T) k_{T+1} = 0. \tag{1.22}$$

Comparing this expression with (1.9), we immediately note that (1.22) is the limit of (1.9) as $T \to \infty$, which indeed corroborates the idea that the tvc plays the role of the terminal condition. The tvc has an intuitive economic interpretation: it rules out policies implying "too fast" a capital accumulation in the long run. To understand this point, assume, for example, that–to allow for a fast capital accumulation–our agent decides to decrease consumption over time. This policy would imply a high and increasing marginal utility of consumption, and a high and increasing value for the product $U'(c_T)k_{T+1}$. This, in itself, does not involve the violation of condition (1.22). Indeed, condition (1.22) allows $U'(c_T)k_{T+1}$ to increase over time *if* such growth is slow enough to be compensated by the convergence to 0 of the discount term β^T. This is why we say that the transversality condition rules out policies implying a "too fast" long-run capital accumulation.

We differentiate (1.21) with respect to c_t, k_{t+1}, and λ_t for $t = 0, 1, ...$ obtaining:

$$U'(c_t) = \lambda_t, \; \forall\, t, \tag{1.23}$$

$$\beta^t \lambda_t = \beta^{t+1} \lambda_{t+1}[f'(k_{t+1}) + (1-\delta)], \; \forall\, t, \tag{1.24}$$

and, of course:

$$k_{t+1} = f(k_t) + (1-\delta)k_t - c_t, \; \forall\, t. \tag{1.25}$$

Note that from Eq. (1.23)–considered for two consecutive periods–and from Eq. (1.24) we immediately obtain that optimality satisfies the Euler equation:

$$U'(c_t) = \beta U'(c_{t+1})[f'(k_{t+1}) + 1 - \delta],$$

that we have already discussed in the finite-lives example.

1.2.1 *Qualitative dynamics*

As is typical in many infinite-horizon frameworks (which almost always lack an analytical solution), a phase diagram is useful for characterizing the solution. Our phase diagram helps visualize the possible time paths along which consumption and capital can evolve and identifies the specific path that represents the solution. This path, which defines a relationship between optimal consumption and capital, depicts the solution to the optimization problem in a qualitative way.

To obtain a two-dimensional phase diagram, we consider that the dynamics of our model are captured by the system comprising the Euler equation (1.10) and the dynamic constraint, Eq. (1.25):

$$\begin{cases} U'(c_t) = \beta U'(c_{t+1})[f'(k_{t+1}) + 1 - \delta] \\ k_{t+1} = f(k_t) + (1-\delta)k_t - c_t. \end{cases} \tag{1.26}$$

We then compute the set of points such that $c_{t+1} = c_t$, and $k_{t+1} = k_t$, which implies $\Delta c_{t+1} = 0$, and $\Delta k_{t+1} = 0$.[12] In the jargon, these sets of points are called "stability loci." The loci $\Delta c_{t+1} = 0$ and $\Delta k_{t+1} = 0$ will help us identify the "stationary states," defined as the points where no variable moves (in our case, the points where we simultaneously have $\Delta c_{t+1} = 0$ and $\Delta k_{t+1} = 0$).

We will then analyze how each variable changes over time whenever it does not lie on one of the stability loci. Such qualitative dynamics are obtained by exploiting the difference equations making up System (1.26). This will allow us to jointly depict the "directions of movement" for both variables.

We start our analysis with consumption. Recall that optimality requires that the Euler equation (1.10) is satisfied. When $c_{t+1} = c_t$, then the marginal utilities must be equal, $U'(c_t) = U'(c_{t+1})$, so that the Euler equation (1.10) implies that consumption is constant when $k_{t+1} = \hat{k}$, where $\hat{k}$ is such that:

$$1 = \beta[f'(\hat{k}) + 1 - \delta]. \tag{1.27}$$

Hence, in Figure 1.1, we plot the locus implying stationarity for consumption as a vertical line drawn at $\hat{k}$. In the steady state–that is, when $k_{t+1} = \hat{k}$ and consumption is constant over time–the impatience parameter β exactly offsets the positive effects on savings driven by the reward provided by the marginal productivity of capital.[13]

Whenever $k_{t+1} < \hat{k}$, the marginal productivity of capital is higher than at $\hat{k}$ (i.e., $f'(k_{t+1}) > f'(\hat{k})$);[14] hence $\beta[f'(k_{t+1}) + 1 - \delta] > 1$. Therefore, the Euler equation is satisfied only for consumption levels such that $U'(c_t) > U'(c_{t+1})$. Hence, it must be true that $c_t < c_{t+1}$. In other words, since the marginal productivity of capital will be high, saving is very rewarding. Therefore, it is sensible to save "a lot" by reducing consumption at the "early" date t. Because the "early" consumption is low, consumption increases over time.

By a similar argument, when $k_{t+1} > \hat{k}$, capital is "abundant" and its marginal productivity becomes low. Therefore $\beta[f'(k_{t+1}) + 1 - \delta] < 1$. Eq. (1.10) is satisfied if $U'(c_t) < U'(c_{t+1})$, which implies that $c_t > c_{t+1}$. Because the marginal productivity of capital is low, saving is poorly compensated. Therefore, it is sensible to choose a high consumption level at t, and to decrease it over time.

In sum, whenever $k_{t+1} < \hat{k}$, it is optimal for our consumer to increase her consumption over time (hence $c_t < c_{t+1}$). When, instead, $k_{t+1} > \hat{k}$, consumption must be shrinking over time ($c_{t+1} < c_t$). This behavior is summarized by the arrows in Figure 1.1.

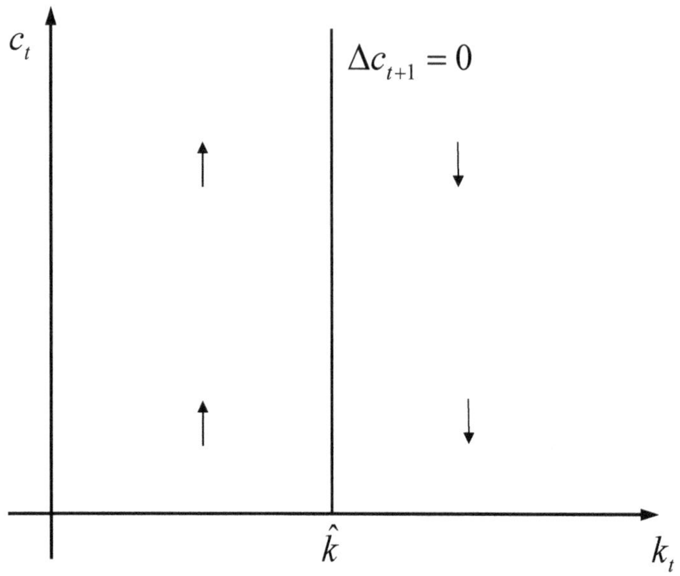

FIGURE 1.1. The $\Delta c_{t+1} = 0$ locus and the dynamics for consumption

We now turn our attention to the $\Delta k_{t+1} = 0$ locus (refer to Figure 1.2). From Eq. (1.25), we see that $\Delta k_{t+1} = f(k_t) - \delta k_t - c_t$. Hence, capital is stationary when:

$$c_t = f(k_t) - \delta k_t. \tag{1.28}$$

Starting at the origin (due to assumption (c)), this relation can be graphically represented as a function peaking at $\underline{k}$ (defined as the capital level such that $f'(\underline{k}) = \delta$), and intersecting again the $c_t = 0$ axis at $\bar{k}$ (which is the capital level such that $c_t = 0$, i.e., it is obtained by solving the equation $f(\bar{k}) - \delta\bar{k} = 0$).[15] The $\Delta k_{t+1} = 0$ locus is depicted in Figure 1.2.

To see what happens when the economic system is not on the stability locus (1.28), pick a capital level $k'' \in [0, \bar{k}]$; the corresponding consumption level guaranteeing stationarity for capital is obviously:

$$c'' = f(k'') - \delta k''.$$

If the consumer chooses a consumption level $c_t > c''$, her capital stock must decrease over time: the consumption is so high that our consumer is using part of her capital to live. More precisely, consumption is higher than the level, c'', that guarantees the difference between gross production, $f(k'')$, and consumption exactly matches capital depreciation $\delta k''$. Therefore

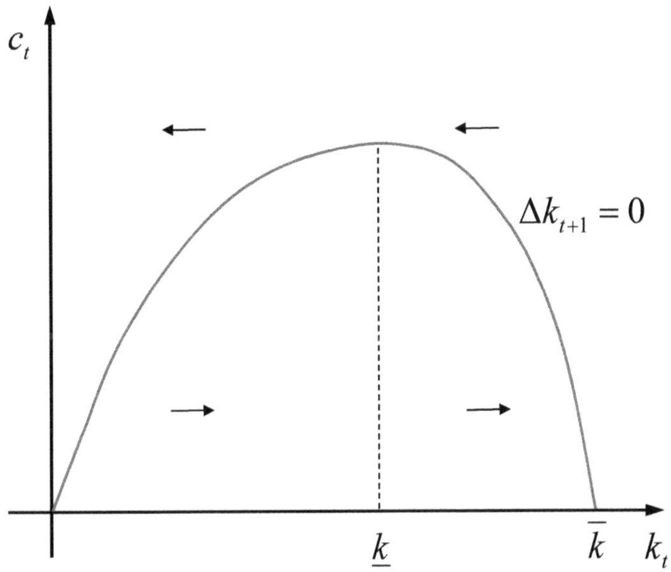

FIGURE 1.2. The $\Delta k_{t+1} = 0$ locus and the dynamics for capital

the capital stock must decrease. The converse happens when our consumer chooses a consumption level c_t that is lower than c'': her capital increases over time because a consumption lower than c'' implies that savings $(f(k'') - c'')$ exceed capital depreciation, and hence there is some net investment. This behavior is summarized by the arrows in Figure 1.2.

By merging Figures 1.1 and 1.2, we obtain Figure 1.3, which depicts the dynamics of the model.

Note that there are three steady states (E, the origin, and I). It is easy to see that E is a steady state: it is the crossing point for the two loci $\Delta k_{t+1} = 0$ and $\Delta c_{t+1} = 0$. From Eqs. (1.3) and (1.10), it is clear that at E both consumption and capital do not change over time when:

$$\begin{cases} 1 = \beta[f'(\hat{k}) + 1 - \delta] \\ \hat{c} = f(\hat{k}) - \delta\hat{k}. \end{cases} \tag{1.29}$$

Hence, the levels of consumption and capital characterizing this steady state can be obtained by solving the system above.

The origin is a resting point because of Assumption (c): if capital is 0, there is no production, and therefore no possibility of further capital accumulation. This resting point is usually considered uninteresting.

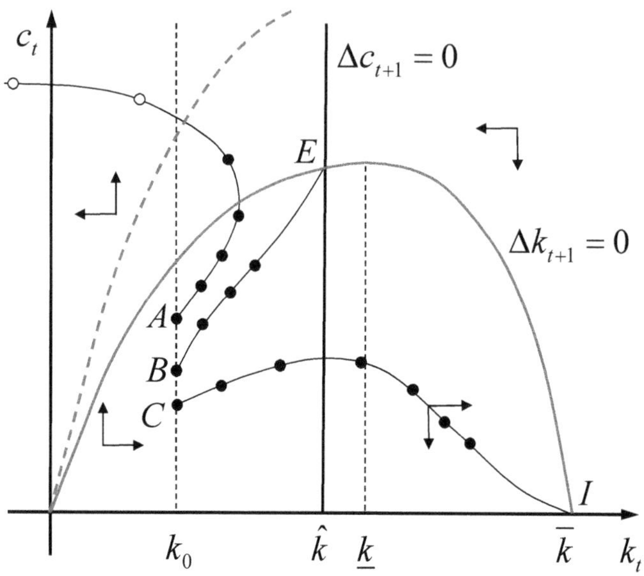

FIGURE 1.3. Phase diagram for the Ramsey model and the dynamics of consumption and capital

Although less obvious, I is also a steady state. To gain some intuition, note that the marginal utility of consumption increases rapidly as consumption approaches 0 (this is because we assumed that $\lim_{c_t \to 0} U'(c_t) = \infty$). Hence, the increase in the marginal utility of consumption prescribed by Eq. (1.10) for $k_t > \hat{k}$ implies smaller and smaller reductions in consumption as c_t approaches 0, so that consumption "glides" toward point I. Hence, consumption does not become negative (which would of course have had no economic meaning) and I is a resting point.[16]

In Figure 1.3, the dashed line represents the maximum level of consumption for period t allowing for a non-negative capital stock in period $t+1$. It is obtained by solving for c_t (for any given k_t) the equation:

$$f(k_t) + (1 - \delta)\, k_t - c_t = 0\,(= k_{t+1})\,. \tag{1.30}$$

Hence, the dashed line represents the maximum feasible consumption for each stock of capital.

Finally, consider that our consumer is endowed with a limited amount of capital (k_0); such a constraint must be taken into account when choosing her optimal consumption path.

In Figure 1.3 we have depicted some of the possible paths that our agent may decide to follow. These paths are designed to satisfy the Euler equation (1.10) and the capital accumulation constraint (1.3).[17] The fact that there are many (actually, infinitely many) trajectories that are compatible with one initial condition should not be surprising: while the capital stock k_0 is given, our consumer is free to pick her initial consumption level, which then determines the path for consumption and capital (via Eqs. (1.10) and (1.3)).

Note as well that each trajectory represents the relationship between the variable controlled by the representative agent (i.e., consumption) and the variable representing the "state of the system" (i.e., capital). Accordingly, the solution–the path maximizing the overall utility–also takes the form of a function that relates the control variable to the state variable.

1.2.2 The optimal path

So far, we have seen that multiple paths are compatible with the same initial condition. Now we need to select the optimal one(s).

First, note that the trajectory starting at A in Figure 1.3 cannot be optimal. Loosely speaking, because consumption is ever-increasing, capital must be entirely depleted within finite time. Since by assumption capital is essential for production, consumption would have to collapse to zero at that point. In this respect, note that in Figure 1.3, the last two points in the sequence starting at A are colored white: this is to highlight that they are a sort of "phantoms." Indeed, they cannot actually be reached. Focusing in particular on the second-to-last point, we note that it is not feasible since the consumption level it identifies implies a negative capital stock for the subsequent period: such consumption exceeds the level defined by Eq. (1.30). Consequently, the actual consumption level must be lower, lying on (or below) the dashed line in Figure 1.3. Therefore, the sequence of points starting at A cannot be optimal: feasibility requires that the consumption levels must abandon this path at a certain point in time, which in turn implies a violation of the Euler equation. Hence, the path starting at A–and all the paths similar to this one–cannot be optimal.[18]

Second, consider the trajectory starting at B. In this case, our consumer chooses *exactly* the consumption level that leads the system to the stationary point E. This path not only satisfies the difference equations (1.10) and (1.3) but also the transversality condition (1.22). In fact, as time goes to infinity (i.e., as $t \to \infty$) capital and consumption approach their steady-state levels, $\hat{k}$ and $\hat{c}$, which are given by System (1.29). The fact that the long run-levels for consumption and capital are constant (and positive) tells us that, in the steady state, the marginal utility of consumption is finite. Hence, $\lim_{t\to\infty} \beta^t U'(c_t)k_{t+1} = \lim_{t\to\infty} \beta^t U'(\hat{c})\hat{k} = 0$ simply because $\beta < 1$. This trajectory is optimal.

Third, consider the trajectory starting at C and leading to I. In this case, both consumption and capital initially increase. However, as capital exceeds $\hat{k}$, consumption begins to shrink while the capital accumulation process continues. In the long run, our optimizing agent finds herself around I, devoting all her productive effort to maintaining an excessive stock of capital, that is actually never used to produce consumption goods. Hence, this trajectory cannot be optimal, and in fact the transversality condition is violated, because the marginal utility of consumption tends to infinity. [19]

To sum up, the solution to our problem is the path that leads to the steady state E; this path–which is unique–relates optimal consumption to the available capital stock in each period, identifying a monotonically increasing relation between them. Although not expressed in an analytical form, this relation is the counterpart of Eqs. (1.18-1.16) in the previous subsection. Note also that in the initial period our consumer (or our economy) "jumps" on this path, adjusting the initial consumption to the level compatible with the existing capital stock, and consistent with the behavior prescribed by our optimal trajectory.

Exercise 3 *In each period, an infinitely-lived individual enjoys consumption according to the utility function* $c_t^{1-\gamma}/(1-\gamma)$, *with* $\gamma \in [0,1) \cup (1,\infty)$, *the dynamic constraint is* $k_{t+1} = (1-\delta)\, k_t + Ak_t^{\alpha} - c_t$, *with* $\delta, \alpha \in (0,1)$, $A \in (0,\infty)$. *The subjective discount rate is positive and constant, so that* $\beta \in (0,1)$. *Provide as many details as possible for the solution.*

Exercise 4 *In each period, an infinitely-lived individual enjoys consumption according to the utility function* $c_t^{1-\gamma}/(1-\gamma)$, *with* $\gamma \in (1,\infty)$, *the dynamic constraint is* $k_{t+1} = (1+\overline{r})\, k_t + \overline{y} - c_t$, *with* $\overline{r}, \overline{y} > 0$ *and constant. Assume further that the subjective discount rate is positive and constant, and that* $\beta\,(1+\overline{r}) < 1$. *Obtain the consumption function and show that the transversality condition is satisfied. (Hint: start by obtaining the consumption function. Note that you may interpret* k *as "financial capital,"* $\overline{r}$ *as a fixed interest rate and* $\overline{y}$ *as labor income.)*

Exercise 5 *A competitive firm sells its output at a price normalized to 1; it uses* y_t *units of input at a total cost of* $cy_t^2/2$, *with* c *being constant; future profits are discounted at the constant factor* $1+r > 1$ *(so that* $\beta \equiv 1/(1+r) < 1$*). The firm's productivity is* $1 + bx_t/2$, *so that its output is*

$y_t\,(1 + bx_t/2)$; productivity evolves over time according to $x_t = y_{t-1}$ (i.e. the firm benefits from some learning by doing). Assume $b < 2c/(1+\beta)$ (why?) and obtain the sequence for input maximizing the firm's value.

Notes

[1]An analysis focusing on a *single* consumer may seem very limited. Indeed, in our setting, a single agent—acting alone—optimizes under the constraint of the aggregate production function. This appears to be in sharp contrast with the real world. In a market economy, agents do not directly manage a production function. Instead, they work to earn a wage, and they receive interest (or dividends) from the financial wealth they have accumulated through past savings. In other words, optimizing agents take into account prices, wages, interest rates ...

However, it can be shown that *if* markets are perfectly competitive, the resource allocation in our analysis is equivalent to the allocation of resources achieved by a decentralized economy. In such an economy, decisions are made by a large number of economic agents based on prices. This equivalence is a fundamental result in economics (and is famously known as the Second Welfare Theorem). When all agents are identical, the proof is straightforward. Therefore, while our *if* is a rather big one, our analysis is less limited than it might appear.

[2]Should you be concerned that capital is the only production input, rest assured that we can integrate the presence of labor into our framework. In particular, this is readily done when the supply of labor is fixed. In this case, we might have specified our production function as $y_t = g(k_t, \bar{l})$, where $\bar{l}$ is the fixed supply of labor, and we could have normalized $\bar{l}$ to unity and then written $f(k_t) \equiv g(k_t, 1)$. An alternative and more sophisticated way of justifying Eq. (1.2) is to assume that output is obtained by means of a production function that exhibits constant returns to scale, being homogeneous of degree one in capital and labor. In this case, one interprets k_t as the capital-labor ratio.

[3]What is really necessary is to accept that $\lim_{k_t \to \infty} f'(k_t) < \delta$, a hypothesis that can hardly be considered restrictive. The assumption in the main text allows for a slightly easier exposition.

[4]A neat interpretation of the role of Lagrange multipliers can be found in Dixit (1990).

[5]Refer, e.g., to Beavis and Dobbs (1990), or to de la Fuente (2000).

[6]An alternative interpretation is that our representative consumer, by forgoing one unit of consumption today, obtains $f'(k_{t+1}) + 1 - \delta$ units of consumption tomorrow. Accordingly, $f'(k_{t+1}) + 1 - \delta$ can also be interpreted as the price of current consumption if the price of future consumption is the numeraire, and hence fixed to 1. According to this interpretation, Eq. (1.10) can be seen as prescribing the equalization of the marginal rate of substitution $U'(c_t)/\beta U'(c_{t+1})$ with the price ratio $[f'(k_{t+1}) + 1 - \delta]/1$.

[7]To denote an arbitrary level for a variable we use a prime (e.g., k') or a double prime (e.g., k''). Stars are reserved for optimal levels (e.g., k^*), and hats for steady states (e.g., $\hat{k}$) of the variables. As we will see, a steady state is a situation where all the variables remain constant over time.

[8]If you do not "see" this, consider that the difference (in terms of period t utility) of the two policies is $U(c_t'' + \xi) - U(c_t'')$. Applying Taylor's theorem to $U(c_t'' + \xi)$ one obtains: $U(c_t'' + \xi) \approx U(c_t'') + U'(c_t'')\xi$.

[9]The higher the value of A, the larger the output for any given level of the available capital stock.

[10]The value for α is sensible, as it represents the capital income share of output, a value typically between 0.25 and 0.4 for most OECD countries. Our motivation for choosing β and A will become clear once we have discussed the infinite-horizon version of the model.

[11]After all, even in sci-fi novels an alien technology is often needed to obtain a potentially infinite life (as in *The Expanse* book series).

[12]Following an often-used convention we denote $\Delta y_{t+1} \equiv y_{t+1} - y_t$ for any variable y_t

[13]Existence and uniqueness of $\hat{k}$ is granted by Assumptions (a), (b), (d) and (e).

[14]This is granted by a positive but *decreasing* marginal productivity of capital, Assumptions (a) and (b).

[15]Existence and uniqueness of $\bar{k}$ are granted by Assumptions (b) and (e).

[16]For a more detailed argument rewrite (1.10) as:

$$U'(c_{t+1}) = U'(c_t)\left[\frac{1}{\beta\left(f'(k_{t+1}) + 1 - \delta\right)}\right].$$

Pick a capital level, k'', belonging to the interval $(\hat{k}, \bar{k})$: it is easy to see that $f'(k'') + 1 - \delta \in (1 - \delta, 1/\beta)$: this comes from (1.27) and from the assumptions $f''(k_t) < 0$, and $\lim_{k_t \to \infty} f'(k_t) = 0$, that is from Assumptions (b) and (e). Therefore, when $k'' \in (\hat{k}, \bar{k})$, the term in the big square brackets in the equation above must be larger than one, since the largest value for the denominator is smaller than one. Therefore, the Euler equation not only tells us that the marginal utility of consumption must increase (and hence that consumption must decrease), but also that the rate of change of marginal utility is limited. Indeed, we have:

$$\frac{U'(c_{t+1}) - U'(c_t)}{U'(c_t)} = \frac{1}{\beta(f'(k'') + 1 - \delta)} - 1,$$

and the value of the right-hand side of the expression above belongs to the interval $(0, 1/\left(\beta(1 - \delta)\right) - 1)$. This has a relevant implication: because the rate of change of the marginal utility is bounded, when we consider a sequence of consumption levels that–starting from a non-negative value–fulfills the Euler equation, we see that this sequence cannot go to zero in finite time. This is because the marginal utility of consumption cannot "reach infinity" in finite time (bear in mind that $\lim_{c_t \to 0} U'(c_t) = \infty$). Because consumption takes an "infinite time" to reach its limiting value (that is, 0), "in the meantime" capital reaches $\bar{k}$ (since consumption decreases, the system must reach at some time the area below the $\Delta k_t = 0$ locus where capital grows, approaching $\bar{k}$). Hence I is a stationary state for our system.

[17]While it is not possible to check that our paths in Figure 1.3 precisely conform to what is prescribed by our difference equation, note that they have been drawn respecting the "arrows", which, in turn, summarize the "direction of movement" obtained from the difference equations (1.10) and (1.3).

[18]Thanks go to Michele Piffer for pushing me to spell out this point in detail.

[19]A less informal argument for the reasons why a path like the one starting at C violates the tvc goes as follows. Imagine that you are "very close" to I. Here, capital is (almost)

$\bar{k}$. Recall that for $k_t \in (\underline{k}, \bar{k})$, $f'(k_t) + 1 - \delta < 1$ (at $\underline{k}$, $f'(\underline{k}) = \delta$, and $f''(k_t) < 0$)), and consider that consumption should evolve according to:

$$U'(c_{t+1}) = U'(c_t)\frac{1}{\beta(f'(k_{t+1}) + 1 - \delta)}.$$

Hence, for a capital stock close to $\bar{k}$, we have that

$$\beta U'(c_{t+1}) = U'(c_t)\frac{1}{f'(k_{t+1}) + 1 - \delta} > U'(c_t).$$

Because "around" $\bar{k}$, $\beta U'(c_{t+1}) > U'(c_t)$, $\lim_{t\to\infty} \beta^t U'(c_t) > 0$. (Indeed, suppose that at a given time T our system is already "very close" to I. In this case, in the following periods, i.e. for $t > T$, $\beta^{t-T}U'(c_t) > U'(c_T)$. Hence $\lim_{t\to\infty} \beta^t U'(c_t) = \lim_{t\to\infty} \beta^T \beta^{t-T} U'(c_t) > \beta^T U'(c_T)$) Consequently, the tvc (1.22) is not fulfilled, so that any trajectory like the one starting at C is not optimal.

2

The Dynamic Programming formulation

ABSTRACT This chapter discusses the dynamic programming approach to solving the infinite-horizon growth model. Section 2.1 takes advantage of our prior knowledge of the Ramsey model to provide an intuitive introduction to this new technique. The more formal Section 2.2 first addresses the existence and uniqueness issues of the solution, and then shows how the envelope theorem can be used to characterize it.

2.1 Introduction to the basic concepts

As before, our representative agent aims at maximizing the intertemporal utility function (1.20). Her problem is to choose the consumption sequence $\{c_t\}_{t=0}^{\infty}$ to maximize her total discounted utility:

$$\max_{\{c_t\}_{t=0}^{\infty}} W_0 = \max_{\{c_t\}_{t=0}^{\infty}} \sum_{t=0}^{\infty} \beta^t U(c_t)$$

under the constraints $k_{t+1} = f(k_t) + (1-\delta)k_t - c_t$, for $t = 0, 1, ...$, and given k_0.

DOI: 10.4324/9781003774051-2

Obviously, our agent's preferences can be written as:

$$W_0 = U(c_0) + \sum_{t=1}^{\infty} \beta^t U(c_t),$$

in which we have "separated" the utility obtained in the present (period 0) from the utility that will be enjoyed in the future. However, there is no change in the meaning of W_0. Note that the expression above can be reformulated as:

$$W_0 = U(c_0) + \beta \left[\sum_{t=1}^{\infty} \beta^{t-1} U(c_t) \right]. \tag{2.1}$$

Here, we have factored out the term β which is common to all the terms capturing future utility. The reason for this manipulation is that the sum within the square brackets represents the consumer's preferences from the perspective of period 1.

Eq. (2.1) allows us to write our problem as:

$$\max_{\{c_t\}_{t=0}^{\infty}} W_0 = \max_{\{c_t\}_{t=0}^{\infty}} \left\{ U(c_0) + \beta \left[\sum_{t=1}^{\infty} \beta^{t-1} U(c_t) \right] \right\}. \tag{2.2}$$

under the constraints $k_{t+1} = f(k_t) + (1-\delta)k_t - c_t$, for $t = 0, 1, ...,$ and given k_0. In plain English, we have proposed a new formulation for the very same problem as that considered in Chapter 1: we wish to determine the optimal consumption c_t^*, and the implied optimal capital level k_{t+1}^*, for $t = 0, 1, \ldots$.

Now consider, in Figure 2.1, the optimal path starting from B and approaching E. This trajectory represents a function, say $\varphi(k_t)$, relating the optimal consumption to the capital stock of the same period. Put differently, c_1^* can be viewed as $c_1^* = \varphi(k_1)$; c_2^* as $c_2^* = \varphi(k_2)$, and so on. The function $c_t^* = \varphi(k_t)$ is unknown, and it can be very complex; actually, only in rare cases the function $\varphi(k_t)$ can be expressed in closed form. Nevertheless, the point is that Figure 2.1 powerfully supports the idea that we have just stated, i.e., that there exists a function relating optimal consumption to the contemporaneous capital stock.

It is also worth underscoring that our function $c_t^* = \varphi(k_t)$ is time invariant, meaning it does not depend on time; in other words it is the same function, regardless of the time period we are considering. The intuition for why $\varphi(k_t)$ is time-independent is that our consumer's perception of the future does not change over time. Because she lives forever, her horizon is

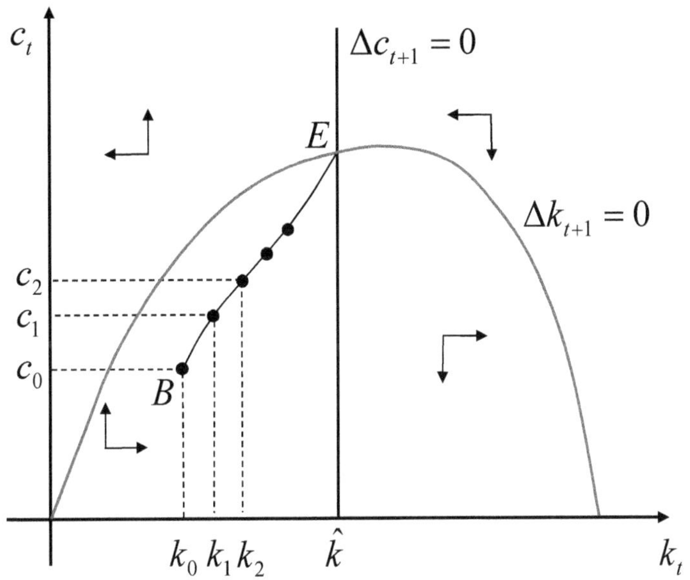

FIGURE 2.1. The equilibrium path as a function relating optimal consumption and capital

infinite at time 0, and remains infinite at time 1. Therefore, her decision should not be based on time, but solely on capital, which is therefore the only state variable in our model.

Note that we have not proved that $\varphi(k_t)$ is continuous and differentiable. However, the evolution of capital and consumption on the optimal path must fulfill Eqs. (1.10) and (1.3), which are based on continuous and differentiable functions. Hence, we have "good reasons to believe" that $\varphi(k_t)$ is actually continuous and differentiable, and we will skip the formal proof for these statements.

Now note that if we can write $c_1^* = \varphi(k_1)$, then we can also express the capital stock at time 2 as a function of k_1. Indeed, from (1.3),

$$k_2^* = f(k_1) + (1 - \delta)k_1 - c_1^*,$$

hence, on the optimal path:

$$k_2^* = f(k_1) + (1 - \delta)k_1 - \varphi(k_1) = \zeta(k_1).$$

The fact that $k_2^* = \zeta(k_1)$ allows us to consider the period-2 consumption as a function of k_1: $c_2^* = \varphi(k_2^*) = \varphi(\zeta(k_1))$. The important point here is that *we can iterate this reasoning to express the whole sequence of optimal consumptions as a function of the period-1 capital stock.* (In fact, in general, $k_{t+1}^* = \zeta(k_t^*)$, and $c_{t+1}^* = \varphi(k_{t+1}^*) = \varphi(\zeta(k_t^*))$, and the substitutions can thus be iterated backwards until the next-to-initial capital level, k_1, is reached.). As a result, when consumption is optimally chosen from period 1 onward, the group of terms in the square brackets in (2.2) can be expressed as a function of k_1 alone:

$$\sum_{t=1}^{\infty} \beta^{t-1} U(c_t^*) = V(k_1).$$

$V(k_1)$ is a "maximum value function," which represents the maximum overall utility that can be obtained in period 1, when the consumption levels are optimally chosen given the available capital stock, k_1, and given the need to fulfill the constraints of the (1.3)-type.

Because the value of all future choices can be summarized in the function $V(k_1)$, we can "translate" our original problem into one in which our consumer, at time 0, chooses only her optimal consumption for that period. This choice must account for the fact that, given the available capital (k_0), an increase in current consumption will reduce the future capital stock (via Eq. (1.3)), which in turn negatively affects the future overall utility $V(k_1)$. Accordingly, the consumer's intertemporal problem can be written as:

$$\max_{c_0} \{U(c_0) + \beta V(k_1)\},$$
$$s.t.\ k_1 = f(k_0) + (1-\delta)k_0 - c_0,$$
$$k_0 \text{ given.}$$

Now, solving her period-0 constrained optimization problem our representative consumer obtains also her period-0 maximum value function, $V(k_0)$, which means that, for any given k_0,

$$V(k_0) = \max_{c_0} \{U(c_0) + \beta V(k_1)\},$$
$$s.t.\ k_1 = f(k_0) + (1-\delta)k_0 - c_0, \tag{2.3}$$

The above problem is said to be expressed in "recursive form" or as a "Bellman equation". While it is easy to understand that Problem (2.3) gets its name from Richard Bellman, the author of the well-known (1957) book, it is not as simple to explain the meaning of the word "recursive" in plain English.

Let us try. A procedure is recursive when one of the steps that makes up the procedure requires a rerunning of the procedure itself. Hence, a recursive procedure involves some degree of "circularity." As a simple example, consider the following recursive definition for the factorial of a positive integer number (denoted by $n!$):

$$\text{«if } n > 1, \text{ then } n! = n(n-1)!; \text{ when } n = 1, \text{ then } 1! = 1\text{»}.$$

The above procedure defines $n!$ by means of $(n-1)!$, which is defined using $(n-2)!$ and so on. This procedure goes on until 1 is reached, at this point, the "termination clause," $1! = 1$, enters into play.

The logic of Problem (2.3) is quite similar: the maximum value $V(k_0)$ is obtained by choosing the current consumption to maximize the sum of the current utility and of the next-period discounted maximum value, which, in turn is obtained by choosing future consumption in order to maximize the sum of the future period utility and of the two periods ahead maximum value, and so on.

The difference between (2.3) and the factorial example lies in the fact that our Bellman equation does not have a termination clause. This is due to the fact that the planning horizon for our representative agent is infinite. If she had to optimize only between period 0 and a given period T, for example because she knew she was going to die at T, it would have been natural to introduce a terminal condition: in this case, the maximum value at time $T+1$ of any capital stock k_{T+1} would have been equal to zero.[1]

Note that the finite-horizon example we have just sketched implies that the maximum value function depends not only on capital, but also on time. In fact, when the agent's time horizon is finite, the maximum value function typically depends on the remaining optimization horizon: how long you are going to live typically matters a lot for you, and it also affects how you evaluate your stock of wealth. Accordingly, at time t the maximum value function is characterized by some terms involving $T-t$ (as it happened in the example in Subsection 1.1.4).

In contrast, in Problem (2.3) the maximum value function depends only on capital. This sometimes strikes attentive students as counterintuitive: the fact that $V(k_t)$ is treated as a function of capital *alone* implies that the functional form of $V(k_t)$ does not change over time. This is despite the fact that–when moving back one period–we discount the future maximum value function and we then add to it the term $U(c_{t-1})$. Indeed, in problem (2.3) we have the very same function $V(k_t)$ both on the left- and on the right-hand sides.

The reason why $V(k_t)$ is independent of time is that our consumer's perception of the future is the same at time 0 and at time 1. This occurs simply because she lives forever. Hence, she bases her consumption decision only on capital, which is therefore the unique state variable in our model. Because the function $V(k_t)$ summarizes the optimal consumption decisions from period t onward, this function likewise depends only on capital.

The time-independence of the maximum value function in infinite horizon frameworks is one of the reasons why these frameworks are so popular: having only one state variable, the maximum value function is less *complex* to compute. Note, however, that the absence of a terminal condition makes the problem of finding a solution conceptually more *difficult.* In fact, when we have a terminal time, we know the value function for that period: this is just the final period utility. Hence, we can always solve the problem for the terminal date, and then work backward toward the present. This simple approach is precluded in infinite-horizon models. Solving a finite-horizon problem is similar to deciding how to send a scientific pod to the surface of the Moon, while the solution to an infinite horizon model is analogous to finding the optimal lunar orbit for the pod. In the former case, you can analyze all possible locations to pick the most convenient one–say, a place in the Sea of Tranquility. Then, working backward, you realize that to send your pod there, you need a lunar module, a spaceship to reach lunar orbit, and finally a Saturn$-V$ rocket to move the spaceship out of the Earth gravitational field. Note that, in this case, you have a clear hint on how to start to work out your sequence of optimal decisions, and your sequence is composed of a finite number of steps. On the contrary, if you need to have the scientific pod orbiting around the Moon, your time horizon is (potentially) infinite, and you need to devise an infinite sequence of decisions. Moreover, because your pod is continuously orbiting, you do not have a clearly specified terminal condition from which to move backward.

The Bellman Equation (2.3) is useful for introducing some of the dynamic programming jargon. The single period payoff (utility) function is most often called the *return function*, the dynamic constraint is referred to as the *transition function*, while a function relating the control variable(s) to the state variable(s) in an optimal way is called the *policy function.* In our example, the policy function is $c_t^* = \varphi(k_t)$, the transition function is $k_{t+1} = f(k_t) + (1-\delta)k_t - c_t$, while the return function is, of course, $U(c_t)$.

Before studying how an infinite horizon problem can be solved, we need to understand the conditions under which the solution to Problem (2.3) exists and is unique. Stokey, Lucas, and Prescott (1989) assure us that

Theorem 1 *If: i) $\beta \in (0,1)$, ii) the return function is continuous, bounded and strictly concave, and iii) the transition function is concave, then the maximum value function $V(k_t)$ not only exists and is unique, but it is also strictly concave, and the policy function is continuous.*

Assumption i) is usually referred to as the "discounting" hypothesis. Assumption ii) requires the utility function $U(c_t)$ to be continuous, bounded and strictly concave, while Assumption iii) constrains the production function to be concave. This ensures that the transition function $k_{t+1} = f(k_t) + (1-\delta)k_t - c_t$ is concave in k_t and–being linear–in c_t.[2]

The above result is neat, but it suffers from a relevant drawback: it does not allow us to work with unbounded utility functions, and hence it does not allow us to assume, for example, that $U(c_t) = \ln(c_t)$. In general, it does not seem easy to justify an assumption that precludes utility from growing without bound (or to be unbounded below as c_t approaches 0).[3]

Unfortunately, there is no general theory that can be applied to optimization problems with unbounded returns. One approach (borrowed from mathematics) is to restrict the maximum value function to belong to a set of continuous functions and then to identify a function that bounds such a set (thereby also bounding $V(k_t)$). When this is possible, the theory developed for bounded returns can be applied with some qualifications.[4] Miao (2014) provides a neat (but not immediate) discussion. Refer, in particular, to his Theorem 7.3.6 and to the example that follows it.[5]

Stokey, Lucas, and Prescott (1989) discuss the case of unbounded returns in some detail, in particular their Theorem 4.14 can be applied to log-utility models so that it is (relatively) easy to show that in these cases the maximum value function exists and is unique. Here we state a more restrictive theorem–originally proposed in Thompson (2004)–that suffices for some applications.

Theorem 2 *(A theorem for unbounded returns). Consider the dynamic problem (2.3). Assume that $\beta \in (0,1)$, and that $\sum_{t=0}^{\infty} \beta^t U(c_t)$ exists and is finite for any feasible path $\{k_t\}_{t=0}^{\infty}$, given k_0. Then there is a unique solution to the dynamic optimization problem.*

Theorem 2 essentially restricts the admissible one-period payoffs to sequences that cannot grow (or decay) too rapidly relative to the discount factor.[6] To see how this theorem applies, consider Figure 1.3. Let $U(c_t)$ be bounded below; when $k_0 < \bar{k}$, capital cannot become larger than $\bar{k}$. Therefore $U(c_t)$ is also bounded above (since c_t is limited by output), and so is $\sum_{t=0}^{\infty} \beta^t U(c_t)$, for any feasible path. This satisfies the theorem's requirements.

While the reasoning about upper boundedness based on Figure 1.3 can be generalized, when the utility function is unbounded below (as in the logarithmic case where $\ln(c_t) \downarrow -\infty$ as $c_t \downarrow 0$), if we can argue that $V(k_0)$ is finite, the theorem gives us "reasons to believe" in the uniqueness of the solution. To verify that $V(k_0)$ is bounded, consider a policy that prescribes consuming a small amount ε–sufficiently low to allow for capital accumulation, given k_0. Note that in finite time the capital stock will reach a level such that $f(k_t) - \delta k_t = \varepsilon$, at which point capital accumulation stops. Such a path yields a finite discounted utility, providing a lower bound for $V(k_0)$.[7]

Finally, let us start considering the problem of finding the solution for the Bellman equation.[8] This is a functional equation, since we need to determine the form of the unknown function $V(.)$.

The first step takes advantage of the fact that Problem (2.3) is an optimization problem. Indeed, it tells us that, to obtain $V(k_0)$, it is necessary to maximize the expression $U(c_0) + \beta V(k_1)$ with respect to c_0. Provided that $V(k_1)$ is continuous and differentiable–as we are ready to accept–the necessary condition for a maximum is obtained by differentiating $U(c_0)+\beta V(k_1)$ with respect to current consumption, which yields:

$$U'(c_0^*) + \beta V'(k_1^*)\frac{\partial k_1}{\partial c_0} = 0, \tag{2.4}$$

where, of course, $\partial k_1/\partial c_0 = -1$ from the capital accumulation equation.

The first-order condition above relates the control variable (current consumption) to the future value of the state variable (k_1). The Bellman equation, the constraint (1.3), and the first-order condition (2.4) form–for given k_0– the following system:

$$\begin{cases} V(k_0) = U(c_0^*) + \beta V(k_1^*) \\ k_1^* = f(k_0) + (1-\delta)k_0 - c_0^* \\ U'(c_0^*) = \beta V'(k_1^*). \end{cases} \tag{2.5}$$

The above system determines the form of the maximum value function $V(k)$, and pins down k_1^* and c_0^* for a given k_0 (thereby also determining the dynamics for capital). Note that the "max" operator in the Bellman equation has disappeared, simply because we have already performed this operation, via Eq. (2.4). Now, consider that when we need to solve a difference or a differential equation–both of which are functional equations–we often (try to) guess the solution. When dealing with a Bellman problem, we can proceed similarly. Chapter 3 provides examples for which this strategy is successful.[9]

2.2 Some more advanced material

At this stage, many students wish to immediately see in which cases, and how, the maximum value function can be obtained in closed form by using the guess-and-verify method; they may then wish to proceed to the analysis of some of the numerical techniques used to obtain the solution when a closed-form solution does not exist. These students can skip the present section, (hopefully) to come back later, and move straight to Chapter 3. Instead, readers with a more theoretical inclination may wish to obtain some details about the reasons why, under appropriate conditions, the maximum value function exists and is unique. They may also wish to know how to identify some of the properties of the solution in cases where an analytical formulation for the maximum value function does not exist.

This section is written for the second group. In particular, Subsection 2.2.1 touches upon the mathematical reasons guaranteeing that the solution to our functional problem exists and is unique; Subsections 2.2.2 and 2.2.3 review the results useful in characterizing the maximum value function.

2.2.1 Existence and uniqueness of the solution for a Bellman problem (*)

In this subsection, we proceed in steps. First, we consider a function defined on the real line and the conditions under which it is a contraction mapping. Then, we state a theorem that guarantees that a contraction mapping has a unique fixed point. The relevance for us lies in the fact that the solution to an equation such as $f(x) = x$ is a fixed point. Subsequently, since the solution to a Bellman equation is a function, not a single point, we state a theorem that allows us to identify a contraction mapping in the space of bounded functions.

The concept of "contraction mapping," which is crucial for proving the existence and uniqueness of the solution to a problem, is introduced by means of a simple example. Consider an agent characterized by the return function $c_t^{1-\gamma}/(1-\gamma)$ with $\gamma \in (1, \infty)$; her subjective discount rate ρ is positive and constant, so that the discount factor $\mu \equiv 1/(1+\rho)$ is lower than 1.[10] She has access to a financial market where she can invest her wealth (and go into debt if optimal), so that the dynamic constraint she faces is $k_{t+1} = (1+\overline{r})\, k_t + \overline{y} - c_t$. Crucially, we assume that the return on capital, $\overline{r}$, is positive, constant over time, and low enough that the condition $\mu(1+\overline{r}) < 1$ holds. The agent's non-capital (labor) income $\overline{y}$, which may be equal to 0, is also constant over time.

The optimal consumption path of our representative agent satisfies:

$$c_t^{-\gamma} = \mu(1+\overline{r})\, c_{t+1}^{-\gamma}. \tag{2.6}$$

Indeed, (2.6) is an Euler equation: the fixed return on investment simply takes on the role of the marginal return on capital, net of depreciation, that we highlighted in Eq. (1.10). Eq. (2.6) quickly becomes:

$$c_{t+1} = (\mu(1+\overline{r}))^{\frac{1}{\gamma}}\, c_t, \tag{2.7}$$

which is a function (a mapping), relating period $t+1$ consumption to period t consumption. It is immediately apparent that there is a unique consumption, $\hat{c}$, such that $c_{t+1} = c_t (= \hat{c})$; this steady-state is $\hat{c} = 0$.

When $\mu(1+\overline{r}) < 1$, Function (2.7) is a *contraction mapping*, as it satisfies the following definition:

Definition 1 *Consider the Euclidean space $\mathbb{R}^n$ and the Euclidean distance d, and let $T : \mathbb{R}^n \to \mathbb{R}^n$ be a function mapping $\mathbb{R}^n$ into itself. T is a contraction mapping with modulus β if for some $\beta \in (0,1)$, $d(Tx, Ty) \leq \beta d(x,y)$, for all $x, y \in \mathbb{R}^n$.*

To verify that Function (2.7) satisfies Definition 1, note that in our case the Euclidean space is simply the real line (more precisely, $\mathbb{R}_+$), and consider two arbitrary consumption levels c_t' and c_t'' (which play the role of the points x, y). Their Euclidean distance is:

$$d(c_t', c_t'') = \sqrt{(c_t'' - c_t')^2}.$$

Applying Function (2.7) to the two consumption levels, we obtain:

$$c_{t+1}' = (\mu(1+\overline{r}))^{\frac{1}{\gamma}}\, c_t',$$

and

$$c_{t+1}'' = (\mu(1+\overline{r}))^{\frac{1}{\gamma}}\, c_t''.$$

Accordingly, we have that

$$d\left(c'_{t+1}, c''_{t+1}\right) = d\left(Tc'_t, Tc''_t\right) = \left(\mu\left(1+\overline{r}\right)\right)^{\frac{1}{\gamma}} \sqrt{\left(c''_t - c'_t\right)^2}.$$

Clearly, $d\left(c'_{t+1}, c''_{t+1}\right) < d\left(c'_t, c''_t\right)$ since $\left(\mu\left(1+\overline{r}\right)\right)^{1/\gamma} < 1$. More precisely, note that we have $d\left(c'_{t+1}, c''_{t+1}\right) \leq \beta d\left(c'_t, c''_t\right)$, where $\beta = \left(\mu\left(1+\overline{r}\right)\right)^{1/\gamma}$ is the modulus of the contraction.

We have defined a contraction mapping in the Euclidean space, but a similar definition applies for every space in which a metric can be defined, as explained, for example, by Stokey, Lucas, and Prescott (1989).

Armed with Definition 1, we now introduce the crucial *Contraction Mapping Theorem,* which is:

Theorem 3 *Consider the Euclidean space $\mathbb{R}^n$ and the Euclidean distance d, and let $T: \mathbb{R}^n \to \mathbb{R}^n$ be a contraction mapping with modulus β, then*

(a) T has exactly one fixed point, $\hat{v}$, in $\mathbb{R}^n$, and

(b) for any $v_0 \in \mathbb{R}^n$, $d\left(T^n v_0, \hat{v}\right) \leq \beta^n d\left(v_0, \hat{v}\right)$, for $n = 0, 1, 2, 3...$

Although the proof of this theorem is simple and elegant, we skip it, referring the interested reader to Theorem 3.2 in Stokey, Lucas, and Prescott (1989), which is formulated for any complete metric space.

Here we check that Theorem 3 holds for Function (2.7), which is a contraction mapping.

As for part (a), note that the unique fixed point of Function (2.7) is $\hat{c} = 0$.

We now verify that applying Function (2.7) over and over again to the initial consumption level moves the result closer and closer to the fixed point (which is part (b)). In our case, the role of v_0 is played by the arbitrary consumption level c'_0, while the fixed point $\hat{v}$ is of course $\hat{c} = 0$. Note that, a single application of Function (2.7) transforms c'_0 into:

$$c'_1 = Tc'_0 = \left(\mu\left(1+\overline{r}\right)\right)^{1/\gamma} c'_0.$$

If we iterate for two periods we obtain:

$$c'_2 = T^2 c'_0 = \left(\mu\left(1+\overline{r}\right)\right)^{2/\gamma} c'_0,$$

and iterating n times:

$$c'_n \left(= T^n c'_0\right) = \left(\mu\left(1+\overline{r}\right)\right)^{n/\gamma} c'_0.$$

Since the fixed point is $\hat{c} = 0$, the distance between $T^n c_0'$ and $\hat{c}$ is:

$$d\left(T^n c_0', \hat{c}\right)\left(= \sqrt{\left(\left(\mu\left(1+\bar{r}\right)\right)^{n/\gamma} c_0' - \hat{c}\right)^2}\right) = \left(\mu\left(1+\bar{r}\right)\right)^{n/\gamma} c_0',$$

so that, with $\beta = \left(\mu\left(1+\bar{r}\right)\right)^{1/\gamma} < 1$, $d\left(c_n', \hat{c}\right) \leq \beta^n d\left(c_0', \hat{c}\right)$ holds with equality. Hence, part (b) of Theorem 3 is verified.

Please take a moment to reflect on the importance of the Contraction Mapping Theorem: it guarantees that if a function is a contraction mapping, iterating the function we "move toward" its unique fixed point, which–importantly–can well be unknown.

Our discussion of a contraction mapping is not per se very helpful in demonstrating the existence and uniqueness of the maximum value *function.* In fact, we have considered a *given* function and we have shown that–under appropriate conditions–applying this function over and over again to an initial condition, we move toward the fixed point. However, when considering a Bellman problem, what we need to find is not a point, but a function. As already remarked, our problem is a *functional* one. Actually, we are dealing with a "space" composed of bounded functions (let us denote it by $B(X)$, in which X is the subset of $\mathbb{R}^n$ for which the set of functions is defined).

This fact has implications for the definition of a "distance." Clearly, the Euclidean distance is no longer appropriate: while it is of immediate use when we deal with "points," we now need to measure the distance between functions. In this case, the most frequently used distance is the "*sup norm,*" which is defined as follows. Consider two functions, $f(x)$ and $g(x)$, defined over a set X. The expression

$$\sup_{x \in X} \{|f(x) - g(x)|\}$$

defines a distance. Specifically, it identifies the largest difference (in absolute value) between the values of the two functions as the "distance" between them. This distance is the *sup norm* (or supremum norm), which can be considered a generalization of the Euclidean distance.

Theorem 3.2 in Stokey, Lucas, and Prescott (1989), which corresponds to our Theorem 3, applies to the space of bounded functions $B(X)$ (and not just to the Euclidean space), using the "sup norm" as the distance between functions. While we once again refer the interested reader to Stokey, Lucas, and Prescott (1989), here we introduce "Blackwell's Sufficient Conditions" for a contraction, relying on their Theorem 3.3:

Theorem 4 *Let $X \subseteq \mathbb{R}^n$, and let $B(X)$ be a space of bounded functions $f : X \longrightarrow \mathbb{R}$, with the sup norm. Let $T : B(X) \longrightarrow B(X)$ be an operator satisfying:*

(a) (monotonicity) $f, g \in B(X)$ and $f(x) \leq g(x)$ for all $x \in X$ imply $Tf(x) \leq Tg(x)$ for all $x \in X$, and

(b) (discounting) there exist some $\beta \in (0,1)$ such that $T(f(x) + a) \leq Tf(x) + \beta a$ for all constants $a > 0$, and for all $f \in B(X)$, $x \in X$,

then T is a contraction mapping with modulus β.

Once again we skip the proof and instead verify that the maximization operator in the Bellman formulation for the growth model is a contraction mapping.

We report our recursive formulation here for convenience:

$$V(k_0) = \max_{c_0} \{U(c_0) + \beta V(k_1)\},$$
$$s.t.\ k_1 = f(k_0) + (1-\delta)k_0 - c_0,$$
$$k_0 \text{ given.}$$

By substituting the intertemporal constraint in the utility function, our problem is reformulated as:

$$V(k_0) = \max_{k_1} \{U(f(k_0) + (1-\delta)k_0 - k_1) + \beta V(k_1)\},$$

so that the operator T is defined as:

$$TV(k_0) = \max_{k_1} \{U(f(k_0) + (1-\delta)k_0 - k_1) + \beta V(k_1)\}. \tag{2.8}$$

To prove that T is a contraction, we need to verify that it fulfills the conditions of Theorem 4.

As for monotonicity, consider two functions, $W(k_0)$ and $V(k_0)$, such that $W(k_0) \leq V(k_0)$ for all $k_0 \geq 0$. Let k_1^* be the optimal next-period capital stock for function $W(k_0)$, that is,

$$TW(k_0) = U(f(k_0) + (1-\delta)k_0 - k_1^*) + \beta W(k_1^*).$$

Because $W(k_0) \leq V(k_0)$ for all k_0, we also have $W(k_1^*) \leq V(k_1^*)$, so that:

$$TW(k_0) \leq U(f(k_0) + (1-\delta)k_0 - k_1^*) + \beta V(k_1^*).$$

Note that k_1^* is the optimal choice for $W(k_0)$, and that the optimal choice for $V(k_0)$, denoted by k_1^{**}, is the value for k_1 that solves:

$$\max_{k_1} \{U(f(k_0) + (1-\delta)k_0 - k_1) + \beta V(k_1)\}.$$

Because the value of $U(f(k_0) + (1-\delta)k_0 - k_1) + \beta V(k_1)$ is maximal at k_1^{**}, it cannot be lower than $U(f(k_0)+(1-\delta)k_0 - k_1^*)+\beta V(k_1^*)$, from which it follows that:

$$\begin{aligned} TW(k_0) \leq U(f(k_0) + (1-\delta)k_0 - k_1^*) + \beta V(k_1^*) \leq \\ \leq U(f(k_0) + (1-\delta)k_0 - k_1^{**}) + \beta V(k_1^{**}) = TV(k_0), \end{aligned}$$

which establishes monotonicity.

As for discounting, consider the candidate maximum value functions $V(k_0)$ and let a be a positive constant. We have that:

$$\begin{aligned} T(V(k_0) + a) &= \max_{k_1} \{U(f(k_0) + (1-\delta)k_0 - k_1) + \beta\,(V(k_1) + a)\} = \\ &= \max_{k_1} \{U(f(k_0) + (1-\delta)k_0 - k_1) + \beta V(k_1) + \beta a\} = \\ &= TV(k_0) + \beta a, \end{aligned}$$

which implies that discounting is satisfied (with equality).

Loosely speaking, the fact that the "max" operator is a contraction mapping is of paramount importance. It guarantees that the solution to the Bellman problem–the maximum value function–not only exists, but it is also unique (part (a) of Theorem 3). Moreover it tells us that starting from an arbitrary function V_0, and solving the maximization problem, we obtain a function which is closer to the true maximum value function (part (b) of Theorem 3). This fact will be exploited in Section 4.1.

2.2.2 *The Envelope Theorem (*)*

In this subsection, we introduce the Envelope Theorem by applying it to the growth model as formulated in Problem (2.3). The results we obtain are not only important but also of general relevance.

To save on notation, we denote the transition function by $k_1 = g(k_0, c_0)$; accordingly, the recursive formulation for our utility-maximization problem becomes:

$$V(k_0) = \max_{c_0} \{U(c_0) + \beta V(k_1)\}, \ \textit{s.t.}\ k_1 = g(k_0, c_0),\ k_0 \text{ given.}$$

We already know that the first-order condition with respect to the control variable is[11] $U_c(c_0^*) + \beta V_k(k_1^*)(\partial k_1/\partial c_0) = 0$. Consider now the Bellman problem above, assuming we are on the optimal path. In this case, we have:

$$V(k_0) = U(c_0^*) + \beta V(k_1^*)$$

(the max operator disappears precisely because we are already on the path along which consumption is optimal). The total differential[12] for the last equation is: $dV(k_0) = dU(c_0^*) + \beta dV(k_1^*)$, or

$$V_k(k_0)dk_0 = U_c(c_0^*)dc_0 + \beta V_k(k_1^*)dk_1.$$

The differential for k_1 can be easily obtained from the dynamic constraint, and is $dk_1 = g_k(k_0, c_0)dk_0 + g_c(k_0, c_0)dc_0$ (where $g_c(k_0, c_0) = -1$).

By exploiting dk_1, the total differential for the Bellman equation becomes:

$$V_k(k_0)dk_0 = U_c(c_0^*)dc_0 + \beta V_k(k_1^*)\left[g_k(k_0, c_0^*)dk_0 + g_c(k_0, c_0^*)dc_0\right].$$

This expression, by using the first-order condition for c_0, reduces to:

$$V_k(k_0) = \beta V_k(k_1^*) g_k(k_0, c_0^*).$$

This is the result of applying the Envelope Theorem: the simplification in the total differential arises precisely because we are on the optimal path, where the first-order condition is satisfied.

Note that we could have expressed the above result as follows:

$$V_k(k_0) = \beta V_k(k_1^*)\frac{\partial k_1}{\partial k_0}, \tag{2.9}$$

where $\partial k_1/\partial k_0$ is the partial derivative $g_k(k_0, c_0^*)$.

Equation (2.9) can be useful in several contexts. In fact, it can be reformulated in a very convenient way. Since the first-order condition states that $U_c(c_0^*) = \beta V_k(k_1^*)$, it also holds that $U_c(c_1^*) = \beta V_k(k_2^*)$. With these facts in mind, we advance equation (2.9) by one period, and we obtain:

$$U_c(c_0^*) = \beta U_c(c_1^*) g_k(k_1^*, c_1^*), \tag{2.10}$$

which is the Euler equation (bear in mind that $g_k(k_1, c_1) = f'(k_1) + 1 - \delta$, and refer to (1.10)). Not only is it often easier to solve numerically Eq. (2.10) than the Bellman one–as we shall see in Section 5.1–but Eq. (2.10) can also be interpreted without referring to the still-unknown maximum value function.

2.2.3 The Benveniste and Scheinkman formula (*)

In this subsection we consider a more general framework, where the return function, now denoted by $Q(.)$, does not depend only on the control variable(s), but it also depends on the state(s). In this case the dynamic programming formulation for our consumption-saving problem is:

$$V(k_0) = \max_{c_0} \{Q(k_0, c_0) + \beta V(k_1)\},$$

$$s.t.\ k_1 = g(k_0, c_0),\ k_0 \text{ given.}$$

The first-order condition with respect to the control variable gives:

$$Q_c(k_0, c_0^*) + \beta V_k(k_1^*) \frac{\partial k_1}{\partial c_0} = 0.$$

Assume, as in the previous subsection, that we are on the optimal path:

$$V(k_0) = Q(k_0, c_0^*) + \beta V(k_1^*).$$

The total differential for the last equation is: $dV(k_0) = dQ(k_0, c_0^*) + \beta dV(k_1^*)$, or:

$$V_k(k_0)dk_0 = Q_c(k_0, c_0^*)dc_0 + Q_k(k_0, c_0^*)dk_0 + \beta V_k(k_1^*)dk_1.$$

The differential for period 1 capital–obtained from the dynamic constraint–is $dk_1 = g_k(k_0, c_0)dk_0 + g_c(k_0, c_0)dc_0$. Hence, the total differential for the Bellman's equation becomes:

$$V_k(k_0)dk_0 =$$
$$= Q_c(k_0, c_0^*)dc_0 + Q_k(k_0, c_0^*)dk_0 + \beta V_k(k_1^*)\left[g_k(k_0, c_0^*)dk_0 + g_c(k_0, c_0^*)dc_0\right].$$

Using the first-order condition, the equation above reduces to:

$$V_k(k_0) = Q_k(k_0, c_0^*) + \beta V_k(k_1^*) g_k(k_0, c_0^*). \tag{2.11}$$

This is the Benveniste and Scheinkman formula, obtained as an application of the Envelope Theorem.

The usefulness of (2.11) can be appreciated by considering that, in many problems, the definition of states and controls is not unique. For example, in the growth model, one could define the control variable not as consumption, but as gross savings (which means that the control is $s_t = f(k_t) - c_t$). When depreciation is complete (i.e., when $\delta = 1$), this modification implies that the next-period state is equal to the current control ($k_{t+1} = s_t$), and the Bellman problem (2.3) becomes:

$$V(k_0) = \max_{s_0} \{U(f(k_0) - s_0) + \beta V(k_1)\},$$
$$s.t.\ k_1 = s_0,\ k_0 \text{ given.} \tag{2.12}$$

The first-order condition is: $U_c\left(f(k_0) - s_0^*\right) = \beta V_k(k_1)$.[13]

Differentiating the Bellman equation "on the optimal path," we obtain:

$$V_k(k_0)dk_0 = U_c\left(f(k_0) - s_0^*\right)\left(df(k_0) - ds_0\right) + \beta V_k(k_1^*)dk_1.$$

Because $dk_1/ds_0 = 1$, using the first order condition the differential simplifies to:

$$V_k(k_0) = U_c\left(f(k_0) - s_0^*\right) f_k(k_0), \tag{2.13}$$

which is how the Benveniste and Scheinkman formula applies to this problem.[14]

Formula (2.13) highlights a relationship between the maximum value function, the return function, and the dynamic constraint. The Benveniste and Scheinkman formula leads to this relation when the transition function is such that the state variable in period $t+1$ does not depend on the state in period t (i.e., when the partial derivative of the dynamic constraint with respect to period t state variable is 0). For this to be true, it is necessary that the current period state variable (k_0) is excluded from the dynamic constraint, as happens in Problem (2.12). The example we have just developed shows that this can be achieved by means of an appropriate variable redefinition.[15]

Notes

[1] Accordingly, the period T maximum value would have simply been $V(k_T) = U(c_T)$ with $c_T = f(k_T) + (1 - \delta)k_T$.

[2] A logarithmic utility and a Cobb-Douglas production function, satisfying Assumptions (i), (ii), (a) and (b) in Chapter 1 meet the concavity requirement in Theorem 1.

[3] Unfortunately, the boundedness of the return function is an essential component of the proof for the results stated in Theorem 1. In fact, to prove existence and uniqueness for $V(k_t)$, one needs to use an appropriate fixed-point theorem, because the function

$V(k_t)$ is the fixed point of Problem (2.3), and the proofs of fixed-point theorems require the boundedness of the functions involved.

[4]Loosely speaking, Theorem 2 can be interpreted as applying this idea to our context.

[5]Miao (2014) provides also a sharp discussion of the literature on this specific issue. The interested reader can also refer to Stachurski (2009).

[6]The proof is based on the idea that *if* the sum $\sum_{t=0}^{\infty} \beta^t U(c_t)$ exists and is finite, then the maximum value function is also finite, allowing the application of an appropriate fixed-point theorem. Some more on this in Subsection 2.2.1.

[7]The conditions stated in Theorem 1 or, alternatively, in Theorem 2 imply the fulfillment of Blackwell's sufficient conditions for a contraction. On this, refer to Theorem 4 in Subsection 2.2.1.

[8]Notice that from the way we have formulated Problem (2.3) it is now natural to look for the function $V(.)$, whereas our discussion in the previous chapter may have induced the belief that the policy function is what is truly important. It will soon become clear that once we have obtained the maximum value function $V(.)$ it is easy to obtain the policy function.

[9]*A caveat lector*: we have been able to reformulate our intertemporal maximization problem into the recursive form (2.3) because the payoff function and the intertemporal constraint are time-separable. Moreover, if our agent's utility depended not only on current but also on future (expected) consumption levels, we would need to tackle a time-inconsistency problem. For a simple introduction to this specific issue, see de la Fuente (2000, Ch. 12).

[10]The (temporary) change in notation for the subjective discount factor is to avoid confusion with the "modulus of the contraction", which will be introduced shortly, and which is commonly denoted by β.

[11]Partial derivatives will soon come into play. Hence, we start denoting derivatives with a subscript. For example, $g_k(k_0, c_0)$ is the partial derivative of $g(k_0, c_0)$ with respect to capital, and so on. This convention will be maintained except for models and exercises in which we only need to differentiate functions with only one argument.

[12]The increase in the state variable k_0 is to be interpreted as hypothetical.

[13]Alternatively, defining $U(c_0) \left(= U(f(k_0) - s_0)\right) \equiv Q(k_0, s_0)$, we obtain

$$Q_s(k_0, s_0^*) + \beta V_k(k_1^*) = 0.$$

[14]Note that:

$$Q_k(k_0, s_0)\, dk_0 = U_c(f(k_0) - s_0)\, df(k_0)$$

and

$$Q_s(k_0, s_0)\, ds_0 = -U_c(f(k_0) - s_0)\, ds_0.$$

Differentiating the Bellman equation on the optimal path we obtain:

$$V_k(k_0)dk_0 = Q_k(k_0, s_0^*)\, dk_0 + Q_s(k_0, s_0^*)\, ds_0 + \beta V_k(k_1^*)dk_1,$$

which coincides with (2.13).

[15]Refer to Sargent (1987) pp. 21-27 for a discussion and an alternative example.

3

Guess and verify

ABSTRACT Only a few functional forms for the payoff function and the dynamic constraint allow for a closed-form expression of the maximum value function. This chapter discusses two well-known cases: logarithmic preferences coupled with the Cobb-Douglas production function and quadratic preferences with a linear constraint.

3.1 Logarithmic preferences and Cobb-Douglas production

In this section, we analyze our standard version of the Ramsey optimal growth model. We will propose a tentative solution and then verify that the guess is correct.

The consumer's time horizon is infinite, and her preferences are logarithmic:

$$W_0 = \sum_{t=0}^{\infty} \beta^t \ln(c_t), \tag{3.1}$$

with $\beta \in (0, 1)$. In the jargon, we analyze the case of a logarithmic return function. The production function is a Cobb-Douglas with $\delta = 1$, hence

DOI: 10.4324/9781003774051-3

capital depreciates completely in one period. Accordingly, we have that:

$$k_{t+1} = Ak_t^{\alpha} - c_t, \tag{3.2}$$

where the "total factor productivity" parameter A is constant and $\alpha \in (0, 1)$.

Our problem is to solve:

$$V(k_0) = \max_{c_0} \{\ln(c_0) + \beta V(k_1)\},$$
$$s.t.\ k_1 = Ak_0^{\alpha} - c_0,$$
$$k_0 \text{ given.}$$

The first-order condition, corresponding to Eq. (2.4), is: $1/c_0^* = \beta V'(k_1^*)$. This condition must be exploited in the problem above to substitute out consumption. This yields:

$$\begin{cases} V(k_0) = \ln([\beta V'(k_1^*)]^{-1}) + \beta V(k_1^*) \\ k_1^* = Ak_0^{\alpha} - (\beta V'(k_1^*))^{-1} \\ k_0 \text{ given.} \end{cases} \tag{3.3}$$

This formulation makes it apparent once again that the Bellman equation is a functional equation: it involves the function $V(k)$ and its derivative $V'(k)$; the constraint incorporates the initial condition for the state variable. Note that because k_0 is given, once $V'(k)$ is known, the constraint determines k_1^* and therefore the evolution of the capital stock. Note also that System (3.3) corresponds to (2.5), except for the fact that here we have directly substituted c_0^* with $[\beta V'(k_1^*)]^{-1}$.

We aim to find the solution to the functional equation problem by means of a tentative solution, which in this case takes the form:

$$V(k_t) = e + f \ln(k_t), \tag{3.4}$$

where e and f are two constants to be determined, i.e., two undetermined coefficients.[1] Spend a few seconds considering the guess (3.4). It is a linear transformation of the utility function in which the control variable has been substituted with the state variable. When trying to devise a tentative solution, it is usually sensible to proceed as we have done–namely, by starting with a guess that is "similar" to the return function.

Using the guess and substituting it in (3.3), we obtain, for a given k_0:

$$\begin{cases} e + f\ln(k_0) = \ln\left(\frac{k_1}{\beta f}\right) + \beta[e + f\ln(k_1)] \\ k_1 = Ak_0^\alpha - \frac{k_1}{\beta f}. \end{cases} \tag{3.5}$$

One immediately notes that the second equation may be solved for k_1:

$$k_1 = \frac{\beta f}{1+\beta f} Ak_0^\alpha, \tag{3.6}$$

so that

$$c_0 = \frac{1}{1+\beta f} Ak_0^\alpha.$$

By substituting (3.6) in the first equation of (3.5), we get:

$$e + f\ln(k_0) = \ln\left(\frac{1}{1+\beta f} Ak_0^\alpha\right) + \beta\left[e + f\ln\left(\frac{\beta f}{1+\beta f} Ak_0^\alpha\right)\right].$$

Taking advantage of the usual properties of logarithmic functions, we obtain:

$$\begin{aligned} e + f\ln(k_0) &= -\ln(1+\beta f) + \ln A + \alpha \ln k_0 + \\ &\quad + \beta e + \beta f \ln(\beta f) - \beta f \ln(1+\beta f) + \beta f \ln A + \alpha\beta f \ln k_0. \end{aligned}$$

The above equation must be satisfied for *any* k_0 and for *any* admissible value of the parameters A, β, and α. Hence, it must be true that:

$$\begin{cases} f = \alpha + \alpha\beta f \\ e = -\ln(1+\beta f) + \ln A + \beta e + \beta f \ln(\beta f) - \beta f \ln(1+\beta f) + \beta f \ln A. \end{cases}$$

From the first equation in the system above we obtain:

$$f = \frac{\alpha}{1-\alpha\beta}.$$

Note that $f > 0$, because $\alpha, \beta \in (0,1)$. This implies $V'(k) > 0$, a sensible result that tells us a richer consumer enjoys a higher overall utility. Substituting f in the second equation gives:

$$e = \frac{1}{1-\beta}\left[\frac{\alpha\beta}{1-\alpha\beta}\ln(\alpha\beta) + \ln(1-\alpha\beta) + \frac{1}{1-\alpha\beta}\ln A\right]. \tag{3.7}$$

The equation above provides intuition as to why we need to assume $\beta < 1$: if this requirement were not fulfilled (i.e., were $\beta = 1$), the maximum value function would "explode" to infinity.

Because f and e are independent of capital, our guess (3.4) is verified.

By substituting f into (3.6), we obtain: $k_1^* = \alpha\beta A k_0^\alpha$, which is the specific form of the function $k_{t+1}^* = \zeta(k_t)$ introduced in Chapter 2.

From the first-order condition, we know that $c_0^* = 1/\left[\beta V'(k_1^*)\right]$. Therefore, using our guess, the value for f, and the fact that $k_1^* = \alpha\beta A k_0^\alpha$, we obtain: $c_0^* = (1-\alpha\beta)Ak_0^\alpha$, which is the function $c_t^* = \varphi(k_t)$ that applies to this example.

The consumption function $c_0^* = (1-\alpha\beta)Ak_0^\alpha$ is a neat but somehow uninteresting result: it prescribes a very simple consumption behavior. The representative agent must consume, in each period, a constant share $1-\alpha\beta$ of her current income, Ak_t^α. Note, however, that this share decreases with both β and α, which makes economic sense: an increase in β implies that the future is more important, while an increase in α, which leads to a higher marginal productivity of capital, increases the incentive to save.

Note also that our consumption function relates the control variable to the state variable: that is what any well-behaved policy function should do. Finally, from $k_1^* = \alpha\beta A k_0^\alpha$, we can easily obtain the steady-state level of capital, that is: $\hat{k} = (\alpha\beta A)^{1/(1-\alpha)}$.

3.1.1 *Is the maximum value function unique? (*)*

Having already obtained a unique maximum value function for our standard version of the Ramsey model, it is certainly weird to ask ourselves whether it is ... unique. Nevertheless, this is what we do in the present subsection, in which we show that the utility and production functions under consideration give rise to a value function that is bounded above. This effort is motivated by the desire to develop a line of reasoning that may be helpful when a closed-form solution for the maximum value function cannot be found. The uninterested reader may skip the subsection and move directly to Exercise 6. The jump has a drawback: Exercise 9 will prove rather difficult.

Recall that $U(c_t) = \ln c_t$, and that $k_{t+1} = Ak_t^\alpha - c_t$. Let us start our analysis in period 0 with an endowment of capital equal to k_0''. Note that the path characterized by the fastest possible growth for capital is obtained by choosing zero consumption in each period. This path is given by $k_1'' = A\left(k_0''\right)^\alpha$, $k_2'' = A\left(k_1''\right)^\alpha$, ... Hence, in general, after t periods, the logarithm of the capital stock on this path is:

$$\begin{aligned}\ln k_t'' &= \ln A + \alpha \ln k_{t-1}'' = \ln A + \alpha \ln A + \alpha^2 \ln k_{t-2}'' + ... = \\ &= \frac{1-\alpha^t}{1-\alpha}\ln A + \alpha^t \ln k_0''.\end{aligned}$$

Note also that–in period t–the maximum one-period utility is obtained by consuming the entire output that the representative agent can produce at that time, that is:

$$U(c_t'') = \ln(Ak_t''^{\alpha}) = \ln A + \alpha \ln k_t''.$$

Therefore, if we follow the policy of saving everything up to period $t-1$ and then consuming the whole output, we obtain:

$$U(c_t'') = \ln A + \alpha \ln k_t'' = \frac{1-\alpha^{t+1}}{1-\alpha} \ln A + \alpha^{t+1} \ln k_0''.$$

Imagine, however absurdly, that the above policy could be followed in *every* period (this would require, at the very least, the intervention of a powerful wizard!). In this case, the lifetime utility for the representative agent would be:

$$\begin{aligned}\sum_{t=0}^{\infty} \beta^t \ln c_t'' &= \sum_{t=0}^{\infty} \beta^t \left(\frac{1-\alpha^{t+1}}{1-\alpha} \ln A + \alpha^{t+1} \ln k_0'' \right) = \\ &= \frac{1}{(1-\beta)(1-\beta\alpha)} \ln A + \frac{\alpha}{1-\beta\alpha} \ln k_0''.\end{aligned}$$

The above expression is obviously finite. Clearly, any *feasible* path would yield a lower lifetime utility; therefore, any feasible sequence of payoffs must be bounded above (in present value). This implies that the maximum value function is also bounded above. Following the reasoning in Section 2.1 we then argue that it is reasonable to assume that the maximum value function is unique.[2]

Exercise 6 is based on a deterministic version of Brock and Mirman (1972).

Exercise 6 *Assume that i) the return function is:* $\ln c_t + \gamma \ln(1-l_t)$, *where* $l_t \in [0,1]$ *is the share of time devoted to labor, and* $\gamma \in (0,\infty)$; *ii)* $\beta \in (0,1)$; *iii) the dynamic constraint is* $k_{t+1} = Ak_t^{\alpha} l_t^{1-\alpha} - c_t$, *with* $A \in (0,\infty)$ *and* $\alpha \in (0,1)$. *Find the value function and the associated policy functions. (Hint: since there are two control variables, the first-order conditions ...)*

Exercise 7 *(Habit persistence) Assume that i) the return function is:* $\ln c_t - \gamma \ln(c_{t-1})$, *where* $\gamma \in (0, 1/\beta)$; *ii)* $\beta \in (0,1)$; *iii) the dynamic constraint is* $k_{t+1} = Ak_t^{\alpha} - c_t$, *with* $A \in (0,\infty)$ *and* $\alpha \in (0,1)$. *Find the value function and the associated policy function.*

(Hint: consider past consumption as a state variable, hence the value function has two arguments: k_t and c_{t-1}...)

Exercise 8 *Assume that i) the return function is: $c_t^{1-\gamma}/(1-\gamma)$, where $\gamma \in [0,1) \cup (1,\infty)$; ii) $\beta \in (0,1)$; iii) the dynamic constraint is $k_{t+1} = Ak_t - c_t$, with $A \in (0,\infty)$. Find the value function and the associated policy function, introducing an appropriate restriction relating A, β and γ.*

The next exercise is based on Subsection 3.1.1.

Exercise 9 *For the return and the transition functions used in the previous Exercise 8, provide a condition on γ such that the the maximum value function is bounded above.*

The next three exercises are based on Subsections 2.2.2 and 2.2.3.

Exercise 10 *Taking advantage of the Envelope Theorem, find as many details as possible of the maximum value function for the version of the Ramsey model discussed in Section 3.1.*

Exercise 11 *Apply the Benveniste-Scheinkman formula to the traditional (Ramsey) growth model (with $\delta = 1$), and discuss under which condition the maximum value function is concave.*

Exercise 12 *By means of an appropriate change of variable, find the equivalent of formula (2.13) for the traditional growth model when $\delta < 1$.*

3.2 Quadratic preferences with a linear constraint

We now consider a consumer, whose time horizon is again infinite, characterized by "quadratic" preferences:

$$W_0 = \sum_{t=0}^{\infty} \beta^t \left(\varepsilon + \gamma c_t - \frac{\eta}{2} c_t^2 \right), \text{ with } \beta \in (0,1). \tag{3.8}$$

Assuming the parameters γ and η are positive,[3] the marginal utility for our consumer is positive for $c_t < \gamma/\eta$, while it is negative for $c_t > \gamma/\eta$. Hence, the return function is at its maximum when $c_t = \gamma/\eta$, which is called the "bliss point" in consumption (with the corresponding utility being $\varepsilon + \gamma^2/(2\eta)$).

The intertemporal constraint is linear in the state variable k_t:

$$k_{t+1} = (1+r)k_t - c_t. \tag{3.9}$$

Note that we may interpret k_t as the consumer's financial assets and $r > 0$ as the interest rate. Note also that, because the utility function is strictly concave and bounded above and the transition function is concave, we assume that the value function is unique (which can be verified e.g. exploiting the transversality condition).

Our problem is to solve:

$$V(k_0) = \max_{c_0} \left\{ \varepsilon + \gamma c_0 - \frac{\eta}{2} c_0^2 + \beta V(k_1) \right\},$$
$$s.t.\ k_1 = (1+r)k_0 - c_0,$$
$$k_0 \text{ given.}$$

As before, we find the first-order condition, which is: $\gamma - \eta c_0^* = \beta V'(k_1^*)$. From the dynamic constraint, we obtain $c_0 = (1+r)k_0 - k_1$, which is used to substitute consumption out of the Bellman equation and the first-order condition. This yields

$$\begin{cases} V(k_0) = \varepsilon + \gamma[(1+r)k_0 - k_1^*] - \frac{\eta}{2}[(1+r)k_0 - k_1^*]^2 + \beta V(k_1^*) \\ \gamma - \eta[(1+r)k_0 - k_1^*] = \beta V'(k_1^*) \\ k_0 \text{ given.} \end{cases} \tag{3.10}$$

Note that System (3.10) corresponds to (2.5), except for the fact that we have substituted out c_0^* by exploiting the linear constraint (3.9).

The logic of the solution method is the same as in the previous example. Accordingly, we now introduce the tentative solution, which takes the same functional form as the return function:

$$V(k_t) = g + hk_t + \frac{m}{2} k_t^2, \tag{3.11}$$

where g, h, and m are the undetermined coefficients. The (small) difference with the example in Section 3.1 is that in the present case we shall set up a three-equations system, because we need to determine three coefficients.

First, exploiting our guess (3.11), we obtain from the second equation in (3.10):

$$k_0 = \frac{1}{1+r} \left[\frac{\gamma - \beta h}{\eta} + \frac{\eta - \beta m}{\eta} k_1 \right]. \tag{3.12}$$

The equation above implies that the transition function is linear:

$$k_{t+1} = \frac{\beta h - \gamma}{\eta - \beta m} + \frac{\eta\,(1+r)}{\eta - \beta m} k_t, \tag{3.13}$$

which requires that $m \neq \eta/\beta$.

By substituting the guess (3.11) for $V(k_0)$ and $V(k_1)$ into the first equation of (3.10), and taking advantage of Eq. (3.12), we obtain a quadratic equation in k_1. Because this equation must be satisfied for any value of k_1, it must be true that:

$$\begin{cases} g + \frac{h}{1+r}\left(\frac{\gamma-\beta h}{\eta}\right) + \frac{m}{2(1+r)^2}\left(\frac{\gamma-\beta h}{\eta}\right)^2 = \varepsilon + \frac{\gamma}{\eta}(\gamma - \beta h) - \frac{(\gamma-\beta h)^2}{2\eta} + \beta g \\ \frac{h}{1+r}\left(\frac{\eta-\beta m}{\eta}\right) + \frac{m}{(1+r)^2}\left(\frac{\eta-\beta m}{\eta}\right)\left(\frac{\gamma-\beta h}{\eta}\right) = -\frac{\gamma\beta m}{\eta} + \frac{(\gamma-\beta h)\beta m}{\eta} + \beta h \\ \frac{m}{2(1+r)^2}\left(\frac{\eta-\beta m}{\eta}\right)^2 = -\frac{(\beta m)^2}{2\eta} + \frac{\beta m}{2}. \end{cases} \tag{3.14}$$

Inspection of the above system reveals that it is convenient to solve the third equation first, as the unique unknown it involves is m. From this equation, we obtain that three sets of possible solutions exist; however, one of the three requires $m = \eta/\beta$ and is therefore discarded.

To examine the other two sets of solutions, it is necessary to distinguish between the case where $\beta\,(1+r) \neq 1$ and the case where $\beta\,(1+r) = 1$.

The former case splits into two sub-cases. First, let $m' = 0$; we immediately obtain $h' = 0$ from the second equation in (3.14), and then, from the first equation, we get $g' = \left(\varepsilon + \gamma^2/(2\eta)\right) / (1-\beta)$. Our tentative solution (3.11) is verified, but the value function it identifies does not depend on the available stock of resources, which is very suspicious. Indeed, one can show that consumption is constant and equal–independently of the available capital stock–to the level corresponding to the "bliss point" (γ/η); accordingly, for any initial stock below the steady state, capital collapses to 0 in finite time.[4] This solution does not represent a maximum. (Prove this.)

Then, consider m'':

$$m'' = \frac{\eta}{\beta}[1 - \beta(1+r)^2]. \tag{3.15}$$

By inserting (3.15) into the second equation in (3.14), we get an equation which can be solved for h, yielding:

$$h'' = \frac{\gamma}{\beta r}\left[\beta(1+r)^2 - 1\right]. \tag{3.16}$$

Finally, we can use (3.16) and (3.15) in the first equation in (3.14) to obtain g'':

$$g'' = \frac{\varepsilon}{1-\beta} + \frac{\gamma^2}{2\eta\beta(1-\beta)}\left[\frac{1-\beta(1+r)}{r}\right]^2. \tag{3.17}$$

From (3.17) we see once again why the assumption $\beta < 1$ is crucial: it prevents the maximum value function from exploding to infinity. Because g'', h'' and m'' are independent of the state variable–that is, capital–our guess (3.11) is correct, and what we need to do is to verify that solution (3.15-3.17) satisfies the transversality condition (tvc).

When $\beta(1+r) = 1$, the parameter values identified by (3.15-3.17), properly simplified, still represent a solution. When instead $m' = 0$, the second equation in (3.14) shows that h' is undetermined. Thus, we have

$$g' = \frac{1}{1-\beta}\left(\varepsilon + \frac{(\gamma - \beta h')^2}{2\eta}\right). \tag{3.18}$$

As mentioned above, to complete the discussion, we need to verify whether the tvc is fulfilled. In this respect, The next subsection considers the particular case $\beta(1+r) = 1$, while the general discussion (for $\beta(1+r) \lessgtr 1$) is left to Exercise 13.[5]

Exercise 13 *In the linear-quadratic example, (a) study the dynamics for c_t and k_t if $\beta(1+r) > 1$ and discuss whether the transversality condition is satisfied; (b) study the dynamics for c_t and k_t if $\beta(1+r) < 1$ and discuss whether the transversality condition is satisfied.*

Exercise 14 *Obtain the maximum value function for the firm's problem described in Exercise 5.*

3.2.1 A particular case: $\beta(1+r) = 1$

The discussion of this case requires an introduction. In a competitive economy, the marginal productivity of capital (net of depreciation) is equal to the interest rate. In fact, when factor markets are competitive, capital is paid its marginal productivity, and competition on financial markets keeps the interest rate and the net marginal productivity of capital aligned. Accordingly, under the assumption of competitive markets, we can interpret the interest rate r_t as $f'(k_t) - \delta$.

Coming back to our linear-quadratic example, we note that for the dynamic constraint to be linear (as assumed in (3.9)), the interest rate, and hence $f'(k_t)$, must not change. With a potentially varying capital stock, this can happen in only two cases: either $f(k_t)$ is linear, or $f'(k_t)$ stays constant because the movements over time of the capital stock are so limited that its marginal productivity is virtually unchanged. The linearity of the production function is a strong assumption because it implies that the marginal productivity of capital does not decrease as the capital stock grows. Hence, we will consider the case of an "almost constant" capital stock.[6] It is then natural to focus on the long-run level of capital, $\hat{k}$. The implication of this choice is that $\beta\left(f'(\hat{k})+1-\delta\right)=1$ (refer to Eq. (1.27)), and hence that $\beta(1+r)=1$. In steady state, the impatience parameter β precisely offsets the positive effects on saving exerted by its reward.

When $\beta(1+r)=1$, which means "around" the steady state, a first solution is made up of $m'=0$, h' undetermined, and g' given by (3.18). In this case, the capital accumulation equation (3.13) reduces to:

$$k_{t+1}=\frac{\beta h'-\gamma}{\eta}+(1+r)\,k_t,$$

so that the capital stock is bound to "explode," unless $h'=(\gamma-r\eta k_0)/\beta$, which contradicts our initial guess. When the capital stock diverges over time, the tvc is not satisfied (show this).

Focusing on the second set of solutions, the value function parameters (3.15-3.17) simplify to:

$$\begin{cases} m''=-\frac{\eta}{\beta}r \\ h''=\frac{\gamma}{\beta} \\ g''=\frac{\varepsilon}{1-\beta}. \end{cases}$$

In this particular—but sensible—case, it is easy to find the policy function: since $k_1^*=k_0(=\hat{k})$, from the dynamic constraint (3.9), we get: $c_0^*=rk_0$. It is also immediate to check that the transversality condition holds. In fact, in this case the tvc is:

$$\lim_{t\to\infty}\beta^t(\gamma-\eta c_0^*)k_0,$$

which converges to 0 simply because $\lim_{t\to\infty}\beta^t=0$.

3.2.2 An application to the growth model

Let us reconsider the growth model with logarithmic preferences, where the consumer's overall utility is given by (3.1). We assume a Cobb-Douglas production function, but with a crucial difference: capital depreciates slowly.

In reality, physical capital does not typically depreciate entirely within a single period (except for perhaps some fancy digital devices in certain high-tech industries). Hence, our intertemporal constraint is:

$$k_{t+1} = Ak_t^\alpha + (1-\delta)k_t - c_t. \tag{3.19}$$

Because there is no way to obtain a closed-form analytic solution, we rely on a linear-quadratic approximation of our model. This, of course, implies the need to choose a point around which to approximate. The standard choice is the steady state, which makes sense if your research project involves, for example, the introduction of some sort of shock and studying its effects on a "mature" economic system.

Hence, we first determine the steady state. With the production function (3.19), the steady-state equations (1.29) become:

$$\begin{cases} \beta\left(\alpha A\hat{k}^{\alpha-1} + 1 - \delta\right) = 1, \\ \hat{c} = A\hat{k}^\alpha - \delta\hat{k}. \end{cases} \tag{3.20}$$

The above system allows us to determine the consumption and capital steady-state levels.[7] We now apply Taylor's theorem to the logarithmic utility function, obtaining:

$$\ln(c_t) \approx \ln(\hat{c}) + \frac{1}{\hat{c}}(c_t - \hat{c}) - \frac{1}{2\hat{c}^2}(c_t - \hat{c})^2. \tag{3.21}$$

As for the capital accumulation constraint, we truncate the Taylor's approximation to the first order, which gives:

$$k_{t+1} \approx A\hat{k}^\alpha + (1-\delta)\hat{k} + \alpha A\hat{k}^{\alpha-1}(k_t - \hat{k}) + (1-\delta)(k_t - \hat{k}) - \hat{c} - (c_t - \hat{c}),$$

which can be simplified as:

$$k_{t+1} \approx A\hat{k}^\alpha + (1-\delta)\hat{k} - \hat{c} + \left(\alpha A\hat{k}^{\alpha-1} + 1 - \delta\right)(k_t - \hat{k}) - (c_t - \hat{c}).$$

Hence, using the steady state restrictions from (3.20):

$$k_{t+1} - \hat{k} \approx \frac{1}{\beta}(k_t - \hat{k}) - (c_t - \hat{c}). \tag{3.22}$$

Equations (3.21) and (3.22) lead to the very same structure as found in (3.8) and (3.9). Hence, we can solve the approximated problem using the tentative solution postulated for the linear-quadratic case, with the relevant variables being the deviations of capital and consumption from the steady state. The details are left to the interested reader.

Unfortunately, the examples and exercises in this chapter almost completely exhaust the list of cases that allow for a closed-form solution. However, knowing these examples is useful: it helps us familiarize with the various concepts and with some features of the value function.

Notes

[1] Note that we are bold: we think we know the correct functional form for the maximum value function. However, we are not arrogant: we do not claim that we can spell out the maximum value function in all its details.

[2] Indeed, uniqueness in this case is guaranteed by Theorem 4.14 in Stokey, Lucas, and Prescott (1989).

[3] We do not take a position about ε: it can be positive, zero, or (moderately) negative. A negative ε implies that our consumer needs a minimum amount of consumption to begin enjoying life (thereby achieving a positive utility).

[4] With $m' = h' = 0$, the steady state for capital, from Eq. (3.13), is $\gamma/(\eta r)$.

[5] Our example has required a good deal of calculations. When a linear-quadratic model involves two (or more) state variables, it has to be solved by means of numerical techniques involving matrix manipulations. Refer to Chow (1997) or to Ljungqvist and Sargent (2018).

[6] Note that, by exploiting the tentative solution (3.11), and the parameter values in (3.15-3.17), the second equation in (3.10) becomes: $\gamma - \eta[(1+r)k_0 - k_1^*] = \gamma - \eta r k_1^*$, which confirms $k_1^* = k_0$.

[7] Which are: $\hat{k} = \left(\frac{\alpha\beta A}{1-\beta(1-\delta)}\right)^{1/(1-\alpha)}$ and $\hat{c} = \left(\frac{1-\beta[1-\delta(1-\alpha)]}{\alpha\beta}\right)\left(\frac{\alpha\beta A}{1-\beta(1-\delta)}\right)^{1/(1-\alpha)}$.

4

A "paper and pencil" introduction to function iteration

ABSTRACT This chapter illustrates several alternative techniques used to approximate the solution to a Bellman equation via iteration. First, it introduces the value function iteration method, which is "global" in the sense that it approximates the maximum value function over a wide range of the state space. The steps needed to build the pertinent numerical routines are thoroughly discussed. The chapter then considers the policy function iteration method and the endogenous grid approach; although similar in spirit to the value function iteration method, they offer ways to save on computing time.

The various approaches are discussed by means of simple examples, based on the version of the Ramsey model solved in Section 3.1. The reason for approximating a well-understood problem with numerical techniques is to allow for a direct comparison of the approximated solution with the exact one.

4.1 Value function iteration

In this section we show how a Bellman problem can be solved numerically by iterating on the maximum value function.

DOI: 10.4324/9781003774051-4

Before stating the problem, we need to consider some preliminaries. In particular, we need to choose appropriate values for the parameters of the model and to discretize the state variable(s).

A sensible value for α is 0.3. In fact, α represents the capital income share of output, which ranges between 0.25 and 0.40 for most OECD countries. As for β, we choose 0.97. From Eq. (1.27) we know that–in the steady state–β is equal to the reciprocal of the marginal productivity of capital plus $1-\delta$, which can be interpreted as the interest factor. Hence, if a period represents a year, $\beta = 0.97$ implies a long-run annual (real) interest factor approximately equal to 1.03, which is a realistic value. As for the total factor productivity parameter A, we choose a value such that–given $\delta = 1$–the steady-state capital level, $\hat{k} = (\alpha\beta A)^{1/(1-\alpha)}$, is unity. Hence, $A \approx 3.43643$. This is a normalization: we measure output using a reference unit such that the steady-state value for capital is exactly equal to one.

As we will see, the numerical technique we use inherently requires the discretization of the state space. Therefore, even when the state variable is continuous (as capital is in our case), we must treat it as discrete. We will choose a specific number of levels for capital, which is then restricted to taking one of the values from this grid. In our preliminary example, we assume we are interested in finding the maximum value function for capital levels that are around the steady state.[1] To fix ideas, we consider only five possible values for capital: $k \in \{0.98,\ 0.99, 1, 1.01, 1.02\}$.

Taking into account the proposed values for the parameters, our problem becomes:

$$
\begin{aligned}
V(k_0) &= \max_{c_0} \{\ln(c_0) + 0.97V(k_1)\}, \\
s.t.\ k_1 &= 3.43643k_0^{0.3} - c_0, \\
&k_0 \text{ given.}
\end{aligned}
\tag{4.1}
$$

Note that if we knew the value function–denoted for the moment as $V(k_1)$–it would be relatively easy to solve Problem (4.1). The solution would be composed of the maximum values provided by the consumption levels c_0^* for $k_0, k_1 \in \{0.98, 0.99, 1, 1.01, 1.02\}$, which is the value function $V(k_0)$. For example, assume that $V(k_1) = 20k_1$. (This choice is completely arbitrary; in fact we know that it is wrong: we just want to illustrate what we mean when we say that–knowing $V(k_1)$–it is easy to solve Problem (4.1)).

Let us start with $k_0 = 0.98$. The problem becomes:

$$V(k_0 = 0.98) = \max_{c_0} \{\ln(c_0) + 0.97 \times 20k_1\},$$
$$s.t.\ k_1 = 3.43643(0.98)^{0.3} - c_0, \tag{4.2}$$
$$k_0 = 0.98.$$

To tackle the problem, we must leave our standard tool–the derivative–on the shelf, because the problem is no longer continuous, as a consequence of our decision to evaluate $V(k_1)$ at only a few points. Instead, we need to perform all the required calculations. First, we express the constraint as: $c_0 = 3.43643(0.98)^{0.3} - k_1 = 3.41567 - k_1$, and we compute the consumption levels that are consistent with each of the five feasible values for k_1. These are:

k_1	0.98	0.99	1	1.01	1.02
c_0	2.43566	2.42566	2.41566	2.40566	2.39566

Second, we consider the postulated maximum value function. When $V(k_1) = 20k_1$ the right-hand side of the maximization Problem (4.2) takes, for the five couples $\{k_1, c_0\}$ computed above, the following values:

$r.h.s.(4.2)$	19.90222	20.09210	20.28197	20.47182	20.66166

According to the above calculations, the highest value is obtained for the consumption choice $c_0 = 2.39566$ (corresponding to $k_1 = 1.02$), hence $V(k_0 = 0.98)$ takes the value 20.66166.

This calculation should be repeated for all the remaining $k_0 \in \{0.99, 1, 1.01, 1.02\}$. This process would provide us with the period-0 maximum value function for each state.

However, there is no particular use in performing all these calculations: in fact, the few we have already presented are enough to conclude that the postulated function, $V(k_1) = 20k_1$, is incorrect. From our analysis in Section 2, we know that–in infinite-horizon models–the maximum value function is time-invariant. Accordingly, the functional form we have assumed for period 1 must also apply to period 0. Hence, we should expect to find that $V(k_0 = 0.98) = 19.6$, which is not the case.

While the above example is useful for understanding the required computations, we must now address the real issue: obtaining the unknown maximum value function.

The strategy to get it requires the following steps:

- (Step 1) Specify a set of arbitrary values for $V(k_1)$, and denote this initial set of values by $V_0(k_1)$.

- (Step 2) Solve Problem (4.1) for each state k_0, finding a new (and hence different) maximum value function (which, of course, results in a new set of values, denoted by $V_1(k_0)$).
- (Step 3) Obtain $V_2(k_0)$, using $V_1(k_1) = V_1(k_0)$ as a new initial guess for the value function, for each value of k on the grid.[2]
- (Step 4) Iterate the steps above until $V_n(k_0)$ and $V_{n+1}(k_0)$ are sufficiently close.

The convergence of the above procedure to a set of values that represent the true maximum value function is guaranteed whenever the hypotheses in Theorem 1 or in Theorem 2 are satisfied. In these cases, successive iterations of the value function converge to the true value function, and this convergence occurs regardless of the starting point, i.e., for any arbitrary initial value function.

We now provide some further details on how to apply the above procedure in our extremely simplified example.

We start by choosing a set of values for $V(k_1)$. A commonly chosen set of initial values is $V_0(k_1) = 0$ for all k_1. This no-frills choice–which amounts to assuming that the future does not matter–has the advantage of avoiding the introduction of differences between the behavior of the initial choice and that of the true value function in some areas of the grid, which could slow down the convergence process. The choice $V_0(k_1) = 0$ for all $k_1 \in \{0.98, 0.99, 1, 1.01, 1.02\}$ is Step 1 in our procedure.

As for Step 2, we start by noting that the above choice implies that we face problems of the following type:

$$V(k_0) = \max_{c_0} \{\ln(c_0)\},$$
$$s.t.\ k_1 = 3.43643 k_0^{0.3} - c_0,$$
$$k_0 \text{ given.}$$

Note also that both k_0 and k_1 must take one of the possible values for capital (i.e., $\{0.98, 0.99, 1, 1.01, 1.02\}$): this restricts the set of feasible consumption levels. For example, if $k_0 = 0.98$, for $k_1 = \{0.98, 0.99, 1, 1.01, 1.02\}$, we compute, as before: $c_0 = \{2.43566, 2.42566, 2.41566, 2.40566, 2.39566\}$; the corresponding utilities are $\{0.89022, 0.88610, 0.88197, 0.87783, 0.87366\}$. The highest utility level is reached for $c_0 = 2.43566$, which is the consumption level implying that the next period capital is $k_1 = 0.98$.

Therefore, the solution for this specific problem is $V_1(k_0 = 0.98) = 0.89022$.

Repeating this reasoning, we obtain: $V_1(k_0 = 0.99) = 0.89449$, $V_1(k_0 = 1) = 0.89871$, $V_1(k_0 = 1.01) = 0.90288$, $V_1(k_0 = 1.02) = 0.90701$. In every problem, the solution corresponds to the maximum feasible consumption level, which is always the one corresponding to $k_1 = 0.98$. In other words, for any $k_0 \in \{0.98, 0.99, 1, 1.01, 1.02\}$, c_0 is such that $k_1 = 0.98$. This is hardly surprising: since we arbitrarily chose $V_0(k_1) = 0$, capital has no future value, and it is therefore sensible to consume as much as possible.[3]

The key point is that our maximization procedure has led to a set of values for $V_1(k_0)$, completing Step 2 in the procedure.

Therefore–Step 3–we use these values as a new guess for the maximum value function. This part of the procedure is inspired by the fact that the true maximum value function is time-independent: at different dates it must take the same values for any given capital stock. Accordingly, we now assume $V_1(k_1) = [0.89022, 0.89449, 0.89871, 0.90288, 0.90701]$.

In this second iteration for the maximization problem, when $k_0 = 0.98$, consumption may again take the values $c_0 = \{2.43566, 2.42566, 2.41566, 2.40566, 2.39566\}$. When c_0 is 2.43566 (that is, when it takes the value guaranteeing $k_1 = 0.98$), the corresponding "overall utility" is $\ln(2.43566)$ plus β times $V_1(k_1 = 0.98)(= 0.89022)$, which yields 1.75373. This is the overall value obtained by choosing the consumption level that allows us to maintain the current capital stock in the next period.

Considering the whole set of choices, $c_0 = \{2.43566, 2.42566, 2.41566, 2.40566, 2.39566\}$, we find that the associated values are:

$$\begin{bmatrix} \ln(2.43566) + 0.97 \times 0.89022 \\ \ln(2.42566) + 0.97 \times 0.89449 \\ \ln(2.41566) + 0.97 \times 0.89871 \\ \ln(2.40566) + 0.97 \times 0.90288 \\ \ln(2.39566) + 0.97 \times 0.90701 \end{bmatrix} = \begin{bmatrix} 1.75373 \\ 1.75376 \\ 1.75372 \\ 1.75362 \\ 1.75346 \end{bmatrix}.$$

Note that the second value in the right-hand column, 1.75376, is the highest (so that $V_2(k_0 = 0.98) = 1.75376$). Hence, the optimal choice is now to select a consumption level such that the next-period capital is 0.99. That is, if the initial capital is 0.98 and we account for the discounted utility of the future period, it is optimal to increase capital by saving 0.01 units. The optimal consumption choice is therefore 2.42566.

Repeating this reasoning for the other capital values in our grid, we obtain that: if $k_0 = 0.99$, the optimal consumption choice is such that k_1 remains at 0.99; if $k_0 = 1$, the optimal consumption choice is such that k_1 is again 0.99; if $k_0 = 1.01$ or 1.02, the optimal consumption choice is such that

$k_1 = 1$. In correspondence to these optimal choices, the value function is: $V_2(k_0) = [1.75376,\ 1.75804,\ 1.76228,\ 1.76649,\ 1.77065]$. Obtaining this set of values concludes Step 3 in our procedure.

Of course, a normal person is already fed up with all these calculations. At this point we let our software handle the computations, thereby performing Step 4. It is easy to write a program in Matlab (or Octave, Julia or Python)[4] that carries out this task.[5] The results of this program are reported in Table 2. Note that, having chosen an example for which we know the analytical solution, in the last line of Table 2 we can report, as a reference point, the exact values of $V(k)$ (rounded to the sixth decimal).

TABLE 2: results for $V_n\,(k)$

iter.#	$V_n(0.98)$	$V_n(0.99)$	$V_n(1.00)$	$V_n(1.01)$	$V_n(1.02)$
0	0	0	0	0	0
1	0.890218	0.894487	0.898707	0.902881	0.907009
2	1.753757	1.758043	1.762281	1.766486	1.770648
3	2.591406	2.595692	2.599944	2.604152	2.608314
4	3.403926	3.408223	3.412478	3.416686	3.420850
5	4.192081	4.196381	4.200636	4.204844	4.209008
6	4.956594	4.960894	4.965149	4.969357	4.973521
7	5.698172	5.702472	5.706727	5.710935	5.715099
8	6.417502	6.421802	6.426058	6.430265	6.434430
9	7.115253	7.119553	7.123808	7.128016	7.132180
10	7.792071	7.796371	7.800626	7.804834	7.808998
20	13.538224	13.542524	13.546779	13.550987	13.555151
50	23.204550	23.208850	23.213105	23.217313	23.221477
100	28.264686	28.268986	28.273241	28.277449	28.281613
200	29.608749	29.613049	29.617304	29.621512	29.625676
300	29.672662	29.676962	29.681218	29.685425	29.689590
375	29.675528	29.679828	29.684084	29.688291	29.692456
376	29.675538	29.679838	29.684093	29.688301	29.692465
true	29.675860	29.680156	29.684409	29.688619	29.692788

Table 2 allows us to observe the Contraction Mapping Theorem (Theorem 3) "in action". The values for $V_n(k_0)$ smoothly converge toward the unique fixed point of the maximum value function (that is, to the true maximum value function $V(k_0)$). Since Blackwell's sufficiency conditions are satisfied (refer to Theorem 4), the function we obtain at each step is slightly closer to the true maximum value function. Technically, the sup norm between the function represented by a row of Table 2 and the true function decreases as the number of iterations increases.[6]

Exercise 15 *Check that the values for $V(k)$ in the last line of Table 2 are correct.*

This leads us to select a convergence criterion that leverages a key fact: as the computed value function converges to the true maximum value function, when the set of values for $V_{n+1}(k_0)$ is almost identical to the one used to represent $V_n(k_0)$, we assume that they are also "almost identical" to the true $V(k_0)$. In our exercise we let the computer calculate the difference between $V_{n+1}(k_0)$ and $V_n(k_0)$ for each gridpoint on k_0. We then take the absolute values of these differences and have the routine select the largest.[7] Our convergence criterion is such that the computer stops refining $V_n(k_0)$ when the largest difference is below 10^{-5}. On a computer with an Intel Core Ultra 7 155H, 1.40 GHz CPU, this happens after about $1/100^{th}$ of a second, at the 376th iteration.

In our case, convergence requires a large number of iterations. This is because β is close to unity: what happens in the future matters a lot. Hence, the initial arbitrary values for $V(k_1)$–which represents the future–are very far from the true function and do not lose their importance quickly.

A nice feature of a value function iteration routine is that it is immediate to change the interval for the state variable and the number of gridpoints, therefore adapting the numerical routine to a new situation. For instance, we can use the program written for the problem above to study what happens for $k \in [0.7, 1.1]$ with 1,600 gridpoints. Panel (a) in Figure 4.1 plots the maximum value function, while Panel (b) shows the differences between the true value function and the approximated one. Note that the computing time increases dramatically, taking about two minutes to achieve convergence. However, as shown in the Appendix, our routine can be optimized–becoming around 10 times faster–by exploiting the matrix manipulation capabilities incorporated in many software packages.

Note also that it is also very handy to feed the routine with a different (and more efficient) initial tentative value function. We will come back to the issue of speeding up the process shortly; for now, we will present a refinement of the value function iteration method.

Our procedure requires that for every point on the k_0 grid, we compute the consumption level consistent with each possible next-period capital stock on the grid, and then select the level that maximizes utility. As the number of points on the grid increases, this requires a large number of calculations.

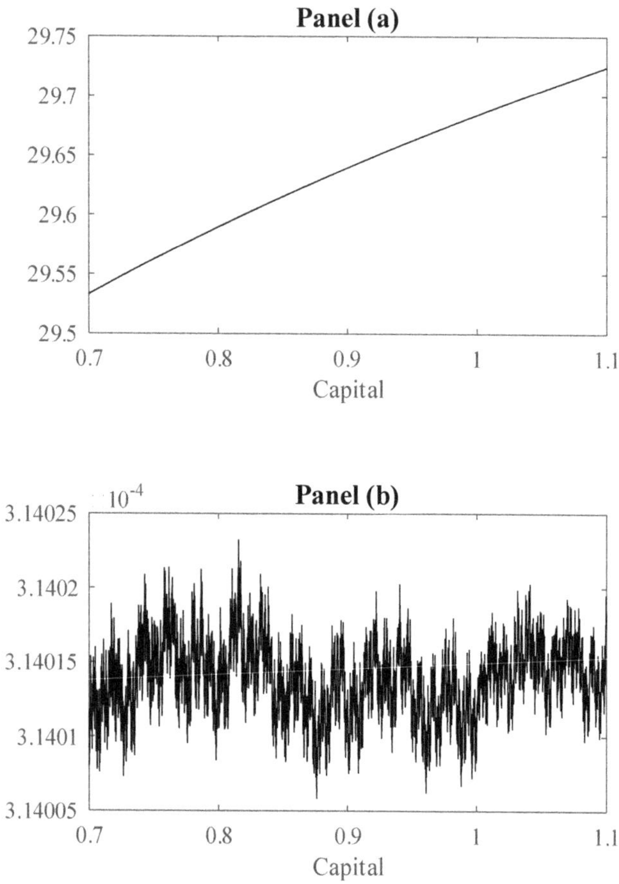

FIGURE 4.1. Value function iteration: maximum value function (Panel a) and approximation errors (Panel b)

There are ways to get around this issue and reduce the computation time by relying on the maximization routine built into our software. Our problem, given the function $V_n(k_1)$, requires solving, for any given k_0:

$$V_{n+1}(k_0) = \max_{c_0} \{\ln(c_0) + \beta V_n(k_1)\},$$
$$s.t.\ k_1 = 3.43643 k_0^{0.3} - c_0.$$

By substituting the constraint in the utility function, our problem becomes that of maximizing with respect to k_1 the function

$$\ln(3.43643 k_0^{0.3} - k_1) + \beta V_n(k_1).$$

If we could specify $V_n(k_1)$ at any point, we could rely on the local maximizer that is embedded in software like Matlab. This routine would find the optimal next-period capital stock, k_1, for each given k_0. Once the optimal next-period capital (and thus the optimal consumption) is obtained, $V_{n+1}(k_0)$ follows. However, while the local maximizer searches over *all* possible values for k_1 (within the limits of the grid), what we actually provide is a set of values $V_n(k)$ defined on our *discrete* grid for k. Moreover, the solution for k_1 (except in extremely unlikely cases) falls *between* two points on the grid. Consequently, to allow the maximization routine to evaluate any k_1, we must supply it with all the possible values of $V_n(k_1)$, and therefore with a method to compute the value function outside the grid. To this end, the values taken by the maximum value function between the points on the grid are approximated by interpolation.

The simplest way is to use a linear interpolation, which is illustrated in Figure 4.2 where $k^{'}$, $k^{''}$, and $k^{'''}$ are points on the grid and x is assumed to be the solution for k_1 corresponding to a given initial capital stock k_0.

The (approximated) maximum value function corresponding to x is obtained according to the formula:

$$V_n(x) = V_n(k^{'}) + \frac{V_n(k^{''}) - V_n(k^{'})}{k^{''} - k^{'}} \left(x - k^{'}\right),$$

that can be seen as a linear combination of $V_n(k^{'})$ and $V_n(k^{''})$.

This approach yields more precise results than the previous one when the number of grid points is chosen to be small, due to limitations in computing power. The drawback, however, is that the use of a maximization routine curbs the gain in computation time. For our standard model, compared to the basic value function iteration routines, an approach that uses

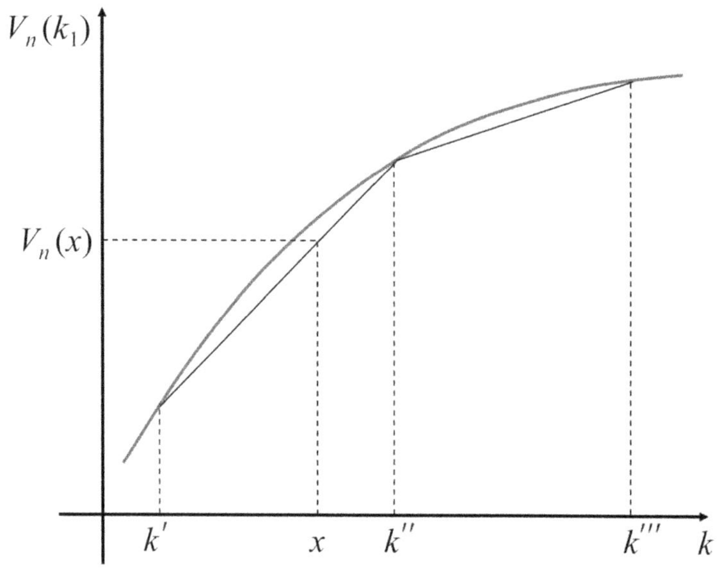

FIGURE 4.2. Linear interpolation of the value function

interpolation saves only about 25% of the computing time using the same convergence criterion (which requires that the largest absolute difference between two successive iterations be below 10^{-5}).

4.2 Speeding up the process

Computing power has become cheaper and cheaper since the mid-1980s, but using efficient techniques is still extremely important. Indeed, we want to use numerical methods to obtain more and more accurate solutions for increasingly complex models. Hence, I will now introduce some ways to save on processing time.

4.2.1 Use of a smart initial guess

The initial value function ($V_0(k) = 0$) used in the previous section is poor because it assumes that the future does not matter for our representative agent, which is obviously not true. A very handy way to speed up the convergence process is to provide a better initial guess.

With this purpose in mind, consider what would happen in our standard growth model if the representative agent were not allowed to change her capital stock. In that case, the maximum value attainable by the representative agent would be, for any given k_0,

$$V(k_0) = \ln(c_0) + 0.97V(k_1),$$
$$\text{with } k_1 = k_0 = 3.43643k_0^{0.3} - c_0.$$

Note that the "max" operator has been omitted, since the representative agent can not make any decisions. Her consumption choice is actually constrained. Accordingly, the maximum value that can be obtained is:

$$V(k_0) = \frac{1}{0.03}\ln(3.43643k_0^{0.3} - k_0),$$

or, in general,

$$V(k) = \frac{1}{1-\beta}\ln(Ak^{\alpha} - k).$$

The expression above is commonly used as an initial guess for the maximum value function because it "respects" the shape of the true value function. Figure 4.3 shows the maximum value function (solid line) and our new initial guess (dashed line). As you can see, the maximum value function lies above the initial guess. This is because the latter was obtained by imposing a constraint on the agent's behavior, whereas the maximum value function is achieved by an unconstrained and fully optimizing agent. Actually, the difference between the two functions can be interpreted as the utility cost imposed by the constraint. In other words, when the capital stock is below the steady state, the figure highlights the present discounted value of the gain in current and future utilities that can be obtained by saving. When the capital stock is above the steady state, Figure 4.3 shows the cost of being obliged to maintain an excessively high capital stock. Unsurprisingly, the two functions take the same value at the steady state, which is the point where the representative agent is unwilling to modify the capital stock, so the constraint is not binding. Interestingly, the computing time collapses to about 0.4 seconds (from around 120).

Note in passing that this logic for obtaining a sound initial guess can be applied to any utility and production function.

4.2.2 Policy function iteration

Another way to save computing time is to iterate on the policy function instead of the value function. This approach is often referred to as the "Howard's improvement algorithm," which generally converges faster than

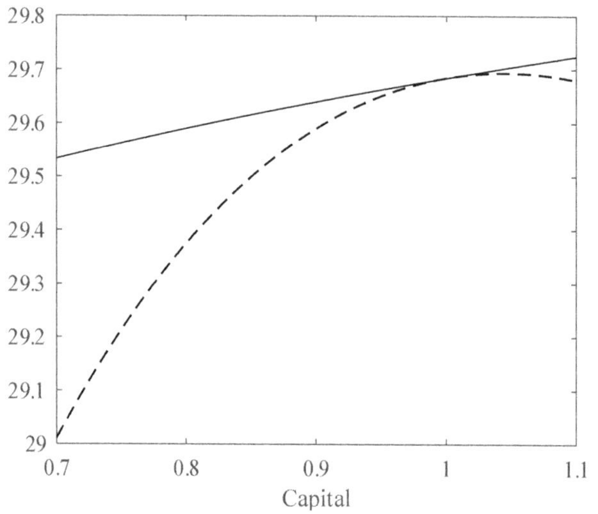

FIGURE 4.3. The cost of rigidity: initial guess (dashed line) versus maximum value (solid line).

value function iteration. Ljungqvist and Sargent (2018) give some prominence to the use of this method and explain why algorithms based on this approach reduce CPU time.

The basic idea behind this method is simple, much like the one we used in the previous section. First, we start with an arbitrary initial guess for the value function. We then find the policy function that is consistent with that guess, and we apply this policy for the entire time horizon of the representative agent. This allows us to get a new interim maximum value function. We repeat the procedure until convergence.

Slightly more formally, from an arbitrary initial guess, $V_0(k_{t+1})$, our representative agent obtains a policy $c_{0,t} = \varphi_0(k_t)$ by solving a maximization problem such as (4.1). The agent can then compute an interim value function, $V_1(k_t)$, by applying the policy function $\varphi_0(.)$ in every period. In other words, the representative agent computes $V_1(k_t)$ as the sum of an infinite number of terms:

$$V_1(k_t) = U(\varphi_0(k_t)) + \beta U(\varphi_0(k_{t+1})) + \beta^2 U(\varphi_0(k_{t+2})) + ...$$

where in every period (i.e., for $i = 0, 1, 2, ..., \infty$): $k_{t+1+i} = Ak_{t+i}^{\alpha} + (1-\delta)\,k_{t+i} -\varphi_0(k_{t+i})$. Then, with the new $V_1(k)$ the representative agent obtains a new policy function $\varphi_1(k_t)$ and then iterates; when $V_{n+1}(k_t)$ and $V_n(k_t)$ are sufficiently close the (approximated) maximum value function is obtained.

Obviously, the point is that the true maximum value function is unknown. However, as in the previous example, the initial guess $V_0(k_{t+1})$ can be chosen arbitrarily–it can even be set to 0 for any period $t+1$ value of the state variable–and then "refined."

While the idea is simple, its practical implementation requires some care. In particular, it is not straightforward to quickly compute the "next iteration" maximum value function, which is the sum of an infinite number of terms.

Our illustration on how to cope with this issue is based on the simple example used in Section 4.1, again with a grid for capital composed of only five elements: {0.98, 0.99, 1, 1.01, 1.02}. For the initial guess on the maximum value function, we choose $V_0(k_{t+1}) = 0$ for each k_{t+1}.

We perform the required optimizations starting with $k_t = 0.98$. In this case, the consumption levels that allow us to obtain, respectively, $k_{t+1} = \{0.98, 0.99, 1, 1.01, 1.02\}$, are: $\{2.43566, 2.42566, 2.41566, 2.40566, 2.39566\}$. The corresponding utilities are $\{0.89022, 0.88610, 0.88197, 0.87783, 0.87366\}$. As before, the highest utility level is reached for $c_t = 2.43566$, which is the consumption level implying $k_{t+1} = 0.98$. The fact that the optimal consumption choice implies no savings is obvious: we have arbitrarily chosen $V_0(k_{t+1}) = 0$, thus the capital stock bears no future value.

Repeating this reasoning for $k_t = \{\ 0.99, 1, 1.01, 1.02\}$, we find that our policy function $\varphi_0(k_t)$ prescribes a consumption that implies $k_{t+1} = 0.98$ for all k_t. Accordingly, the consumption levels are {2.43566, 2.44608, 2.45643, 2.46670, 2.47691} for $k_t = \{0.98, 0.99, 1, 1.01, 1.02\}$, respectively. Note that we have just described the policy function and its implications for the dynamics of the state variable. In plain words, the policy can be summarized by the catchphrase "reduce capital to the lowest feasible level, consuming all you can." In the first period such policy would guarantee the representative agent a utility equal to $U_0(k_t) = \ln(\varphi_0(k_t)) = \{0.89022, 0.89449, 0.89871, 0.90288, 0.90701\}$. If this policy is adopted for two periods, in the first period the agent would choose the consumption level prescribed by $\varphi_0(k_t)$. As mentioned, this would reduce capital to $k_{t+1} = 0.98$; since this is the lowest admissible value, applying the same policy in the second period would imply no net savings, and therefore a next-period capital level kept at $k_{t+2} = 0.98$, a second period consumption equal to 2.43566, and an overall utility given by:

$$\begin{aligned}&[1.75373, 1.75800, 1.76222, 1.76639, 1.7705] \simeq \\ &\quad \simeq [0.89022, 0.89449, 0.89871, 0.90288, 0.90701] + 0.97 \times 0.89022. \qquad (4.3)\end{aligned}$$

The numbers in square brackets on the right-hand side represent the initial period's utility for the five feasible levels of capital. The final term is the discounted second-period utility, which is the same for every initial level. This is precisely because our policy dictates always moving to $k_{t+1} = 0.98$.

Our policy can be summarized by means of a matrix, as follows:

$$
\begin{array}{cc}
 & \overbrace{\begin{array}{ccccc} 0.98 & 0.99 & 1 & 1.01 & 1.02 \end{array}}^{k_{t+1}} \\
k_t \left\{ \begin{array}{c} 0.98 \\ 0.99 \\ 1 \\ 1.01 \\ 1.02 \end{array} \right. &
\begin{bmatrix} 1 & 0 & 0 & 0 & 0 \\ 1 & 0 & 0 & 0 & 0 \\ 1 & 0 & 0 & 0 & 0 \\ 1 & 0 & 0 & 0 & 0 \\ 1 & 0 & 0 & 0 & 0 \end{bmatrix}
\end{array}.
$$

Each row represents one of the period t levels of capital on the grid. The entries are all zeros, except for a 1 that corresponds to the next-period capital level prescribed by the policy. From now on, this matrix will be referred to as the matrix J_0.

In matrix format, the utility enjoyed over two periods (refer to Eq. 4.3) is given by $[\ln(\varphi_0(k_t))]' + \beta J_0 [\ln(\varphi_0(k_t))]'$. Extending our horizon to three periods, we obtain the following utility levels: $[\ln(\varphi_0(k_t))]' + \beta J_0 [\ln(\varphi_0(k_t))]' + \beta^2 J_0^2 [\ln(\varphi_0(k_t))]'$. These observations allow us to express the value attainable through the proposed policy as:

$$V_1(k_t) = \left[I + \beta J_0 + \beta^2 J_0^2 + \beta^3 J_0^3 + \beta^4 J_0^4 + \ldots\right] [\ln(\varphi_0(k_t))]'$$

which leads to the conclusion that[8]

$$V_1(k_t) = [I - \beta J_0]^{-1} [\ln(\varphi_0(k_t))]' .$$

One can compute the matrix $[I - \beta J_0]^{-1}$, which is:

$$[I - \beta J_0]^{-1} = \begin{bmatrix} 33.\bar{3} & 0 & 0 & 0 & 0 \\ 32.\bar{3} & 1 & 0 & 0 & 0 \\ 32.\bar{3} & 0 & 1 & 0 & 0 \\ 32.\bar{3} & 0 & 0 & 1 & 0 \\ 32.\bar{3} & 0 & 0 & 0 & 1 \end{bmatrix},$$

so that:

$$\begin{aligned} V_1(k_t) &= [I - \beta J_0]^{-1} [\log(\varphi_0(k_t))]' = \\ &= \begin{bmatrix} 29.67400 & 29.67827 & 29.68249 & 29.68666 & 29.69079 \end{bmatrix}'. \end{aligned}$$

We now move to the second iteration of the procedure. For $k_t = 0.98$, the consumption levels that yield $k_{t+1} = \{0.98,\ 0.99,\ 1,\ 1.01,\ 1.02\}$ are $c_t = \{2.43566,\ 2.42566,\ 2.41566,\ 2.40566,\ 2.39566\}$, respectively. As before, let $V_1(k_{t+1}) = V_1(k_t)$, so that the corresponding utilities are given by:

$$\begin{aligned} &\ln c_t + \beta V_1(k_{t+1}) = \\ &= \begin{bmatrix} 0.890220 & 0.886106 & 0.881975 & 0.877826 & 0.873661 \end{bmatrix}' + \\ &+ 0.97 \times \begin{bmatrix} 29.67400 & 29.67827 & 29.68249 & 29.68666 & 29.69079 \end{bmatrix}' = \\ &= \begin{bmatrix} 29.67400 & 29.67403 & 29.67399 & 29.67389 & 29.67373 \end{bmatrix}'. \end{aligned}$$

In this case, the highest utility level is reached for $c_t = 2.42566$, which is the consumption level that results in $k_{t+1} = 0.99$. This helps you to see where the first row of matrix J_1 comes from.

$$J_1 = \begin{bmatrix} 0 & 1 & 0 & 0 & 0 \\ 0 & 1 & 0 & 0 & 0 \\ 0 & 1 & 0 & 0 & 0 \\ 0 & 0 & 1 & 0 & 0 \\ 0 & 0 & 1 & 0 & 0 \end{bmatrix}.$$

The other rows of J_1 can be obtained by repeating the reasoning above for $k_t = \{\ 0.99,\ 1,\ 1.01,\ 1.02\}$.

As already mentioned, the procedure iterates until $V_{n+1}(k_t)$ and $V_n(k_t)$ are sufficiently close.

We solved our standard version of the Ramsey model with a routine using an evenly spaced grid of 1600 levels for $k \in [0.7, 1.1]$, and stopped when the maximal difference between $V_{n+1}(k_t)$ and $V_n(k_t)$ (in absolute terms) was less than or equal to 10^{-8}. Figure 4.4 shows the differences between the true value function and the approximated one.

The remarkable point is that our routine produced the above result, which is better than that portrayed in Figure 4.1, in less than one second. In general, exploiting the logic of policy function iteration can save almost 99% of CPU time.[9]

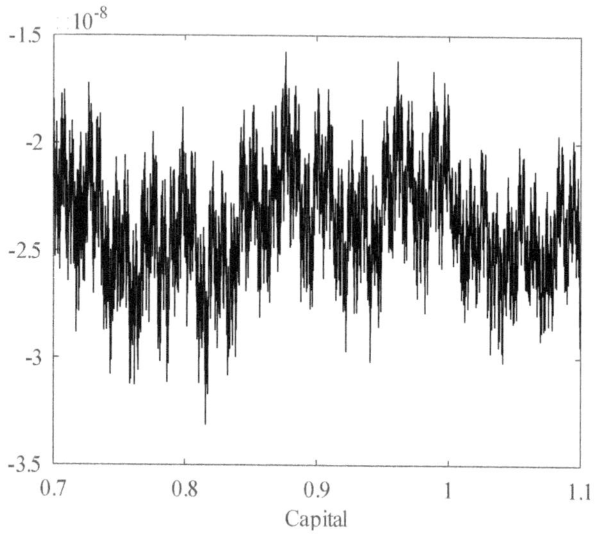

FIGURE 4.4. Approximation errors for the policy iteration routine

4.2.3 Endogenous grid methods

This approach, originally proposed by Carroll (2006), suggests considering a grid defined for k_1. Instead of analyzing what the agent should do at time 0 given her existing stock of capital, the endogenous grid method focus on what an agent must have done, assuming she acted optimally, to arrive at a capital stock level belonging to the grid. Accordingly, the period-0 grid is endogenous, as it depends on the optimal behavior of the agent.

The growth model with full capital depreciation provides a particularly neat illustration based on the computation of the policy function.

Let $\bar{k}_1$ be a point on the grid, and "guess" a policy function; our initial tentative is denoted by the superscript (0). A sensible choice is to assume that the representative agent consumes a share μ of output:

$$\bar{c}_1^{(0)} = \mu A \bar{k}_1^{\alpha}. \tag{4.4}$$

The "sensible" nature of this policy function will soon become apparent.

As mentioned, we assume that the representative agent acts optimally at time 0, which means that the Euler equation is satisfied. Hence we have:

$$\bar{c}_0^{(0)} = \bar{c}_1^{(0)} \left(\beta \alpha A \bar{k}_1^{\alpha-1} \right)^{-1}, \tag{4.5}$$

which also allows us to compute, from the intertemporal budget constraint, the endogenous grid point for period 0, $\bar{k}_0^{(0)}$, corresponding to $\bar{k}_1$. The grid point $\bar{k}_0^{(0)}$ is obtained by starting from:

$$A\left(\bar{k}_0^{(0)}\right)^{\alpha} - \bar{c}_0^{(0)} = \bar{k}_1,$$

which gives:

$$\bar{k}_0^{(0)} = \left(\frac{\bar{c}_0^{(0)} + \bar{k}_1}{A}\right)^{1/\alpha}. \tag{4.6}$$

Using the policy rule (4.4) in (4.5) we obtain $\bar{c}_0^{(0)}$ as an analytical function of $\bar{k}_1$, and thus from (4.6):

$$\bar{k}_0^{(0)} = \left(\frac{\mu + \beta\alpha}{\beta\alpha A}\bar{k}_1\right)^{1/\alpha}. \tag{4.7}$$

Note that $\bar{k}_0^{(0)}$ is a point on the period-0 endogenous grid, and keep in mind that it has been obtained from the exogenous grid point $\bar{k}_1$. By repeating the procedure for all the points of the period-1 grid we obtain our first attempt at the period-0 endogenous grid. Then, importantly, consider that $\bar{c}_0^{(0)}$ can be seen as a function of the state, $\bar{k}_0^{(0)}$, and that $\bar{c}_0^{(0)}$ has been chosen optimally (given $\bar{k}_1$, and the tentative solution $\bar{c}_1^{(0)}$). This suggests that a better "tentative" period-1 consumption function can be obtained by "replicating" period-0 behavior. This new "tentative" function, $c_1^{(1)}$, is a function of the period-1 capital stocks (and hence of a point on the grid). Every period-1 consumption level is obtained by interpolation. Consider, for example, $\bar{c}_1^{(1)}$, corresponding to the period-1 stock of capital $\bar{k}_1$ and let k_0' and k_0'' ($k_0'' > k_0'$) be two consecutive points on the endogenous grid such that $k_0' \leq \bar{k}_1 \leq k_0''$. Then, linear interpolation yields:

$$\bar{c}_1^{(1)} = c_0'^{(0)} + \frac{c_0''^{(0)} - c_0'^{(0)}}{k_0'' - k_0'}\left(\bar{k}_1 - k_0'\right). \tag{4.8}$$

Having obtained a new policy function, we use it to update our period-0 policy, using (4.5), and we iterate until convergence is achieved.

Our simple example is useful to understand why the endogenous grid method can be very convenient: it avoids finding the optimal consumption for every point on the grid by comparing all possible choices, as we did in Section 4.1. This fact becomes more compelling when we consider stochastic models, where evaluating choices will require obtaining expected values, and therefore becomes computationally more demanding.

Two further considerations are in order.

First, note that Eq. (4.8) is useful for explaining why $\bar{c}_1^{(0)} = \mu A \bar{k}_1^{\alpha}$ is "sensible." Recall from Eq. (1.27) that, when $\delta = 1$, the steady-state level of capital is $\hat{k} = (\alpha\beta A)^{1/(1-\alpha)}$. Let $\underline{\underline{k}}_1$ and $\overline{\overline{k}}_1$ be the lowest and highest point on the grid for k_1, and let $\underline{\underline{k}}_0$ and $\overline{\overline{k}}_0$ be the corresponding period-0 capital values obtained using (4.7). When $\underline{\underline{k}}_0 < \underline{\underline{k}}_1$ and $\overline{\overline{k}}_0 > \overline{\overline{k}}_1$, any point on the exogenous period-1 grid (i.e., any $\bar{k}_1$) lies within the range $[\underline{\underline{k}}_0, \overline{\overline{k}}_0]$. This avoids the need to extrapolate some values for the period-1 consumption function. Extrapolation is "dangerous" in the sense that the resulting loss of precision can induce numerical errors and even prevent convergence. Some algebraic manipulation shows that $\underline{\underline{k}}_0 < \underline{\underline{k}}_1$ and that $\overline{\overline{k}}_0 > \overline{\overline{k}}_1$ if $\underline{\underline{k}}_1 < \hat{k}\,(\mu + \alpha\beta)^{-1/(1-\alpha)} < \overline{\overline{k}}_1$. Accordingly, if one is interested, for example, in studying the behavior of the economy for $k \in \left[0.6\hat{k}, 1.1\hat{k}\right]$ and $\alpha = 0.3$, $\beta = 0.97$, one only needs to set $\mu = 1$.[10]

Second, let us consider what happens when depreciation is not complete. The Euler equation (4.5) is:

$$\bar{c}_0^{(0)} = \bar{c}_1^{(0)} \beta^{-1} \left(\alpha A \bar{k}_1^{\alpha-1} + 1 - \delta\right)^{-1},$$

and therefore Eq. (4.6) becomes:

$$A\left(\bar{k}_0^{(0)}\right)^{\alpha} + (1-\delta)\,\bar{k}_0^{(0)} = \bar{c}_0^{(0)} + \bar{k}_1.$$

which cannot be solved explicitly for $\bar{k}_0^{(0)}$, and therefore calls for a numerical solution. This can be (easily) found, but it comes at the cost of slowing down the process.

Summing up, the endogenous grid procedure prescribes the following steps:

- (Step 1) Having specified a grid for period-1 capital $\{k_1\}$, provide a tentative period-1 policy function, $\{c_1^{(0)}\}$.

- (Step 2) Obtain the period-0 optimal choices, $\{c_0^{(0)}\}$, based on the period-1 grid for the state variable and on the tentative policy function.

- (Step 3) Obtain the period-0 endogenous grid for capital $\{k_0^{(0)}\}$ consistent with the grid $\{k_1\}$ and the associated vector of choices $\{c_0^{(0)}\}$.
- (Step 4) Obtain a new period-1 policy function $\{c_1^{(1)}\}$ based on the relation between endogenous grid $\{k_0^{(0)}\}$ and policy function $\{c_0^{(0)}\}$.
- (Step 5) Iterate the steps above until $\{c_1^{(n+1)}\}$ and $\{c_1^{(n)}\}$ are "sufficiently close."

Some additional material and a nutshell guide to the literature are provided in Subsection 8.1.4.

4.3 The curse that strikes function iteration

This is probably the right time to become aware of one of the sad facts of life, often referred to as "the curse of dimensionality." The convergence time for procedures like the ones we have discussed increases more than proportionally with the number of state variables. To understand why, remember that to find the value function by iteration, we had to discretize the state space. In our current case, the state space is simply a line because we only have one state variable: physical capital.

If we had two state variables–such as physical and human capital–our state space would be two-dimensional (a plane). In this case, it would be necessary to divide the state space into small "squares." If we use the same number of grid points, n, for each state variable, the number of these squares (or grid cells) becomes $(n-1)^2$. This implies that the number of evaluation points increases exponentially with the number of state variables. Consequently, the required computational time grows exponentially with the dimension of the state space.[11] For example, in a model where the representative agent makes decisions regarding her consumption level and her schooling effort based on both human and physical capital, the value function must be computed for every combination of human and physical capital on a two-dimensional grid.

In short: if our model is large, a more efficient technique is required, which will be the focus of the next chapter. Nevertheless, the value function iteration method can be quite useful when one or more dimensions of the state space are naturally discrete.

This is the case in problems where an agent might be employed or unemployed, decide whether to pursue a degree, or choose to retire, and so on. This method can also be useful if the transition function is subject to a constraint. Suppose, to mention the most relevant example for growth theory, that investment is irreversible. By this, we mean that capital cannot be converted back into consumption goods, so that the additional constraint $k_1 \geq k_0(1-\delta)$ must be satisfied. This problem is easily dealt with in our framework: it is sufficient to rule out consumption levels that imply an infringement of the irreversibility constraint.[12]

4.4 Appendix

4.4.1 Function iteration routines for the basic growth model

In this Appendix we detail the tasks performed by the Matlab routines we have used in Sections 4.1 and 4.2.

The routines have been written for didactic purposes, they aim at being transparent, and they are inefficient (and sometimes very inefficient). In particular, we have used the "for ... end" loop many times, which slows down the execution of the routines.

We present the routines in the order they were used in the main text.

valfun_iter0.m
This is the script (i.e., a list of commands) that produces Table 2.

```
clear;

format('long');
% This lets Matlab display results in the Command Window using the
% "long" format for numbers (precision of calculations is unaffected).

% parameter values.
alpha=0.3;
beta=0.97;
A=1/(alpha*beta);
kstar=(alpha*beta*A)^(1/(1-alpha)); % steady-state capital stock.

states=5; % Number of states.
kmin=0.98; % Lowest capital level.
kmax=1.02; % Highest capital level.

deltak = (kmax-kmin)/(states-1);
kvec=kmin:deltak:kmax;
% These two lines compute the 'grid' for the state variable.
```

```
vini=zeros(1,states);
% Initial guess for the value function (0 for all gridpoints).

vfin=zeros(1,states);
% This creates the value function which will be obtained at the end
% of one optimization "cycle".

cons=zeros(1,states); % Consumption vector.
opt_choice=zeros(1,states);
% Vector used to store in each cycle the maximum utility,
% inclusive of the discounted value of future utilities.

err=10;
% "err" substantiates the convergence criterion. When "err" is below
% a threshold (specified below), the routine has converged.

tic % This starts the timer.

z=0;
% Initialization of the counter for the value iterations.
while err > 10^(-5)
% Convergence criterion.
  z=z+1;
    for i=1:states
      for j=1:states
        cons(j)=A*kvec(i)^alpha-kvec(j);
        % For any given state (i), this computes the consumption
        % consistent with the next period state (j).
      end

    opt_choice(i)=max((log(cons)+beta*vini)');
    % This is the optimal choice among consumption values (and their
    % related next-period capital stock, summarized by the values in
    % "vini"). Notice that i indexes the current state

    end

  vfin=opt_choice;
  % The maximum value function is the optimal choice for every stock
  % of capital.
  delta=abs(vini-vfin);
  % This computes the difference between the maximum value before
  % and after the optimization cycle, in absolute value.
  err=max(delta');
  % The "convergence variable" takes the maximum absolute difference
  % between the value function before and after the optimization cy-
```

```
  % cle.

  vini=vfin; % the new cycle shall start with this new guess.

  Table2(z,:)=[z vfin(1) vfin(2) vfin(3) vfin(4) vfin(5)];
  % Values in Table 2
end
% This 'closes' the cycle for z.

toc % Shows the used cpu time (when used with 'tic').

% The next lines compute the true maximum value function - refer to
% Chapter 3
par =alpha*beta;
cost1=1/(1-beta)*(par/(1-par)*log(par)+log(1-par)+1/(1-par)*log(A));
cost2=alpha/(1-alpha*beta);
true_val=cost1+cost2*log(kvec);
true_val % These are the values for the true value function.
```

Note that Table 2(:,:) contains the values used to produce the corresponding table in the main text.

valfun_iter1.m
This script is essentially identical to valfun_iter0.m, except for the fact that we consider a grid of 1600 points; the state variable ranges from 0.7 to 1.1. This routine produces Figure 4.1. For specific comments, please refer to the previous script.

```
% For additional comments, refer to file valfun_iter0.
clear;

format('long');

alpha=0.3;
beta=0.97;
A=1/(alpha*beta);

kstar=(alpha*beta*A)^(1/(1-alpha));
states=1600; % Number of points on the grid.

kmin=.7*kstar;
kmax=1.1*kstar;
deltak = (kmax-kmin)/(states-1);
```

```
kvec=kmin:deltak:kmax;
vini=zeros(1,states);
vfin=zeros(1,states);
consV=zeros(1,states);
opt_choice=zeros(1,states);

tic

err=10;
z=0;

while err > 10^(-5)
    z=z+1;
    for i=1:states
        for j=1:states
            consV(j)=A*kvec(i)^alpha-kvec(j);
        end
        opt_choice(i)=max((log(consV)+beta*vini)');
    end
    vfin=opt_choice;
    delta=abs(vini-vfin);
    err=max(delta');
    vini=vfin;
end

toc

% The lines below compute the "true" maximum value function.
par=alpha*beta;
cost1=1/(1-beta)*( par/(1-par)*log(par)+log(1-par)+1/(1-par)*log(A));
cost2=alpha/(1-alpha*beta);
true_val=cost1+cost2*log(kvec);
err_approx=true_val-vfin;
% Approximation errors as differences between the true values and
% those approximated by "vfin".

% ======== The lines below produce the two panels Figure 4.1 ========
size=11; % size of font (in points)
subplot1 = subplot(2,1,1,'FontSize',10,'FontName','Times␣New␣Roman');
plot(kvec',vfin');
% This builds Panel (a)
xlim([0.7 1.1]);
ylim([29.5 29.75]);
% This creates xlabel
xlabel('Capital','FontSize',size,'FontName','Times␣New␣Roman');
% This creates ylabel
ylabel('Maximum␣value','FontSize',size,'FontName','Times␣New␣Roman');
```

```
% This creates title
title('Panel␣(a):␣Maximum␣Value␣Function','FontSize',size+3,...
'FontName','Times␣New␣Roman')
subplot2 = subplot(2,1,2,'FontName','Times␣New␣Roman');
plot(kvec',err_approx'); % this builds Panel (b)
xlim([0.7 1.1]);
% This creates xlabel
xlabel('Capital','FontSize',size,...
'FontName','Times␣New␣Roman');
% This creates ylabel
ylabel('Approximation␣errors','FontSize',size,...
    'FontName','Times␣New␣Roman');
% This creates the title
title('Panel␣(b):␣Approximation␣Errors','FontSize',size+3,...
'FontName','Times␣New␣Roman')
```

valfun_iter1bis.m

This routine produces the same results obtained by valfun.iter1.m in a much more efficient way: in the main loop (lines from 24 to 30) consumption and overall utility are dealt with as vectors, which exploits the Matlab matrix manipulation capabilities. This script also exploits the "smart" initial guess described in Subsection 4.2.1.

```
1 clear;

3 alpha=0.3;
  beta=0.97;
5 A=1/(alpha*beta);
  delta=1;
7 k_ss= (alpha*beta*A/(1+beta*(delta-1)) )^(1/(1-alpha));

9 err=10;

11 states=1600;
   kvec0=linspace(0.7*k_ss,1.1*k_ss,states);
13 % Computes the 'grid' for k.

15 vini=1/(1-beta)*log(A*kvec0.^alpha-delta*kvec0);
   % Initial guess for V(kt), speeds up the solution.
17 % Note that vfin is not declared, since it is not required in the
   % current version of Matlab.
19
   iter=0;
21
   tic
```

```
while err>10^(-5)

    for i=1:states
        cons=A*kvec0(i)^alpha+(1-delta)*kvec0(i)-kvec0;
        util=log(cons);
        [vfin(i),ind(i)]=max(util+beta*vini);
    end

    err=max(abs(vini-vfin));
    vini=vfin;
    iter=iter+1;
    disp(iter) % This displays the iteration number.
end

toc
```

vfi_interp.m

This provides an example of value function iteration with interpolation of the value function. Note that it calls a function, written in a separate file (also called a "function m-file"). This is the "valfunlog.m" file, which describes the value function and to which we will come back shortly.

```
% Value function iteration with interpolation.
clear;

global vini beta delta alpha A kvec i
% 'global' declares variables as valid for all the functions used in
% this script. Usage of global variables is not advisable, since it
% tends to make more difficult the detection of errors. Nonetheless,
% here you have an example.

% Parameter values.
alpha = 0.3;
beta = 0.97;
delta = 1;

A=(1-beta*(1-delta))/(alpha*beta);
% This allows to normalize the steady-state capital to 1 for any
% delta.

k_hat=(alpha*beta*A/(1+beta*(delta-1)) )^(1/(1-alpha));
% Steady-state for capital.

states=1600;
```

```
kmin = 0.7*k_hat;
kmax = 1.1*k_hat;
delta_k = (kmax-kmin)/(states-1);
kvec=kmin:delta_k:kmax;
kvec=kvec';

vini = zeros(states,1);

err=10;
z=0;
maxiter=1000;
% Exit clause for the case that the main loop fails to converge.

tic

while err > 10^(-5) && z<maxiter
z=z+1;

for i = 1:states
    k1 = fminbnd(@valfunlog,kmin,kmax);
    % fminbnd finds the local minimum of the single-variable function
    % "valfunlog" (which is log(c) + beta*vini) in the interval
    % [kmin, kmax].

    vfin(i,1) = - valfunlog(k1);
    % This updates the value of the function in state i.

    cons0_opt(i,1) = A*kvec(i)^(alpha)+(1-delta)*kvec(i)-k1;
    % This updates the optimal consumption at time 0 in state i.
end

v_old=vini;

delta_v=abs(vini-vfin);
err=max(delta_v);
vini = vfin;
% norm(delta_v)
% This computes the euclidean norm of the errors which can be used as
% an alternative convergence criterion.

disp(z) % This shows the # of the iteration.
end

toc
```

valfunlog.m

Here we show the file valfunlog.m. Since it is a function file, it can be used by any Matlab script.

```
function val=valfunlog(k)
% This contains the value function for the neoclassical growth model
% with log utility.

global vini beta delta alpha A kvec i
% The script vfi_interp.m declares the above variables as 'global'.

k_low=max(sum(k>kvec),1);
k_high=k_low+1;
v_interp = vini(k_low) + (k-kvec(k_low))* ...
    (vini(k_high) - vini(k_low))/(kvec(k_high) - kvec(k_low));

% This identifies the gridpoints that falls just below and above the
% choice for k and then does the interpolation.

% v_interp = interp1(kvec,vini,k);
% Alternative: this performs the interpolation using the in-built
% Matlab function.

cons = A*kvec(i)^alpha - k + (1-delta)*kvec(i);
% This computes the consumption corresponding to k
if cons<=0
    val = -1000000;
    % imposes a large negative value if consumption is negative
else
    val = log(cons) + beta*v_interp;
end
val = -val;
% Since the script vfi_interp.m uses "fminbnd" which is a minimiza-
% tion routine, the value is turned negative.
```

policyfn_ iter.m

This provides a simple policy function iteration routine for our deterministic model.

```
% Policy function iteration routine
clear;

alpha=0.3;
beta=0.97;
```

```
A=1/(alpha*beta);
k_ss=1;

err=10;

states=1600;
kvec0=linspace(0.7*k_ss,1.1*k_ss,states);
states=max(size(kvec0));

vini=zeros(1,states);
% vini=1/(1-beta)*log(A*kvec0.^alpha-delta*kvec0);
% Above there is the alternative initial guess for V(kt) used to
% speed up the solution.

vfin=zeros(1,states);
iter=0;

tic

while err>10^(-8)
     for i=1:states
       cons=A*kvec0(i)^alpha-kvec0;
       util=log(cons);
       [vfin(i),ind(i)]=max(util+beta*vini);
     end
       % 'ind' indicates the position on the grid for kt+1 that is
       % consistent with the optimal choice.

   knew=kvec0(ind); % This is kt+1 in paper.
   consnew=A*kvec0.^alpha-knew;
   utilnew=log(consnew);

J=zeros(states,states);

   for i=1:states
       J(i,ind(i))=1;
   end
   % This obtains matrix J from utility maximization.

   vfin=( (inv(eye(states)-beta*J))*utilnew' )';
   % This gives V1(kt) in main text (recall that vfin has been defi-
   % ned as a row vector).
err=max(abs(vini-vfin));
vini=vfin;

iter=iter+1;
disp(iter)
```

```
end
toc

% This computes the true maximum value function - refer to Chapter 3.
cost1=1/(1-beta)*( alpha*beta/(1-alpha*beta)*log(alpha*beta)+ ...
    log(1-alpha*beta)+1/(1-alpha*beta)*log(A));
cost2=alpha/(1-alpha*beta);
vtrue=cost1+cost2*log(kvec0);

% =============== The lines below produces Figure 4.4 ===============
figure
fontsize=13; % Size of font (in points).
plot(kvec0, vfin-vtrue);
xlim([0.7 1.1]);
% This creates xlabel.
xlabel('Capital','FontSize',fontsize,'FontName','Times␣New␣Roman');
% This creates ylabel.
ylabel('Approximation␣errors','FontSize',fontsize,...
'FontName','Times␣New␣Roman');
% This creates title.
title({'Policy␣Iteration:'; 'Approximation␣Errors'},'FontSize',...
fontsize+3, 'FontName','Times␣New␣Roman')
```

endogrid_det.m

This obtains the policy function using the endogenous grid method.

```
% Endogenous grid for the policy function in deterministic Ramsey
clear;
options = optimoptions('fsolve','Display','none');
% Options for the non-linear solver.

alpha=0.3;
beta=0.97;
delta=1;

A=(1-beta*(1-delta))/(alpha*beta);
% This allows to normalize the steady-state capital to 1 for any
% delta.

k_hat=(alpha*beta*A/(1+beta*(delta-1)) )^(1/(1-alpha));

states=1601;
kmin=.6*k_hat;
kmax=1.1*k_hat;

delta_k = (kmax-kmin)/(states-1);
```

```
kvec=kmin:delta_k:kmax;

cons1=A*kvec.^alpha;
% This is our 'sensible' initial guess for consumption.

err=10;
z=0;

tic

while err > 10^(-6)
    z=z+1;
    cons0 = cons1./ (alpha*beta*A*kvec.^(alpha-1)+beta*(1-delta)) ;
    % Consumption in period 0 satisfies the Euler equation.

    if delta == 1
        kvec0=((kvec+cons0)/A).^(1/alpha);
        % When delta=1 solution for period 0 capital is explicit.
    else
    kvec0=fsolve(@endo_k0,kvec,options,kvec,cons0,A,delta,alpha);
    % Numerical solution for period 0 capital (in vector form); note
    % that initial condition is kvec, which is reasonably efficient.
end
disp(z)

cons1new=interp1(kvec0,cons0,kvec,'linear','extrap');
% Interpolation for consumption. It also allows for extrapolation
% should the interval for kvec be too small.

resid=cons1-cons1new;
err=max(abs(resid));

cons1=cons1new;

end
toc
```

endo_k0.m

This is the function file storing the capital accumulation constraint.

```
% This function obtains kvec0 (here called x), in vector notation
function F = endo_k0(x,kvec,cons0,A,delta,alpha)
F=A*x.^alpha+(1-delta)*x-kvec-cons0;
```

4.4.2 Your coding exercises

Consider the Ramsey model with return function $U(c_t) = \ln c_t$ and dynamic constraint $k_{t+1} = k_t + Ak_t^\alpha - c_t$. Let $A = 1$, $\alpha = 0.25$, and $\beta = 0.98$. Assume that the irreversibility constraint $k_{t+1} \geq k_t$ applies. Find the value function by means of a value function iteration routine, and compare your results with those you obtain in the absence of the irreversibility constraint.

Consider the Ramsey model with return function $U(c_t) = \ln c_t$; output is given by $y_t = Ak_t^\alpha$. Let $A = 1$, $\alpha = 0.25$, and $\beta = 0.98$. Assume capital does not depreciate, and that a unit of investment costs $i_t + \varphi i_t^2/2$, with $\varphi = 0.20$. Find the value function by means of a value function iteration routine.

Assume that the return function is $U(c_t, l_t) = \ln(c_t - \phi l_t^\psi)$, where l_t is labor time; the dynamic constraint is $k_{t+1} = (1 - \delta)\, k_t + Ak_t^\alpha l_t^{1-\alpha} - c_t$. The parameter values are: $\phi = 1$, $\psi = 2$, $A = 1$, $\delta = 0.15$, $\alpha = 0.25$, and $\beta = 0.98$. Find the value function and the policy functions by means of a value function iteration routine.

Consider a deterministic version of the Brock and Mirman model with return function $U(c_t, l_t) = \ln c_t + \gamma \ln(1 - l_t)$, $\gamma = 3\,(1 - \alpha)\,/\,(1 - \alpha\beta)$ (why?). The dynamic constraint is $k_{t+1} = (1 - \delta)\, k_t + Ak_t^\alpha l_t^{1-\alpha} - c_t$, with parameter values $A = 1$, $\delta = 0.15$, $\alpha = 0.25$, and $\beta = 0.98$. Find the value function and the policy functions by means of a value function iteration routine.

Consider a deterministic version of the Brock and Mirman model with return function $U(c_t, l_t) = \ln c_t + \gamma \ln(1 - l_t)$, $\gamma = 3\,(1 - \alpha)\,/\,(1 - \alpha\beta)$ (why?). The dynamic constraint is $k_{t+1} = (1 - \delta)\, k_t + Ak_t^\alpha l_t^{1-\alpha} - c_t$. with parameter values $A = 1$, $\delta = 0.15$, $\alpha = 0.25$, and $\beta = 0.98$. Find the policy functions using the endogenous grid method.

Notes

[1] After reading the current section, justify this choice.

[2] If you feel confused by this, just go on reading.

[3] Here the logic is the same we used in Subsection 1.1.4 to argue that $k_{T+1} = 0$.

[4]Jesse Perla, Thomas J. Sargent and John Stachurski maintain two websites, focusing on Python and on Julia, respectively, that present lectures and examples on dynamic programming and its applications to many economic models.

You can refer to `https://quantecon.org/about-python-lectures` and to `https://julia.quantecon.org/intro.html`.

[5]The Matlab routines used to solve our examples can be found in the Appendix.

[6]Those who have read Subsection 2.2.1 may recall that we have defined contraction mappings for the Euclidean space and for the Euclidean distance. Then, invoking Stokey, Lucas, and Prescott (1989), we have stated that the definition of a contraction mapping applies also for the space of bounded functions, when the sup norm is chosen as the distance measure between any two functions. Consider that each row in Table 2 representes a function; and recall that it is the application of (2.8) to row n that generates row $n+1$. One can now verify that the sup norm between rows n and m is higher than the sup norm between rows $n+1$ and $m+1$.

[7]Note that our convergence criterion is actually based on the sup norm.

[8]Since the sum of the elements in each row of matrix βJ_0 is equal to $\beta < 1$ the matrix $[I - \beta J_0]$ is invertible, by application of the Perron-Frobenius Theorem.

[9]However, when using a policy iteration procedure, the further savings granted by the use of a smarter initial guess are not great: they hardly reach 45% (Why?).

[10]More precisely, any $0.644460 < \mu < 1.138862$ would do the job. Indeed, for example note that

$$\underline{\underline{k}}_0 = \left(\frac{\mu + \beta\alpha}{\beta\alpha A} \underline{\underline{k}}_1 \right)^{1/\alpha} < \underline{\underline{k}}_1$$

when

$$\underline{\underline{k}}_1 = 0.6\hat{k} < \hat{k}\,(\mu + 0.291)^{-1/0.7} .$$

[11]If one chooses a different number of grid points for the two state variables–therefore dividing the plane into small rectangles–the argument in the main text must be properly adapted.

[12]The presence of an irreversibility constraint is much more interesting in a stochastic model than in a deterministic one. Figure 1.3 suggests that whenever the initial capital stock is below the steady-state, capital grows over time until it reaches its steady state value. Accordingly, an irreversibility constraint can bind only if our representative agent receives, as a gift, a capital level that is so much higher than the steady-state one, that she wants to decumulate it at a fast rate. Instead, in a stochastic model, a shock may be sufficient to make the irreversibility constraint binding.

Note that, when the irreversibility constraint is binding, our consumer is forced to consume less than what would be optimal. This means she would like to avoid finding herself in this situation. Therefore, the awareness that the irreversibility constraint may be binding, even if with a low probability, can be sufficient to deeply influence the representative agent's behavior. We shall briefly return to models with stochastically binding constraints in Section 8.4.

5

Collocation and perturbation with paper and pencil

ABSTRACT This chapter discusses two well-known and widely used alternatives to function iteration methods. First, it shows how to obtain a global solution using the collocation method, which usually reduces the computation time. The collocation method is introduced as a way to "interpolate" a function; it is then shown how it can be used to approximate the solution of a simple differential equation. The final step is the solution of a Bellman problem using the very convenient Chebyshev polynomials, which allow for the efficient solution of a large class of dynamic problems. Next, the chapter discusses the perturbation method, which essentially involves obtaining a solution around the steady state. The approach is introduced to approximate the solution to a simple quadratic equation, and it is gradually extended to obtain a second-order approximation to the solution of the consumption-growth problem.

Before starting, a word of warning. Collocation techniques usually provide a global solution with significant savings in computational time, compared to function iteration methods. However, as is almost always the case, there is a price to pay, which is collected in terms of additional coding time. In contrast–if one is willing to focus on the vicinity of the steady state–the perturbation method is very handy. Dynare, for example, allows us to obtain an approximated solution for a general equilibrium model simply by writing the equilibrium conditions in an appropriate form.[1] Thanks to the efforts of

DOI: 10.4324/9781003774051-5

Michel Juillard and his collaborators, Dynare runs on Matlab, Octave and Julia.[2] Readers interested in a general overview on how Dynare works can directly jump to Section 5.2.

5.1 Collocation techniques

The methods explained in Chapter 4 require the evaluation of the value function at a large number of points. If we could compute it at a smaller set of points without losing the accuracy of the approximation, we would travel a significant way down the road to efficiency. This is what collocation techniques achieve. They are usually considered efficient for providing approximate solutions for dynamic models (and not only for them).

To understand the idea underlying this technique, we need to introduce the Weierstrass Theorem, which states:

Theorem 5 *Any continuous real function $f(x)$ can be approximated in a closed and bounded interval X by a polynomial $p_n(x) = \sum_{i=0}^{n} a_i x^i$.*

The words "can be approximated" mean that for any number $\nu > 0$, there is a polynomial, of a suitable degree, $p_n(x)$, such that $\max_{x \in X} |f(x) - p_n(x)| < \nu$. A reduction in ν, i.e. in the approximation error, usually requires an increase in the degree of the polynomial.[3]

This is interesting and rather intuitive, but it does not tell us how to proceed in practice. Since the application of the collocation technique to a Bellman equation is relatively complex, we will approach its practical implementation in small steps, beginning with an application to a trigonometric function.

5.1.1 *Approximation of a trigonometric function using a standard polynomial*

Let us choose a relatively challenging function: suppose we need to approximate $\sin(x)$ over the interval $X = [0, 2\pi]$. Let us start with a third degree polynomial, $p_3(x) = a_0 + a_1 x + a_2 x^2 + a_3 x^3$. Our problem is to determine the four coefficients (the a_i) so that our polynomial behaves "as closely as possible" to $\sin(x)$ in the interval X.

For the polynomial to mimic $\sin(x)$, we impose equality between the two functions at some points, called "collocation points." In fact, the approximation of a function using the collocation method is similar to what one can do with some pins and a flexible plastic stick: one takes the stick (the polynomial) and the pins (the values of the function at the collocation points), and uses the pins to fix the stick onto the function.

Because we need to determine four unknown coefficients, we choose four points in X. By imposing equality between $\sin(x)$ and $p_3(x)$ at these points, we obtain four equations for the a_i, which can be solved for the unknown coefficients. For example, let us choose $x = \{0, 2\pi/3, 4\pi/3, 2\pi\}$.[4] At these points, the collocation method forces the approximating polynomial to be identical to the function being approximated. This gives:

$$\begin{cases} 0 = a_0 \\ 0.86603 = a_0 + a_1 2.09440 + a_2 4.38649 + a_3 9.18704 \\ -0.86603 = a_0 + a_1 4.18879 + a_2 17.54596 + a_3 73.49636 \\ 0 = a_0 + a_1 6.28319 + a_2 39.47842 + a_3 248.05021 \end{cases} \tag{5.1}$$

Solving for the a_i in this linear system, we obtain:

$$\begin{cases} a_0 &= 0 \\ a_1 &= 1.860735 \\ a_2 &= -0.888436 \\ a_3 &= 0.094266 \end{cases} .$$

Therefore, the approximating third-degree polynomial is:

$$p_3(x) = 0 + 1.860735x - 0.888436x^2 + 0.094266x^3.$$

For a "first-impression judgment" of the goodness of fit, we plot our polynomial and the $\sin(x)$ function over the interval $[0, 2\pi]$. In Figure 5.1, the solid line represents $\sin(x)$, while the dashed line is its third-degree approximation. Some further calculations show that the largest difference between the two functions is 0.255346. Although this is a large number, we can be fairly satisfied with our exercise: we were able to approximate a trigonometric function using a simple third-degree polynomial.

However, you must be aware that our approximation deteriorates rapidly as we move outside of the interval $X = [0, 2\pi]$–compute $p_3(x)$ at $x = 2.5\pi$!. The rapid deterioration of the approximation outside the interval is a general feature of the results obtained using this approach. As noted, it is similar to fitting a flexible plastic stick to a desired shape: using a decent number of pins, we can easily do a good job within the interval between the first and the last pin; outside this interval, the plastic stick retains its original shape.

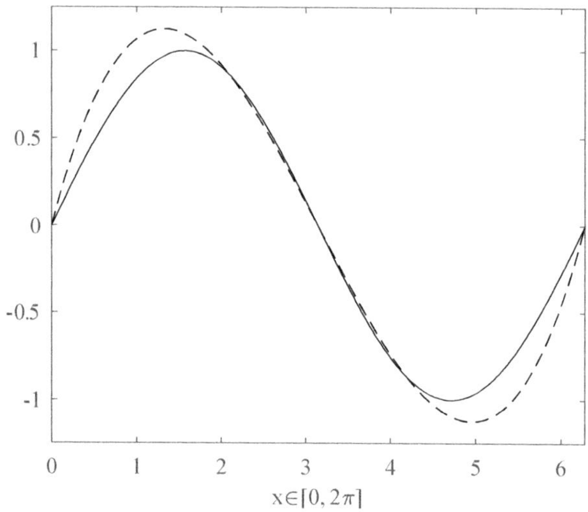

FIGURE 5.1. $sin(x)$ (solid line) versus its 3rd degree approximation (dashed line)

It is now time to put aside paper and pencil once again. By choosing, for example, eleven collocation points, and therefore using a tenth-degree polynomial, we can easily build a system of eleven equations. We can then use the matrix manipulation tools built into software platforms such as Matlab, Octave, or Julia to solve the system.[5] With Matlab, this should take less than $1/100^{th}$ of a second.[6] You can deal with this problem using Mathematica or Maple as well.

Figure 5.2 shows the approximation errors for this exercise. An approximation error is defined as the difference between the actual value for $\sin(x)$ and the corresponding value of the approximating polynomial, for $x \in [0, 2\pi]$. The bright side is that we are really doing a decent job; the somehow dark side is that the errors are definitely higher than average at the beginning and at the end of the interval. This is usually regarded as a sign that we can improve our approximation.

5.1.2 *Approximation of the solution to a linear differential equation*

It is now possible to climb a step of the ladder that is bringing us to the solution of the dynamic optimization problem. Thus far, we have shown that we can approximate a function using a polynomial. The solution to a difference or differential equation *is* itself a function (in our next example,

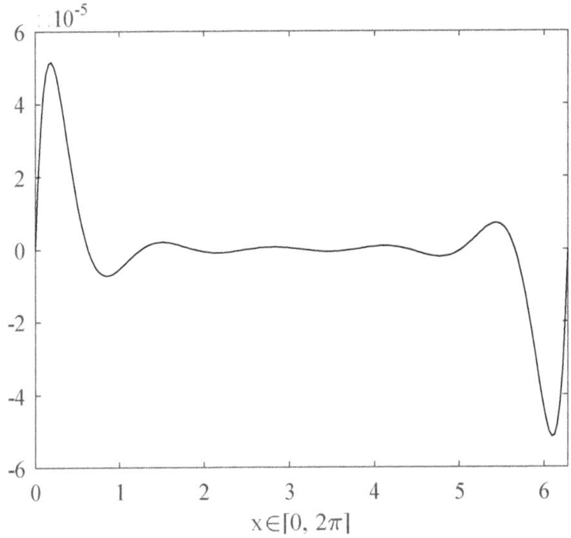

FIGURE 5.2. Approximation errors for $sin(x)$ using a 10th degree standard polynomial

the solution will be a function of time, which acts as the state variable). This suggests that our collocation technique can be used to approximate the solution of a functional equation.

As before, we will begin with a simple example, specifically, a differential equation that is easily solved analytically. This will let us evaluate the goodness of fit of our approximation.

Suppose that we need to solve the first-order linear differential equation

$$\frac{dx(t)}{dt} = 0.1x(t) + 1, \tag{5.2}$$

over the interval $t \in [0, 4]$, given $x(0) = 2$. Assume that the solution $x(t)$ must be approximated by a second-degree polynomial. Denoting the approximated solution with an overbar, we have:

$$\bar{x}(t) = a_0 + a_1 t + a_2 t^2. \tag{5.3}$$

A good approximation, one that behaves "almost like" the true solution $x(t)$, must satisfy Eq. (5.2). Since the true solution fulfills Eq. (5.2) for any t, it is more than reasonable to require that $\bar{x}(t)$ satisfies (5.2) at least somewhere–specifically, at the collocation points. At these points the approximation must be such that:

$$\frac{d\bar{x}(t)}{dt} = 0.1\bar{x}(t) + 1.$$

By using the polynomial form (5.3) on both sides of the last equation, it must be that at the collocation points:

$$a_1 + 2a_2t = 0.1(a_0 + a_1t + a_2t^2) + 1.$$

To determine the three coefficients we now collocate the above equation at *two* points. The two collocation points are the extrema of the interval (0 and 4): had we chosen two different points, we would have induced large errors in parts of the interval of interest.[7] The third equation for our system is provided by the initial condition $\bar{x}(0) = a_0 = 2$. This is an important feature of the solution that we do not want to overlook. Accordingly, the system that determines the coefficients is:

$$\begin{cases} a_1 = 0.1a_0 + 1 \\ a_1 + 8a_2 = 0.1a_0 + 0.4a_1 + 1.6a_2 + 1 \\ a_0 = 2. \end{cases} \tag{5.4}$$

A few calculations are all we need to get the approximating function: $\bar{x}(t) = 2 + 1.2t + 0.075t^2$. In Figure 5.3, the dashed line represents the approximating function, while the solid line shows the exact solution, which is: $x(t) = -10 + 12e^{0.1t}$.

We could now compute the approximation errors as the difference between $x(t)$ and $\bar{x}(t)$. However, the analysis of these errors is of no practical interest: why should we bother with the errors from a numerical solution when we can compute the exact one? Knowing the errors of an approximation is instead of great interest when an analytic solution does not exist. This observation leads us to a crucial question: when the analytic solution for a functional equation is unknown, how can we judge the goodness of the approximation?

The standard answer is grounded in Eq. (5.2): since the true function satisfies this equation for any t, a good approximation should do the same. We therefore compute the "residual function:"

$$R(t) = \frac{d\bar{x}(t)}{dt} - 0.1\bar{x}(t) - 1, \; t \in [0, 4],$$

and we inspect it. If this function takes values that are "almost zero," the approximation is good.[8]

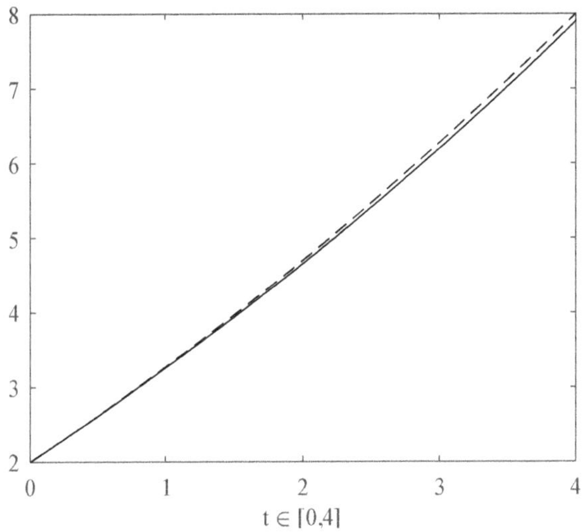

FIGURE 5.3. Exact solution for $dx(t)/dt = 0.1x(t) + 1$ (solid line) versus its approximation using a 2nd degree polynomial (dashed line)

In our example, the residual function is given by:

$$R(t) = 1.2 + 0.15t - 0.2 - 0.12t - 0.0075t^2 - 1 = 0.03t - 0.0075t^2.$$

Instead, the approximation errors, computed as the difference between the exact solution and the approximated one, are given by:

$$x(t) - \bar{x}(t) = -10 + 12e^{0.1t} - \left(2 + 1.2t + 0.075t^2\right) = \\ = 12e^{0.1t} - 12 - 1.2t - 0.075t^2.$$

Figure 5.4 shows the errors we make when we let our computer approximate the solution using an eight-degree polynomial.[9] The solid line represents the "true" errors, while the residual function is shown by the dashed line. Both the errors and the residuals are computed for 200 equally spaced points in the interval $t \in [0, 4]$.

While the approximation is very good, it can be further improved: again, note that the residuals are higher than average at the beginning and especially at the end of the interval, suggesting that some improvement is possible.

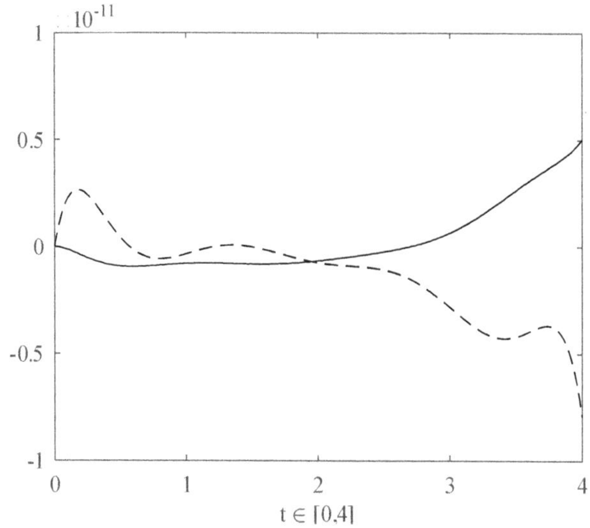

FIGURE 5.4. Approximating $dx(t)/dt = 0.1x(t) + 1$ using an 8th degree polynomial: approximation errors (solid line) and residuals (dashed line)

5.1.3 Approximate solution for the Ramsey model using a standard polynomial

Finally, we are ready to tackle the problem we are really interested in. We will now solve:

$$V(k_0) = \max_{c_0} \{\ln(c_0) + 0.97V(k_1)\},$$
$$s.t.\ k_1 = 3.43643k_0^{0.3} + 0.85k_0 - c_0,$$

for $k_0 \in [0.5\hat{k}, \hat{k}]$, where $\hat{k}$ is the steady-state level of capital (currently standing at around 12.01). Note that this is the same problem we analyzed in Section 4.1, but with the difference that the depreciation parameter now takes the much more sensible value $\delta = 0.15$. Note also that we are dealing with a quite large interval for the state variable.

First, suppose the maximum value function is approximated by an ordinary $n-th$ degree polynomial: $V(k) = \sum_{i=0}^{n} a_i k^i$. Exploiting the first-order condition, $1/c_0 = 0.97V'(k_1)$, we immediately obtain that:

$$c_0 = \frac{1}{0.97 \sum\limits_{i=1}^{n} i\ a_i k_1^{(i-1)}}.$$

Substituting the approximating function and the first-order condition above into the original problem, we obtain:

$$\sum_{i=0}^{n} a_i k_0^i = -\ln(0.97) - \ln\left(\sum_{i=1}^{n} i\ a_i k_1^{(i-1)}\right) + 0.97 \sum_{i=0}^{n} a_i k_1^i.$$

There are $n+2$ unknowns in this equation. Specifically, for any given collocation point k_0 we need to determine the next-period state, k_1, and the $n+1$ coefficients (the a_i).

If we couple the equation above with the dynamic constraint, we get a system of two equations with $n+2$ unknowns (the $n+1$ a_i and the next-period state), which is:

$$\begin{cases} \sum_{i=0}^{n} a_i k_0^i = -\ln(0.97) - \ln\left(\sum_{i=1}^{n} i\ a_i k_1^{(i-1)}\right) + 0.97 \sum_{i=0}^{n} a_i k_1^i \\ \\ k_1 = 3.43643 k_0^{0.3} + 0.85 k_0 - \left(0.97 \sum_{i=1}^{n} i\ a_i k_1^{(i-1)}\right)^{-1}. \end{cases} \tag{5.5}$$

Note that the number of extra equations needed to get a determined system is n.

Now, let us consider *two* levels for k_0 (i.e., two collocation points). In this case, we have a system of four equations with $n+3$ unknowns: the $n+1$ coefficients and two next-period states. Note that we have narrowed the gap toward closing the system: the number of "missing equations" is now $(n+3)-4 = n-1$. Therefore, if we choose $n+1$ collocation points (which means $n+1$ values for $k_0 \in [0.5\hat{k}, \hat{k}]$), we have $2n+2$ unknowns: the $n+1$ coefficients and the $n+1$ values for k_1 (one for each collocation point). Thus, we can build a system composed of $2n+2$ equations. For each of the $n+1$ collocation points, we create a two-equation system like (5.5), and then we assemble all of these into a larger system of $2n+2$ equations. In other words, System (5.5) is the building block for the large system we need to solve to determine the $n+1$ a_i coefficients and the $n+1$ k_1 values.

Besides being large, such system is also nonlinear, so we need to rely on the nonlinear equation solver built into Matlab.[10] Moreover, a glance at (5.5) is enough to convince oneself that our system is *highly* nonlinear. Hence, one might run into troubles with the nonlinear equation solver.[11]

An often-used way out is to determine the consumption function from the Euler equation. This escape route is convenient but suffers from a significant drawback: since the computation of the policy function does not rely directly on the contraction mapping theorem, the attainment of the solution is not guaranteed. From a practical point of view, when computing a policy function it is often advisable to use any extra information about the solution, such as the value of consumption in the steady state.

In our specific case the Euler equation readily gives

$$c_1 = c_0 \left(k_1^{-0.7} + 0.8245\right),$$

hence, assuming $c_t = \sum_{i=0}^{n} d_i k_t^i$, (and recalling that $\alpha\beta A = 1$), we have, for each collocation point, a system of the form:

$$\begin{cases} \sum\limits_{i=0}^{n} d_i k_1^i = \sum\limits_{i=0}^{n} d_i k_0^i \left(k_1^{-0.7} + 0.8245\right) \\ k_1 = 3.43643 k_0^{0.3} + 0.85 k_0 - \sum\limits_{i=0}^{n} d_i k_0^i, \end{cases} \tag{5.6}$$

The system above involves two equations and $n+2$ unknowns: the $n+1$ coefficients (d_i) and the next-period state, k_1, which is related to the value of k_0 pertaining to our collocation point.

It is tempting to conclude that we can now choose $n+1$ collocation points and solve a $(2n+2)$-equation system (composed of $n+1$ blocks like 5.6) for the $n+1$ values of k_1 and the $n+1$ coefficients d_i. However, this is not the best way to proceed. As mentioned earlier, it is helpful to incorporate into the system the knowledge that, in the steady state,

$$\hat{c}\left(= \sum_{i=0}^{n} d_i \hat{k}^i\right) = 3.43643\hat{k}^{0.3} - 0.15\hat{k}. \tag{5.7}$$

Loosely speaking, if we do not consider this information, our routine might give us a solution that characterizes consumption on one of the (infinite) non-optimal paths where the Euler equation is satisfied (refer to Figure 1.3). To incorporate the piece of information provided by the steady state, when we use a nth degree polynomial we choose only n collocation points instead of $n+1$. In this way, we have $2n+1$ unknowns: $n+1$ coefficients and n values for k_1). Recall that for each collocation point we have two equations (refer to System 5.6), which gives us $2n$ equations. The steady-state equation above closes the system, which can actually be solved rather easily (with a nonlinear equation solver). Figures 5.5a and 5.5b show the consumption function and the residuals.[12] These were obtained using an eighth-degree polynomial; the computation time was about $9/100^{th}$ of a second.

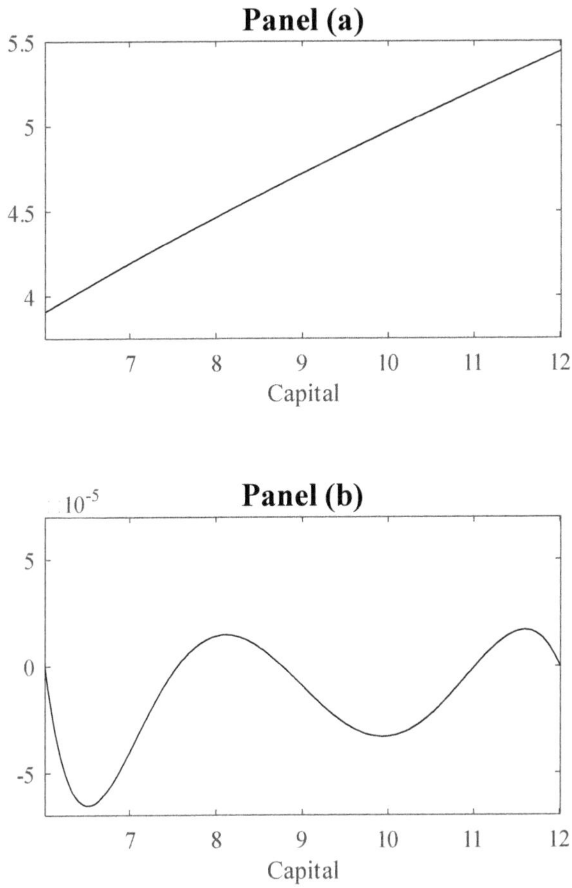

FIGURE 5.5. Consumption function (Panel a) and Euler equation residual (Panel b) using an 8th degree standard polynomial

Our exercises have been based on standard power polynomials. This choice is usually considered very inefficient, as standard polynomials exhibit some unpleasant characteristics that will be highlighted in the next subsection. Furthermore, we have always chosen evenly spaced collocation nodes. There is no reason to believe that this is the optimal choice for the nodes. Indeed, this can cause the residuals to be much higher than average in subintervals of the state variable's range, typically close to its boundaries (in our case, this occurred when capital was roughly between 6.2 and 7.2). These issues are addressed in the next subsection, where we introduce a different type of polynomials–the Chebyshev ones–which are of great help from several perspectives.

5.1.4 Collocation using Chebyshev polynomials

Standard polynomials are a very inefficient choice. The most important reason for this inefficiency is illustrated in Figure 5.6, which shows the behavior of the standard monomials x, x^2, x^3, x^4, x^5, and x^6 for $x \in [-1, 1]$. The behavior of the even-degree monomials, and also of the odd-degree ones starting from the third degree, is very similar. Therefore, adding more terms to the polynomial may not reduce the approximation errors.[13]

There are several possible alternatives to deal with this problem; the most common one is based on Chebyshev polynomials.

In this subsection, we first introduce the Chebyshev polynomials and illustrate their properties. Then we define the Chebyshev nodes, which are the grid points used for the Chebyshev polynomial approximation. Finally–having sketched how to approximate an exponential function using the Chebyshev polynomials–we show how to use them to obtain the consumption function in the standard growth model.

A Chebyshev polynomial is defined as $T_i(x) = \cos(i \arccos(x))$.[14] Note in passing that while each $T_i(x)$ plays a role analogous to a monomial, it is nonetheless referred to as a polynomial in its own right. Furthermore, the set $\{T_i(x)\}_{i=0}^{n}$ is said to form a "basis" for the approximation.

We use as an approximating function a linear combination of Chebyshev polynomials $T_i(x)$ of degree up to n, such that:

$$P_n(x, \mathbf{d}) = \sum_{i=0}^{n} d_i T_i(x) = \sum_{i=0}^{n} d_i \cos(i \arccos(x)), \tag{5.8}$$

where x is a real number such that $x \in [-1, 1]$ and $\mathbf{d}$ is a vector of constants (a vector composed of the coefficients d_i for $i = 0, 1, ..., n$). For example,

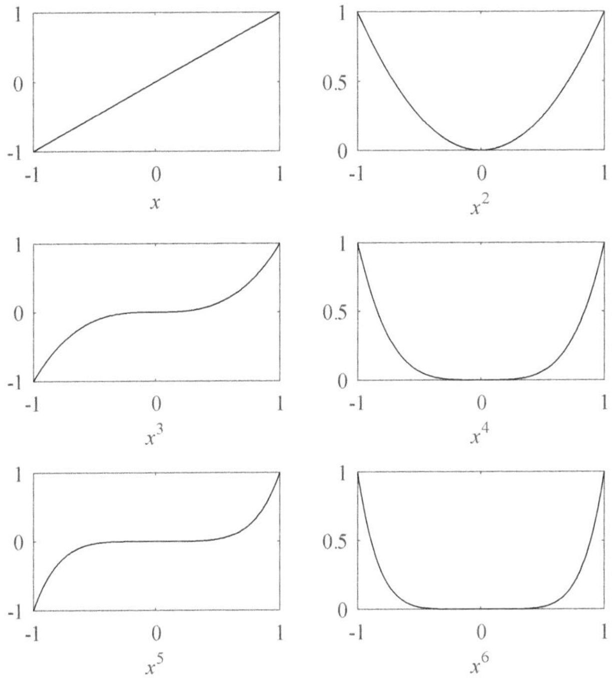

FIGURE 5.6. Behavior of the standard monomials in $[-1, 1]$, degrees ranging from 1 to 6

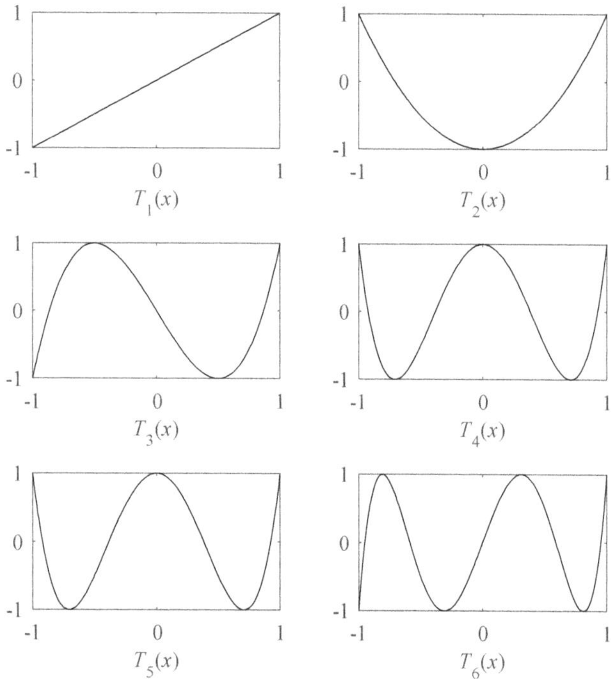

FIGURE 5.7. Behavior of the Chebyshev polynomials in $[-1,1]$, degrees ranging from 1 to 6

choosing $n = 3$ we have that:

$$P_3(x, \mathbf{d}) = \\ = d_0 + d_1 \cos(\arccos(x)) + d_2 \cos(2 \arccos(x)) + d_3 \cos(3 \arccos(x)).$$

Figure 5.7 shows $T_i(x)$ for $i = 1, 2, 3, 4, 5, 6$ and $x \in [-1, 1]$, providing some insight into why the Chebyshev basis is particularly convenient for approximating functions. A quick glance suggests that Chebyshev polynomials allow for a larger number of "bends," making them more flexible than the standard monomials (compare with Figure 5.6).

In Figure 5.8 we arbitrarily set $d_i = 1$ for $i = 0, 1, ..., 4$, and we compare $P_4(x, \mathbf{1})$ (solid line) with the standard polynomial $1 + x + x^2 + x^3 + x^4$ (dashed line), for $x \in [-1, 1]$. This exercise confirms our intuition: Chebyshev polynomials indeed allow for richer shapes! This occurs because with standard polynomials the highest-order element "prevails," whereas this is

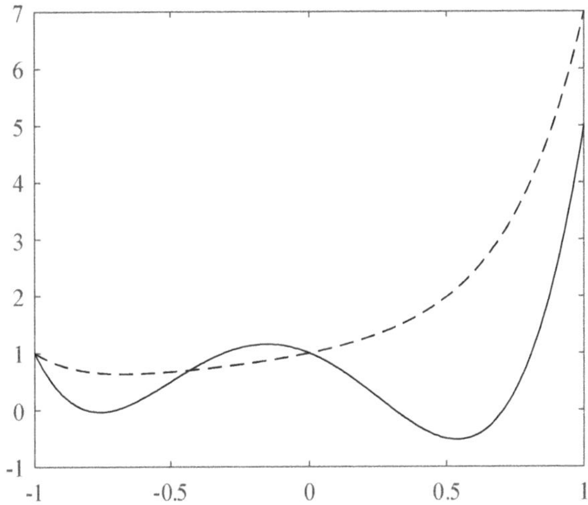

FIGURE 5.8. Sum of monomials up to 4th degree: Chebyshev (solid line) versus ordinary (dashed line)

not the case with Chebyshev polynomials. Of course, one might think that, when approximating a function with a standard polynomial, one can just set the coefficients for the highest powers to a low value. But the flip side is that this "kills" the contribution of the higher degrees of the polynomial.

Approximations based on the Chebyshev polynomials are usually "collocated" at a specific set of points, called the Chebyshev nodes. First, we introduce such nodes, and then we illustrate their important property, which helps us to understand why the use of Chebyshev polynomials (and nodes) is widespread.

To obtain m nodes (m being of course an integer) compute the points:

$$x_s = -\cos\left(\frac{2s-1}{2m}\pi\right) \text{ for } s = 1, 2, ..., m. \tag{5.9}$$

Since $(2s-1)/(2m) \in (0,1)$, $x_s \in (-\cos(0), -\cos(\pi))$, and hence $x_s \in (-1, 1)$. For $m = 9$, the nodes are shown in Figure 5.9.

The Chebyshev polynomials, when evaluated at the Chebyshev nodes, enjoy an important property. Consider a degree n for the basis; then choose two of the polynomials that make up the Chebyshev approximation, say

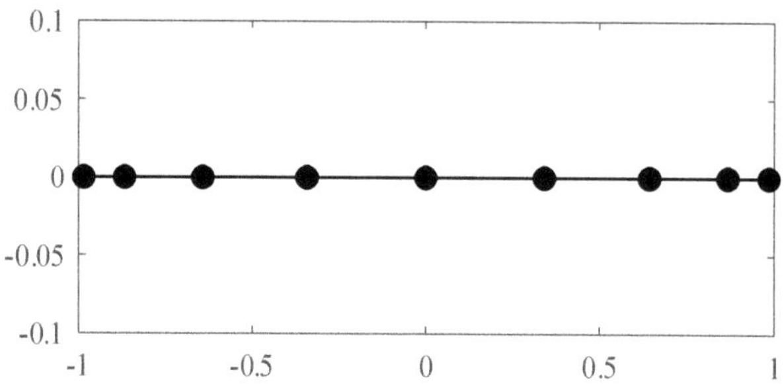

FIGURE 5.9. Chebyshev nodes for $m = 9$

$T_i(x)$ and $T_j(x)$, with $i, j = 0, 1, ..., n$. It is possible to verify that:

$$\sum_{s=1}^{m} T_i(x_s)T_j(x_s) = \begin{cases} 0 \text{ if } i \neq j \\ m \text{ if } i = j = 0 \\ m/2 \text{ if } i = j > 0, \end{cases} \tag{5.10}$$

where m can be different from n.

This property is extremely useful for quickly computing the approximation of a function.

To illustrate this, assume, as in Subsection 5.1.1, that we need to approximate a function $y = f(x)$ over the interval $[-1, 1]$. We use a linear combination of Chebyshev polynomials up to degree n as the approximating function, and we choose m Chebyshev nodes as our collocation points. At these points, it must be true that:

$$\begin{aligned} f(x_1) &= \sum_{i=0}^{n} d_i T_i(x_1) \\ f(x_2) &= \sum_{i=0}^{n} d_i T_i(x_2) \\ \dots &= \dots \\ f(x_m) &= \sum_{i=0}^{n} d_i T_i(x_m). \end{aligned}$$

Obviously, we can multiply both sides of the equations above by any nonzero constant. Let us choose (arbitrarily) the $j - th$ polynomial that makes up the Chebyshev approximation, to obtain:

$$\begin{aligned} T_j(x_1)f(x_1) &= T_j(x_1)\sum_{i=0}^{n} d_i T_i(x_1) \\ T_j(x_2)f(x_2) &= T_j(x_2)\sum_{i=0}^{n} d_i T_i(x_2) \\ \ldots &= \ldots \\ T_j(x_m)f(x_m) &= T_j(x_m)\sum_{i=0}^{n} d_i T_i(x_m). \end{aligned}$$

Summing over the collocation equations yields:

$$\sum_{s=1}^{m} T_j(x_s)f(x_s) = \sum_{s=1}^{m}\left(T_j(x_s)\sum_{i=0}^{n} d_i T_i(x_s)\right).$$

Because the $T_j(x_s)$ are independent of i, the above equation becomes

$$\sum_{s=1}^{m} T_j(x_s)f(x_s) = \sum_{i=0}^{n} d_i \sum_{s=1}^{m} T_i(x_s)T_j(x_s).$$

We are now in the position of exploiting Property (5.10): considering $j = 0, 1, \ldots, n$, we obtain:

$$\begin{aligned} \sum_{s=1}^{m} T_0(x_s)f(x_s) &= \sum_{i=0}^{n} d_i \sum_{s=1}^{m} T_i(x_s)T_0(x_s) = md_0 \\ \sum_{s=1}^{m} T_1(x_s)f(x_s) &= \sum_{i=0}^{n} d_i \sum_{s=1}^{m} T_i(x_s)T_1(x_s) = \frac{m}{2}d_1 \\ \ldots &= \ldots \\ \sum_{s=1}^{m} T_n(x_s)f(x_s) &= \sum_{i=0}^{n} d_i \sum_{s=1}^{m} T_i(x_s)T_n(x_s) = \frac{m}{2}d_n, \end{aligned}$$

which is a system that allows us to get the vector $\mathbf{d}$ quickly and reliably. In fact, each d_i is determined by a single equation![15]

These brief notes strongly support the use of Chebyshev polynomials for approximating smooth functions. Decades of experience have shown that they work well, usually better than other basis functions.[16]

We are now almost ready to use Chebyshev polynomials to solve our standard growth model. However, there is still one small technical issue that we must address. Chebyshev polynomials are defined on the interval $[-1, 1]$, whereas we use a collocation method precisely when we are interested in studying the behavior of an economic system over a large interval of the capital stock, $[\underline{k}, \overline{k}]$. Accordingly, an appropriate variable transformation is required. To illustrate this, suppose we need to approximate the exponential function $y = exp(az)$ over the interval $[\underline{z}, \bar{z}]$. The variable z can be seen as a function of x, and x is defined on the interval $[-1, 1]$. The values for x are transformed into the values for z by the mapping:

$$z = \underline{z} + \frac{\bar{z} - \underline{z}}{2}(x + 1). \tag{5.11}$$

Choosing an approximation of degree n, one can set up a system, similar in principle to (5.1), composed of $n + 1$ equations:

$$P_n(x_s, \mathbf{d}) = \exp\left(a\left(\underline{z} + \frac{\bar{z} - \underline{z}}{2}(x_s + 1)\right)\right), \quad s = 1, 2, ..., \; n + 1,$$

in which the x_s are the $n + 1$ Chebyshev nodes. Solving the above system for vector $\mathbf{d}$ we obtain our approximation for the exponential function.

Eventually, we can solve the Ramsey model. In particular, we will obtain the consumption function from the Euler equation, as we did in Subsection 5.1.3.

We determine $n + 1$ collocation nodes, x_s, using (5.9); we then approximate the aggregate period-0 consumption using a linear combination of Chebyshev polynomials, so that at each node we have the following:

$$c_0(k_{0,s}) \approx P_n(x_s, \mathbf{d}).$$

Note that each node x_s is related to a capital stock (use 5.11)

$$k_{0,s} = \underline{k} + \frac{\bar{k} - \underline{k}}{2}(x_s + 1),$$

so that consumption is a function of capital. Also note that for each Chebyshev node there is a corresponding time-1 capital stock, which is:

$$k_{1,s} = Ak_0(x_s)^{\alpha} + (1 - \delta)\, k_0(x_s) - P_n(x_s, \mathbf{d}).$$

Finally, consider that, to compute time-1 consumption, we need to transform the capital level into the $[-1, 1]$ interval using the inverse of (5.11), which is:

$$x'_s = \frac{2}{\bar{k} - \underline{k}}\left(k_{1,s} - \underline{k}\right) - 1.$$

To summarize, for each collocation point x_s, we have a system in the form:

$$\begin{cases} P_n(x_s', \mathbf{d}) = P_n(x_s, \mathbf{d})\beta\left(\alpha A k_{1,s}^{\alpha-1} + 1 - \delta\right) \\ k_{1,s} = A k_0(x_s)^\alpha + (1-\delta)\, k_0(x_s) - P_n(x_s, \mathbf{d}), \end{cases} \tag{5.12}$$

in which the unknowns are the $n+1$ components of vector $\mathbf{d}$, and $k_{1,s}$ (the relationship between x_s' and $k_{1,s}$ is taken as understood). Choosing $n+1$ collocation points we have $2n+2$ equations determining $\mathbf{d}$ and $k_{1,s}$, for $s = 1, 2, ..., n+1$.

When (as in the previous subsection), $\alpha = .3$, $\beta = .97$, and $\delta = .15$, using an eighth-degree Chebyshev approximation we obtain a consumption function characterized by Euler equation errors that are in the order of $1/100^{th}$ of those reported in Subsection 5.1.3, despite the fact that we have omitted to consider the steady state. Figures 5.10a and 5.10b show the consumption function and the residuals; the computation time is about $3/100^{th}$ of a second.[17]

Before concluding the section, a word of warning: Chebyshev polynomials like smooth functions. When a function has kinks, as it can be the case in the presence of binding constraints, the approximation around these points can be poor.

Having understood the collocation technique, dealing with "finite element" methods should not be prohibitive. While as interpolating function the collocation technique uses a polynomial which can take non-zero values over the entire approximation interval, a finite element method uses interpolating functions that are *defined* to be zero over a large part of the approximation interval, taking the form of a (low-degree) polynomial only over a specific subinterval–refer again to Judd (1998) or to Miranda and Fackler (2002).

The logic of the collocation methods bears some resemblance also to that of the "minimum weighted residuals" technique. In fact, this method is based on the choice of some nodes and of an interpolating function, too. In this case, however, the coefficients of the polynomial are chosen to minimize the (weighted) differences between the value of the function and of the polynomial at the nodes. On this, see again Judd, or McGrattan (1999).

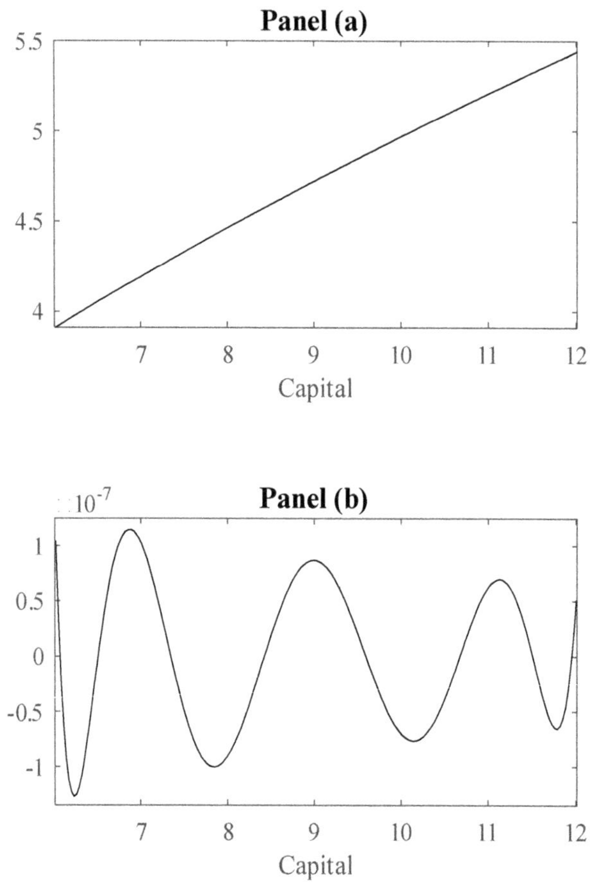

FIGURE 5.10. Consumption function (Panel a) and Euler equation residual (Panel b) using an 8th degree Chebyshev polynomial

5.2 Local approximation: the "perturbation" method

Both value function iteration and collocation are global in the sense that they approximate the value function over a wide range of values for the state variables. In many applications, however, such an effort is not warranted, as the researcher is only interested in what happens in a relatively narrow interval of the state space (for example, around the steady state in a growth model). When this is the case, if the functions making up the model are differentiable (a critical condition) then one can use a linear-quadratic approximation of the model and then proceed as in our Section 3.2. Indeed, this is quite feasible, but the curvature of the relevant functions would be altered or lost. Perturbation techniques allow for the inclusion of higher-order terms in the approximation, so that the non-linear aspects of the optimal behavior are taken into account.

The general idea is as follows: if our original problem—whether it is condensed into an algebraic equation, a differential equation, a stochastic difference equation, or a system of such equations—has no explicit solution, we consider a related, simpler problem for which an analytical solution exists. This related problem is then slightly modified (i.e., it is "perturbed") to make it more similar to the original one. This induces changes in the solution, but if the problem is differentiable with respect to the parameter(s) capturing the change, the solution can be expressed as a "deviation" from the exact solution of the related problem. Such a solution is closer to that of the original problem than the (exact) solution for the associated simpler problem. As we will see shortly, several "rounds" of approximation are usually possible, leading to solutions that are increasingly closer to the true one.

The idea will appear much simpler than it seems now, once illustrated through a simple example. Accordingly, we will now approximate the solution of a quadratic equation using the perturbation method; once the "fog of technicalities" has dispersed, we will apply the method to our workhorse optimal growth model.

5.2.1 *Basic example*

Suppose that we are interested in the non-negative solutions of the following quadratic equation:

$$(1+\epsilon)x^2 - 2(1-\epsilon)\,x - 8 = 0, \tag{5.13}$$

in which, by assumption, ϵ is a non-negative number.

Suppose also that we have forgotten the standard formula for solving quadratic equations, but that we are smart enough to factorize the above equation in the case $\epsilon = 0$, which is particularly easy. Performing this task, we obtain:

$$x^2 - 2x - 8 = (x - 4)(x + 2) = 0,$$

so that it is immediate to see that the solution we are interested in (the positive one) is unique, namely $x = 4$.

To approximate the solution for $\epsilon > 0$, note that we can conceive of the solution for x as a function of ϵ. Henceforth, we will denote it as $x(\epsilon)$. Moreover, we can think that the solution, when ϵ is not too large, can be approximated by means of a Taylor series. Denoting the approximated solution with an overbar, we have that:

$$\bar{x}(\epsilon) = x(0) + \left.\frac{dx(\epsilon)}{d\epsilon}\right|_{\epsilon=0} \epsilon + \frac{1}{2}\left.\frac{d^2x(\epsilon)}{(d\epsilon)^2}\right|_{\epsilon=0} \epsilon^2 + \frac{1}{6}\left.\frac{d^3x(\epsilon)}{(d\epsilon)^3}\right|_{\epsilon=0} \epsilon^3 + ... \tag{5.14}$$

Note that, to compute $\bar{x}(\epsilon)$—beside knowing $x(0)$—we need to compute the derivatives up to the desired order and to evaluate them at $\epsilon = 0$.

At first glance, this appears to be a puzzling problem: how can we compute $dx(\epsilon)/d\epsilon$ if we do not know the function $x(\epsilon)$?

The way out, however, is conceptually simple. For convenience, let us write Eq. (5.13) as:

$$(1 + \epsilon)x(\epsilon)^2 - 2(1 - \epsilon)x(\epsilon) - 8 = 0,$$

let $x'(\epsilon) = dx(\epsilon)/d\epsilon$, and note that the total derivative of the equation above satisfies:

$$x(\epsilon)^2 + 2(1 + \epsilon)x(\epsilon)x'(\epsilon) + 2x(\epsilon) - 2(1 - \epsilon)x'(\epsilon) = 0. \tag{5.15}$$

At $\epsilon = 0$ we have

$$x(0)^2 + 2x(0)x'(0) + 2x(0) - 2x'(0) = 0,$$

which gives:

$$x'(0) = \frac{2x(0) + x(0)^2}{2(1 - x(0))} = -4.$$

In words, we have computed $x'(0)$ by exploiting the implicit function theorem and our knowledge of the fact that $x(0) = 4$.

The Taylor series (5.14), truncated at the first-order term, is then:

$$\bar{x}_1(\epsilon) = x(0) + \left.\frac{dx(\epsilon)}{d\epsilon}\right|_{\epsilon=0} \epsilon = 4 - 4\epsilon.$$

To obtain the second-order terms, we compute the derivative of Eq. (5.15), which yields:

$$\begin{aligned} 2x(\epsilon)x'(\epsilon) + 2x(\epsilon)x'(\epsilon) + 2(1+\epsilon)\left(x'(\epsilon)\right)^2 + 2(1+\epsilon)x(\epsilon)x''(\epsilon) + \\ + 2x'(\epsilon) + 2x'(\epsilon) - 2\left(1-\epsilon\right)x''(\epsilon) = 0, \end{aligned} \quad (5.16)$$

and therefore, collecting terms,

$$2\left[(1+\epsilon)x(\epsilon) - (1-\epsilon)\right]x''(\epsilon) + 4\left[1 + x(\epsilon)\right]x'(\epsilon) + 2(1+\epsilon)x'(\epsilon)^2 = 0,$$

so that, at $\epsilon = 0$,

$$x''(0) = -\frac{4\left[1 + x(0)\right]x'(0) + 2x'(0)^2}{2\left[x(0) - 1\right]} = 8.$$

Accordingly, our second-order approximation for the solution is:

$$\bar{x}_2(\epsilon) = 4 - 4\epsilon + 4\epsilon^2. \quad (5.17)$$

Note that (at least in principle) it would be easy to obtain $x'''(0)$ starting from Eq. (5.16). Since this would not add anything to our understanding of the procedure, we accept (5.17) as our approximation; that is, we truncate the Taylor series at the second term.

Now, assume that the formula for solving a quadratic equation has come back to our minds, so we know that:

$$x(\epsilon) = \frac{4}{1+\epsilon}. \quad (5.18)$$

Using Eq. (5.18), it is immediate to verify that $\bar{x}_1(\epsilon)$ and $\bar{x}_2(\epsilon)$ from (5.17) are identical to the first- and second-order Taylor approximations, respectively, obtained from the true solution.

Figure 5.11 shows the true solution (solid line), and both the first-order (dashed line) and the second-order (dotted line) approximation for $\epsilon \in [0, 1]$. The approximations are "quite good" when ϵ is small, but they then rapidly deteriorate. This is unsurprising, since we are essentially working with Taylor series, which suffer from the same problem. Also, when ϵ is small, the

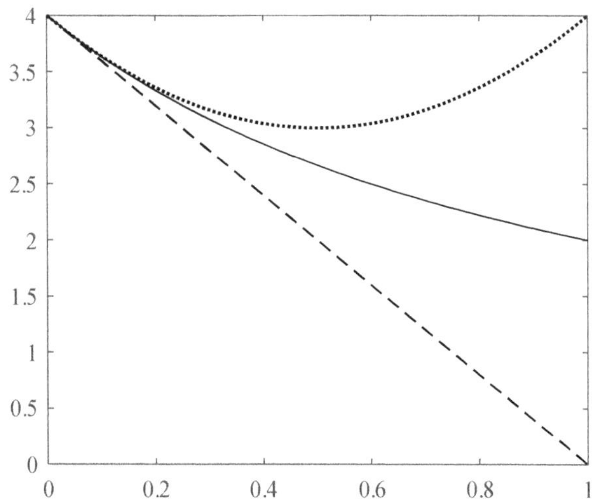

FIGURE 5.11. Exact solution of a quadratic equation (solid line) versus first-order (dashed line) and second-order approximations (dotted line)

second-order approximation is better than the first order one, precisely because it is able to capture some of the curvature required by the solution to our problem. Moreover, note that the second-order approximation deteriorates more rapidly than the first-order one as ϵ increases, precisely due to its quadratic term.

The statement according to which our approximations are "quite good" when ϵ is small is obviously very sloppy. To move one step in the direction of rigor, we can proceed as in Section 5.1 and compute the residual function, which is:

$$R(\epsilon) = abs\left[(1+\epsilon)\bar{x}(\epsilon)^2 - 2\,(1-\epsilon)\,\bar{x}(\epsilon) - 8\right],$$

in which the absolute value facilitates the comparison because the residual may be of different signs. Figure 5.12 shows the residuals for both the first-order (dashed line) and the second-order (dotted line) approximations of the solution.

5.2.2 The neoclassical growth model once again

We now apply these ideas to the Ramsey model, focusing, as usual, on its deterministic discrete-time version. The perturbation ideas are easily employed to obtain its approximate solution. Indeed, the Euler equation relates consumption–which, loosely speaking, plays the role of $x(\epsilon)$ in Eq.

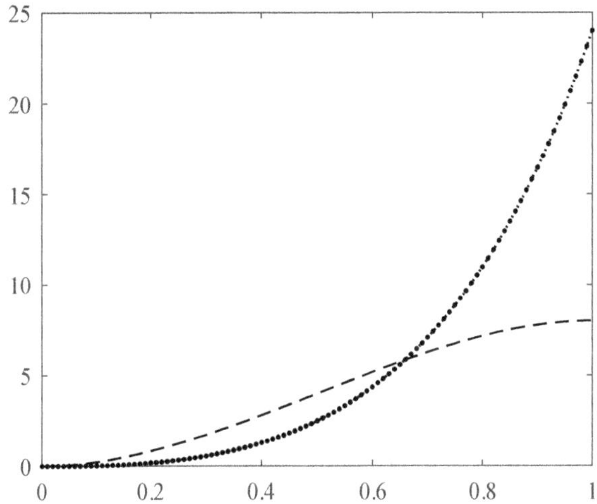

FIGURE 5.12. Solution of a quadratic equation: first-order residuals (dashed line) versus second-order residuals (dotted line)

(5.13)–to capital–which takes the role of ϵ. Moreover, there is a natural reference point around which to perturb the equation, namely the steady state, for which we are able to obtain a solution.

Equipped with these ideas, we can proceed. Our solution amounts to finding the policy function, which is denoted by:

$$c_t = \varphi(k_t). \tag{5.19}$$

The dynamic nature of the Euler equation complicates the procedure a bit, as we need to consider not only the effect of capital on c_t, but also its impacts on c_{t+1} and on k_{t+1}. To address this issue, we find it convenient to set (for brevity) $h(k_t) \equiv Af(k_t) + (1-\delta)\, k_t$, so that the Euler equation is written as:

$$U_c(c_t) = \beta U_c(c_{t+1}) h_k(k_{t+1}). \tag{5.20}$$

Note that the next-period state, k_{t+1}, can be expressed as:

$$k_{t+1} = h(k_t) - \varphi(k_t). \tag{5.21}$$

We now "perturb" Eq. (5.20). Its total derivative is:

$$U_{cc}(c_t)\varphi_k(k_t) = \beta U_{cc}(c_{t+1})\varphi_k(k_{t+1})\left[h_k(k_t) - \varphi_k(k_t)\right] h_k(k_{t+1}) + \\ + \beta U_c(c_{t+1}) h_{kk}(k_{t+1})\left[h_k(k_t) - \varphi_k(k_t)\right]. \quad (5.22)$$

First, let us briefly consider the left-hand side of the equation above. The marginal utility of consumption $U_c(c_t)$ is differentiated with respect to c_t (which gives $U_{cc}(c_t)$); we then consider the change in consumption in response to the change in k_t (via Eq. (5.19), which gives $\varphi_k(k_t)$). The same goes for the first term on the right-hand side, except for the fact that consumption and capital must be considered at time $t+1$, so that the relation between k_{t+1} and k_t must be taken into account (by means of Eq. (5.21)), which explains the term $h_k(k_t) - \varphi_k(k_t)$. While conceptually this is a simple application of the chain rule for differentiation, some care is clearly needed.

Since in the steady state $\beta h_k(\hat{k}) = 1$, Eq. (5.22) readily becomes:

$$\varphi_k(\hat{k}) = \varphi_k(\hat{k})\left[h_k(\hat{k}) - \varphi_k(\hat{k})\right] + \frac{U_c(\hat{c})}{U_{cc}(\hat{c})} h_{kk}(\hat{k})\left[1 - \beta\varphi_k(\hat{k})\right],$$

which can be solved for $\varphi_k(\hat{k})$, the only unknown. In fact, we have:

$$\varphi_k(\hat{k})^2 + \left[1 - h_k(\hat{k}) + \beta\frac{U_c(\hat{c})}{U_{cc}(\hat{c})} h_{kk}(\hat{k})\right]\varphi_k(\hat{k}) - \frac{U_c(\hat{c})}{U_{cc}(\hat{c})} h_{kk}(\hat{k}) = 0,$$

and therefore:

$$\varphi_k(\hat{k}) = \frac{1}{2}\left[-\left[1 - h_k(\hat{k}) + \beta\frac{U_c(\hat{c})}{U_{cc}(\hat{c})} h_{kk}(\hat{k})\right] + \right. \\ \left. + \sqrt{\left(1 - h_k(\hat{k}) + \beta\frac{U_c(\hat{c})}{U_{cc}(\hat{c})} h_{kk}(\hat{k})\right)^2 + 4\frac{U_c(\hat{c})}{U_{cc}(\hat{c})} h_{kk}(\hat{k})}\,\right]. \quad (5.23)$$

Note that we have considered the positive root of the quadratic equation as the only relevant solution. There are good reasons for this. First, on economic grounds, it makes no sense for an increase in the capital stock to reduce consumption: given that the marginal utility of consumption is positive, a wealthier agent should consume more. Second, it can be shown that if $\varphi_k(\hat{k})$ were negative, a deviation from the steady-state capital stock at time t would induce a larger deviation at time $t+1$, implying that capital would diverge from the steady state.[18]

To provide a quantitative assessment of the first-order perturbation based on (5.23), we once again consider the traditional growth model with $U(c_t) = \ln(c_t)$, $y_t = Ak_t^{\alpha}$, $\alpha = 0.3$, $\beta = 0.97$, $\delta = 1$, and $A = 3.436426$ (so that $\hat{k} = 1$ and $\hat{c} = 2.436426$). Some straightforward calculations allow us to get $U_c(\hat{c}) = 0.410437$, $U_{cc}(\hat{c}) = -0.168459$, $h_k(\hat{k}) = 1.030928$, and $h_{kk}(\hat{k}) = -0.721649$. Accordingly, we obtain that $\varphi_k(\hat{k}) = 0.730928$, and hence the first-order approximation is:

$$\overline{\varphi}(k_t) = 2.436426 + 0.730928\,(k_t - 1)\,. \tag{5.24}$$

But, of course, we wish to move to a second-order approximation.

Proceeding as in the previous subsection, we now consider the total derivative of Eq. (5.22), which gives:

$$\begin{aligned}
&U_{ccc}(c_t)\varphi_k(k_t)^2 + U_{cc}(c_t)\varphi_{kk}(k_t) = \\
&\quad = \beta U_{ccc}(c_{t+1})\varphi_k(k_{t+1})^2\,[h_k(k_t) - \varphi_k(k_t)]^2\, h_k(k_{t+1}) + \\
&\quad + \beta U_{cc}(c_{t+1})\varphi_{kk}(k_{t+1})\,[h_k(k_t) - \varphi_k(k_t)]^2\, h_k(k_{t+1}) + \\
&\quad + \beta U_{cc}(c_{t+1})\varphi_k(k_{t+1})\,[h_{kk}(k_t) - \varphi_{kk}(k_t)]\, h_k(k_{t+1}) + \\
&+ \beta U_{cc}(c_{t+1})\varphi_k(k_{t+1})\,[h_k(k_t) - \varphi_k(k_t)]\, h_{kk}(k_{t+1})\,[h_k(k_t) - \varphi_k(k_t)] + \\
&+ \beta U_{cc}(c_{t+1})\varphi_k(k_{t+1})\,[h_k(k_t) - \varphi_k(k_t)]\, h_{kk}(k_{t+1})\,[h_k(k_t) - \varphi_k(k_t)] + \\
&\quad + \beta U_c(c_{t+1}) h_{kkk}(k_{t+1})\,[h_k(k_t) - \varphi_k(k_t)]^2 + \\
&\quad + \beta U_c(c_{t+1}) h_{kk}(k_{t+1})\,[h_{kk}(k_t) - \varphi_{kk}(k_t)]\,.
\end{aligned} \tag{5.25}$$

Note that the first four lines on the right-hand side of Eq. (5.25) come from the first term in Eq. (5.22), while the last three lines come from the second term. Complex as it may seem, this is just an application of the product and chain rules for differentiation. We now evaluate Eq. (5.25) at the steady state, obtaining:

$$\begin{aligned}
&U_{ccc}(\hat{c})\varphi_k(\hat{k})^2 + U_{cc}(\hat{c})\varphi_{kk}(\hat{k}) = \\
&= U_{ccc}(\hat{c})\varphi_k(\hat{k})^2 \left[h_k(\hat{k}) - \varphi_k(\hat{k})\right]^2 + U_{cc}(\hat{c})\varphi_{kk}(\hat{k}) \left[h_k(\hat{k}) - \varphi_k(\hat{k})\right]^2 + \\
&+ U_{cc}(\hat{c})\varphi_k(\hat{k}) \left[h_{kk}(\hat{k}) - \varphi_{kk}(\hat{k})\right] + 2\beta U_{cc}(\hat{c})\varphi_k(\hat{k}) \left[h_k(\hat{k}) - \varphi_k(\hat{k})\right]^2 h_{kk}(\hat{k}) + \\
&+ \beta U_c(\hat{c}) h_{kkk}(\hat{k}) \left[h_k(\hat{k}) - \varphi_k(\hat{k})\right]^2 + \beta U_c(\hat{c}) h_{kk}(\hat{k}) \left[h_{kk}(\hat{k}) - \varphi_{kk}(\hat{k})\right].
\end{aligned} \tag{5.26}$$

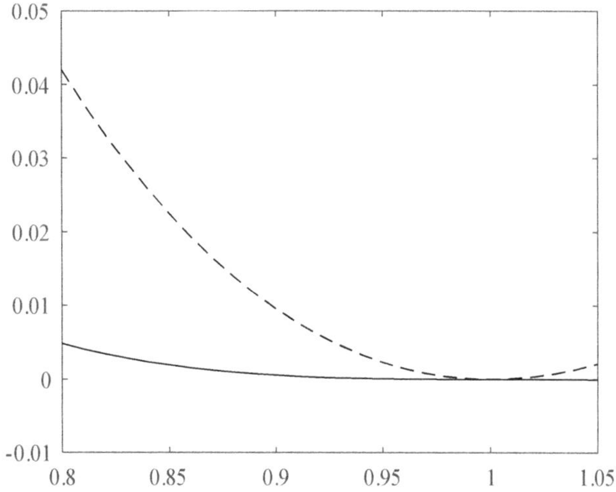

FIGURE 5.13. First- (dashed line) and second-order (solid line) approximation errors for the policy function around the steady state (normalized to 1)

The equation above is linear in $\varphi_{kk}(\hat{k})$; with the proposed parameterization, we have that $U_{ccc}(\hat{c}) = 0.138283$, and $h_{kkk}(\hat{k}) = 1.226804$. By also exploiting $\varphi_k(\hat{k})$, it is straightforward to obtain $\varphi_{kk}(\hat{k}) = -0.511649$, so that the second-order approximation for the policy function is:

$$\overline{\overline{\varphi}}(k_t) = 2.436426 + 0.730928\,(k_t - 1) - 0.511649\frac{(k_t - 1)^2}{2}. \tag{5.27}$$

Because this specification of the model is endowed with a closed-form solution, it is now easy to compute the approximation errors. From Eq. (5.24) we obtain $\varphi(k_t) - \overline{\varphi}(k_t)$, while Eq. (5.27) allows us to compute $\varphi(k_t) - \overline{\overline{\varphi}}(k_t)$. The errors are reported in Figure 5.13, where the first-order errors are represented by the dashed line. Our figure is of interest because it confirms the remarkable improvement achieved with second-order perturbation. It also visually confirms that this approach provides essentially local approximations: the errors rapidly increase as we move away from the steady state.

However, various researchers have documented that perturbation methods often display good properties over a wide range of values for the state variables. In this vein, see Judd (1998), Aruoba *et al.* (2006), and Caldara *et al.* (2012). Nevertheless, it is important to bear in mind that the use of the perturbation approach is problematic (or, as a minimum, requires a lot of care) if one aims to study the implications of significant policy changes (e.g., the introduction of a distortionary tax, or a labor market reform), or of large and permanent "structural" shocks (e.g., an oil shock): in these cases, it is the steady state that is altered.

The fact that this method requires differentiability of the "core" equations becomes relevant in presence of binding constraints. Consider, for example, that our representative agent is required to invest a minimum share of income. At the border between the constrained and the unconstrained regions for capital, the constraint may create a kink in the consumption function, rendering it non-differentiable. This issue precludes a simple analysis of models with binding constraints.

Despite these disadvantages, perturbation methods are simple to code, since in the last twenty years, several algorithms have been developed to provide high-order expansions of the equilibrium conditions of general equilibrium models. Researchers can usually rely on software differentiation toolboxes–the best known of which is the aforementioned Dynare–which require low coding and computing time and thus prove to be very useful when the number of state variables is high.

Judd (1998) is a pioneer in the literature concerning the perturbation approach and presents the general method for both deterministic and stochastic discrete-time growth models.

5.3 Appendix

5.3.1 Collocation routines for the basic growth model

In this appendix we detail the tasks performed by the Matlab routines used in Section 5.1.

prim.m

The file "prim(x,num)" is a function called by the script colloc_0.m (to be discussed below).

The function file prim.m stores the function prim(x,num). This file produces a row vector of length *num*, the elements of which take values x^0, x^1, x^2, ..., $x^{(num-1)}$. For example, if a script file calls prim(2,5), the output of the file prim.m will be $[1, 2, 4, 8, 16]$. Note that if we multiply the output of prim.m by a column vector of parameters (of appropriate dimension), we obtain the value of the polynomial of degree $num - 1$, characterized by the parameters' values stored in the column vector, and computed at x. Typically, in our exercises, x will be a collocation point.

```
% this function gives the standard monomials up to degree n-1
function F=prim(x,num)

for i=1:num
    F(i)=x^(i-1);
% This creates the row vector of length num, evaluated at x.
end
```

colloc_0.m

This script approximates $\sin(x)$ in the interval $[0, 2\pi]$ using first a third-, and then a tenth-degree polynomial. Figure 5.1 and 5.2 are the output of this script. Note that this script calls the function "prim(x,num)."

```
% Approximation of sin(x) - collocation routine
clear;

max_pi=2*pi;
% The approximation range is [0,2*pi].

num=4;
% Number of coefficient of the approximating polynomial.

incr=max_pi/(num-1);
cp=0:incr:max_pi;
% The two lines above determine the collocation points (cp), which
% are equally spaced (the distance between two neighboring points
% being "incr").

A=[prim(cp(1),num);prim(cp(2),num);prim(cp(3),num);prim(cp(4),num)];
b=sin(cp)';
% A and b are used to write System (5.1) in matrix form.
z0=A^(-1)*b;
% This solves linear system; z is vector of parameter for the
% approximating polynomial.

% The next lines create the data for Figure 5.1;
bignum=200;
% Number of points where the true and the approximating functions are
% computed (note that "bignum" is much larger than "num").
real_line=0:max_pi/(bignum-1):max_pi;
% Vector "real_line" discretizes the independent variable in the
```

```
% interval [0, 2*pi].
sin_x=sin(real_line);
% Vector "sin_x" discretizes the dependent variable in the interval
% [0, 2*pi].
for i=1:bignum
    approx_funz(i) = prim(real_line(i),num)*z0;
    % Approximating polynomial in the interval [0, 2*pi].
end

plot_funz=[sin_x;approx_funz];
% This stores sin(x) and the approximating polynomial in a matrix.
% Below, we repeat the above exercise with a 10th degree polynomial.

% main loop
tic

num=11;
% Number of coefficient in the approximating polynomial is increased
% to 11
incr=max_pi/(num-1);
cp=0:incr:max_pi;
% This creates matrix A (which is 11x11) by concatenation. Each row
% represents the values taken by the powers composing the polynomial
% at a collocation point.
A=[prim(cp(1),num)];
% 'prim' is stored in a function m-file;

for i=2:num
    A=[A;prim(cp(i),num)];
end

% Vector b (which is 11x1) stores the values of the function to be
% approximated.
b=sin(cp)';
z=A^(-1)*b;
% z is vector of parameter for the approximating polynomial.

toc

% The lines below create the data for Figure 5.1;
for i=1:bignum
    approx_funz10(i) = prim(real_line(i),num)*z;
    % Approximating polynomial.
end
err_approx10=sin_x-approx_funz10;
% Approximation error as difference between true and approximated
% function.
```

```
% The lines below create Figure 5.1;
fontsize=11; % Size of font (in points).
figure;
plot(real_line,plot_funz(1,:),'-',real_line,plot_funz(2,:),'--');
% First series (which is Sin(x)), is a solid line, second (which is
% the 3rd degree approximation) is a dashed line.
xlim([0 2*pi])
ylim([-1.25 1.25])
xlabel('x␣\in␣[0,2\pi]','FontSize',fontsize,...
'FontName','Times␣New␣Roman');
title('3^{rd}␣degree␣approximation␣for␣Sin(x)','FontSize',...
    fontsize+3,'FontName','Times␣New␣Roman')
% The lines below create Figure 5.2;
figure;
plot(real_line,err_approx10);
xlim([0 2*pi])
xlabel('x␣\in␣[0,2\pi]','FontSize',fontsize,...
'FontName','Times␣New␣Roman');
ylabel('Approximation␣errors','FontSize',fontsize,...
'FontName','Times␣New␣Roman');
title('Approximation␣errors␣for␣Sin(x)','FontSize',fontsize+3,...
'FontName','Times␣New␣Roman')
```

der_1.m

This file stores the function der_1(x,num). This file produces a row vector of length num, the elements of which take values 0, 1, $2x$, ..., $(num-1)$ $x^{(num-2)}$. For example, if a script file calls der_1(2,5), the output will be $[0, 1, 4, 12, 32]$. Note that if we multiply the output of der_1.m by a column vector of parameters (of appropriate dimension), we obtain the first derivative of the polynomial of degree $num-1$, characterized by the parameters' values stored in the column vector, and evaluated at x.

```
function F=der_1(x,num)
F(1)=0;
% This is the first element of the row vector of length num.
for i=2:num
    F(i)=(i-1)*x^(i-2);
% This builds the rest of the row vector of length num, evaluated
% at x.
end
```

colloc_1.m
This script approximates the differential Equation (5.2) for $t \in [0, 4]$ using first a second-, and then an eighth-degree polynomial. It also produces Figures 5.3 and 5.4. This script uses the functions "prim(x,num)" and "der_1(x,num)."

```
% Collocation routine approximating the solution of a linear diffe-
% rential equation
clear;

aa=0.1;
bb=1;
% aa and bb are the parameters of the differential equation.

x0=2; % initial condition.

tmin=0;
tmax=4;
% [tmin, tmax] is the approximation interval.

% The lines below solve for a 2nd degree polinomial (3 coefficients);
num=3; % Number of coefficients

incr=(tmax-tmin)/(num-2);
vt=tmin:incr:tmax; % Vector representing calendar time.

A=[der_1(vt(1),num)-aa*prim(vt(1),num); ...
der_1(vt(2),num)-aa*prim(vt(2),num)];
% 'prim' and 'der_1' are the functions stored in function m-files.

A=[A;prim(0,num)];
bvec=[bb;bb;x0];
% The lines above stores System 5.4, written in matrix notation. No-
% tice that the last row in A and bvec comes from the initial condi-
% tion.

z0=A^(-1)*bvec;
% This solves the linear system; z0 is vector of parameters for
% the approximating polynomial.

% The line below build the data for Figure 5.3;
bignum=200;
% Number of points where the true and the approximating functions are
% computed (note that "bignum" is much larger than "num").
```

```
check_time=tmin:(tmax-tmin)/(bignum-1):tmax;
% Vector of gridpoints for the state variable (which is time in
% the interval [0,4]).

true_funz = -bb/aa+(x0+bb/aa)*exp(aa*check_time);
% Exact solution for the differential equation.

for i=1:bignum
    approx_funz(i) = prim(check_time(i),num)*z0;
    % Approximated solution for the differential equation at "bignum"
    % points. It exploits again the function m-file "prim.m".
end
plot_funz=[true_funz;approx_funz];
% This passes the relevant data to Figure 5.3.
% The lines below solve for an 8th degree polynomial (which implies 9
% coefficients).
num=9;
incr=(tmax-tmin)/(num-2);
vt=tmin:incr:tmax;
Anew=der_1(vt(1),num)-aa*prim(vt(1),num);

tic

for i=2:num-1
    Dnew=der_1(vt(i),num)-aa*prim(vt(i),num);
    Anew=[Anew;Dnew];
    % Notice that matrix Anew is created by concatenation.
end
Anew=[Anew;prim(0,num)];
bvecnew=[bb*ones(num-1,1);x0];
% This incorporates condition x0=2.
z=Anew^(-1)*bvecnew;
% This solves linear system; z is vector of parameter for the 8th
% degree approximating polynomial.

for i=1:bignum
    approx_funz8(i) = prim(check_time(i),num)*z;
    % Approximated solution for the differential equation.
    true_check(i)=der_1(check_time(i),num)*...
    z-bb-aa*prim(check_time(i),num)*z;
    % Approximation error as difference between true and approximated
    % function.
end

fake_check=true_funz-approx_funz8;
% "Fake" check, obtained as difference between true (analytical) so-
% lution and approximated solution.
```

```
plot_funz2=[fake_check;true_check];
% Used to pass the relevant data to Figure 5.4.

toc

% The lines below build Figure 5.3;
font=11; % size of font (in points)
figure;
plot(check_time,plot_funz(1,:),'-',check_time,plot_funz(2,:),'--');
% First series, which is Sin(x), is continuous, second one is dashed
xlim([0 tmax])
xlabel('t␣\in␣[0,4]','FontSize',font,'FontName','Times␣New␣Roman');
title('Approximation␣for␣dx(t)/dt=0.1x(t)+1','FontSize',font+3,...
'FontName','Times␣New␣Roman')

% The lines below build Figure 5.4;
font=11;
figure;
plot(check_time,plot_funz2(1,:),'-',check_time,plot_funz2(2,:),'--');
xlim([0 tmax]);
ylim([-10*10^-12 10*10^-12]);
xlabel('t␣\in␣[0,4]','FontSize',font,'FontName','Times␣New␣Roman');
ylabel('Approximation␣errors␣and␣residuals','FontSize',font,...
'FontName','Times␣New␣Roman');
title('Errors␣of␣an␣8^{th}␣degree␣polynomial','FontSize',font+3,...
'FontName','Times␣New␣Roman')
```

colloc_2.m

This file solves system (5.6-5.7). This routine exploits the Matlab built-in nonlinear equation solver by calling the command fsolve(.). System (5.6-5.7) is stored in the file system0.m; Figure 5.5 represents the output for this script.

```
% Collocation routine using standard polinomial to approximate the
% policy function in the log-utility Ramsey model.

clear;

options = optimset('display','off','MaxFunEvals',500);
% Options for the nonlinear equation solver (refer to Matlab help).

al=0.3;
de=0.15;
be=0.97;

```

```
A=1/(al*be); % Normalization.

kss=(A*al*be / (1+be*(de-1)) )^(1/(1-al));
% Steady-state capital stock.

kmin=0.5*kss; % lowest capital level.
kmax=1.0*kss; % highest capital level.

num=2;
% Number of parameters of the initial polynomial.

for i=1:num
    ck(i)=kmin+(i-1)/(num)*(kmax-kmin);
    % This computes the (equally spaced) collocation points (the
    % steady-state capital (kss) is not a collocation point).
end

x1=[-4;.2;.0];
% Initial guess for the parameter vector (not a smart one).

z=fsolve(@system0,x1,options,num,ck,A,al,be,de,kss);
% Solves the nonlinear system. z is a vector of parameters (vector d
% in system (5.6)). 'system0' is a function m-file.

tic

for num=3:8 % This gradually increases the degree of the polynomial.
   for i=1:num
      ck(i)=kmin+(i-1)/(num-1)*(kmax-kmin);
      % Computes the (equally spaced) collocation points.
   end

x1=[z;0];
% The initial condition is given by the vector of parameters computed
% for the polynomial of degree num-1, and by a 0. This often is a fa-
% ir guess.

z=fsolve(@system0,x1,options,num,ck,A,al,be,de,kss);
% z is vector of parameter d in System (5.6).
end

toc

% The following lines are useful to build Figure 5.5.
bignum=200;
% Number of points where the true and the approximating functions are
% computed.
```

```
incr=(kmax-kmin)/(bignum-1);
chk_k=kmin:incr:kmax;
% Vector of gridpoints for the state variable.

for i=1:bignum
    approx_cons(i) = prim(chk_k(i),num+1)*z;
    % This computes the approximation for consumption.
    chk_k1(i)=A*chk_k(i)^al+(1-de)*chk_k(i)-prim(chk_k(i),num+1)*z;
    % This computes k(t+1) for every k(t) in chk_k.
    resid(i)=prim(chk_k(i),num+1)*z*be*...
    ( al*A*chk_k1(i)^(al-1)+(1-de) )-prim(chk_k1(i),num+1)*z;
    % Residuals in the Euler equation.
end

% ======== The lines below produce the two-panel Figure 5.5 ========
font=11; % Size of font (in points).

subplot1 = subplot(2,1,1,'FontSize',10,'FontName','Times␣New␣Roman');
plot(chk_k,approx_cons); % This builds Panel (a).
xlim([kmin kmax]);
ylim([3.75 5.5]);
xlabel('Capital','FontSize',font,'FontName','Times␣New␣Roman');
ylabel('Consumption','FontSize',font,'FontName','Times␣New␣Roman');
title('Panel␣(a):␣Consumption␣function','FontSize',font+3,...
'FontName','Times␣New␣Roman')

subplot2 = subplot(2,1,2,'FontName','Times␣New␣Roman');
plot(chk_k,resid); % This builds Panel (b).
xlim([kmin kmax]);
ylim([-8*10^(-5) 8*10^(-5)]);
xlabel('Capital','FontSize',font,'FontName','Times␣New␣Roman');
ylabel('Residuals','FontSize',font,'FontName','Times␣New␣Roman');
title('Panel␣(b):␣Euler␣equation␣residuals␣','FontSize',font+3,...
'FontName','Times␣New␣Roman')
```

system0.m

In this function file, we store seventeen equations, nine of which are for the d_i coefficients to be determined, and eight for the collocation points (the values for k_1). Eight equations are of the type

$$\sum_{i=0}^{8} d_i k_1^i = \sum_{i=0}^{8} d_i k_0^i \left(k_1^{-0.7} + 0.8245 \right).$$

Because the nodes k_1 are endogenous (recall the second equation in (5.6)), each of them is determined as a function of the corresponding k_0 and

$c_0 \left(= \sum_{i=0}^{8} d_i k_0^i\right)$, which provides eight further equations. The last equation is the steady state relation $\sum_{i=0}^{8} d_i \hat{k}^i = 3.43643\hat{k}^{0.3} - 0.85\hat{k}$.

```
function F=system0(x,num,ck,A,al,be,de,kss)
for i=1:num
    kap(i)= A*ck(i)^al+(1-de)*ck(i)-prim(ck(i),num+1)*x;
    % This is the second group of equations composing System 5.6;
    % kap(i) is determined by the i-th k0 (which is, the i-th element
    % of the vector ck), the parameters (A, al, de), and the vector
    % of parameters d(i), represented by the vector of unknowns (x).

    F(i) = prim(ck(i),num+1)*x*be*( al*A*kap(i)^(al-1)+(1-de) )- ...
    prim(kap(i),num+1)*x;
    % This is the first group of equations composing System 5.6.
end
F(num+1) = prim(kss,num+1)*x-A*kss^al+de*kss;
% This incorporates the steady state relation 5.7.
```

chebypoly_1.m

This function file generates a unidimensional Chebyshev polynomial (Equation 5.8). Note that, with (x, num) as the function's inputs, it generates a polynomial of degree $num - 1$ computed at x.

```
% This function gives the Chebychev monomials up to degree n-1.
function z=chebypoly_1(x,n)
for i=1:n
    z(i)=cos(acos(x)*(i-1));
end
```

chebynodes.m

With num as the function's input, this file generates num Chebyshev nodes (Equation 5.9)

```
% The output of this function is a vector composed of n Chebychev
% nodes.
function z=chebynodes(n)
for i=1:n
    z(i)=-cos((2*i-1)/(2*n)*pi);
end
```

colloc_3.m
This file solves System (5.12) exploiting the Matlab built-in nonlinear equation solver. System (5.12) is stored in the file system_cheby.m; Figure 5.10 represents the output for this script.

```
% Collocation routine based on Chebychev polynomials used to approxi-
% mates the polcy function for the non-stochastic Ramsey model.

clear;

options = optimset('display','iter','MaxFunEvals',500);
% Options for the nonlinear equation solver.

al=0.3;
de=.15;
be=0.97;

A=1/(al*be);
kss=(A*al*be / (1+be*(de-1)) )^(1/(1-al)); %steady state capital

kmin=0.5*kss;
kmax=1.0*kss;
% Limits for the interval of interest.

    num=2; % Number of parameters of the initial polynomial.

css=A*kss^al-de*kss;
x1=[css; css/10;];
% Initial guess for the vector of coefficients of the consumption
% function (vector d in the main text).

coeff=fsolve(@system_cheby,x1,options,num,A,al,be,de,kmin,kmax);
% This solves the nonlinear system. z is vector d in the main text.

tic;

for num=3:8
    % This gradually increases the degree of the Chebychev polynomial.
    x1=[coeff;0];
    % The initial condition is given by the vector of parameters
    % computed for the polynomial of degree num-1, and by a 0.
    coeff=fsolve(@system_cheby,x1,options,num,A,al,be,de,kmin,kmax);
    % This solves the nonlinear system for 'num' coefficients.
end

toc
```

```

bignum=200;

incr=(kmax-kmin)/(bignum-1);
check_kap=kmin:incr:kmax;
% Vector of gridpoints for the state variable.

for j=1:bignum
    approx_cons(j) = chebypoly_1((2*check_kap(j)-...
        (kmax+kmin))/(kmax-kmin),num)*coeff;
    % Approximation for consumption.
    check_k1(j)=A*check_kap(j)^al+(1-de)*check_kap(j)-chebypoly_1 ...
        ((2*check_kap(j)-(kmax+kmin))/(kmax-kmin),num)*coeff;
    % This computes k(t+1) for every k(t) in check_kap
    error(j)=chebypoly_1((2*check_kap(j)-(kmax+kmin))/(kmax-kmin),...
        num)*coeff*be*( al*A*check_k1(j)^(al-1)+(1-de) ) - ...
        chebypoly_1((2*check_k1(j)-(kmax+kmin))/(kmax-kmin),num)*...
        coeff;
    % Residuals in the Euler equation.
end

% ======= The lines below produce the two panels Figure 5.10 =======
figure;
font=11; % Size of font (in points).
subplot1 = subplot(2,1,1,'FontSize',10,'FontName','Times␣New␣Roman');
plot(check_kap,approx_cons);
xlim([kmin kmax]);
xlabel('Capital','FontSize',font,'FontName','Times␣New␣Roman');
ylabel('Consumption','FontSize',font,'FontName','Times␣New␣Roman');
title('Panel␣(a):␣Consumption␣function','FontSize',font+3,...
    'FontName','Times␣New␣Roman')

subplot2 = subplot(2,1,2,'FontName','Times␣New␣Roman');
plot(check_kap,error);
xlim([kmin kmax]);
xlabel('Capital','FontSize',font,'FontName','Times␣New␣Roman');
ylabel('Residuals','FontSize',font, 'FontName','Times␣New␣Roman');
title('Panel␣(b):␣Euler␣equation␣residuals␣','FontSize',font+3,...
    'FontName','Times␣New␣Roman')
```

system_cheby.m

In this function file we store the $2 \times num$ equations composing System (5.12).

```
function F=system_cheby(x,num,A,al,be,de,kmin,kmax)

T=chebynodes(num);
```

```
% Creates the Chebychev nodes in (-1,1).
k0=(kmax-kmin)/2*T+(kmax+kmin)/2;
% Translates the Chebychev nodes in (kmin,kmax).

for i=1:num
k1(i)= A*k0(i)^al+(1-de)*k0(i)-chebypoly_1(T(i),num)*x;
% Second equation of the pertinent system.

T1(i)=2*(k1(i)-kmin)/(kmax-kmin)-1;
% Creates the time-1 Chebychev nodes in (-1,1).
cons0(i)=chebypoly_1(T(i),num)*x;
cons1(i)=chebypoly_1(T1(i),num)*x;
F(i) = cons0(i)*be*( al*A*k1(i)^(al-1)+(1-de) )-cons1(i);
% First equation of the pertinent system.
end
```

5.3.2 Your coding exercises

Approximate the function $y = exp(1.17z)$ in the interval $z \in [2, 5]$ by a collocation routine based on the Chebyshev polynomials. Compute the approximation errors and the residuals.

Consider the Ramsey model with return function $U(c_t) = \ln c_t$ and dynamic constraint $k_{t+1} = (1 - \delta) k_t + Ak_t^\alpha - c_t$. The parameter values are: $A = 1$, $\delta = 0.15$, $\alpha = 0.25$, and $\beta = 0.98$. Find the value function by means of a collocation routine based on the Chebyshev polynomials. Inspect the residuals.

Consider a deterministic version of the Brock and Mirman model with return function $U(c_t, l_t) = \ln c_t + \gamma \ln(1 - l_t)$ and dynamic constraint $k_{t+1} = (1 - \delta) k_t + Ak_t^\alpha l_t^{1-\alpha} - c_t$. The parameter values are: $\gamma = 3$, $A = 1$, $\delta = 0.15$, $\alpha = 0.25$, and $\beta = 0.98$. Find the policy functions by means of a collocation routine based on the Chebyshev polynomials. Inspect the residuals.

Notes

[1] Dynare also allows for the estimation of general equilibrium models, as explained in Adjemian *et al.* (2024).

[2] Besides Dynare, one can also take advantage of Dynare++, a standalone application that allows one to find a perturbation solution to a model up to an arbitrary order efficiently. Additional information can be found at `http://www.dynare.org`.

[3]Bear in mind, however, that the relationship between ν and the degree of the approximating polynomial is not always monotonic.

[4]Using the jargon, we say that we have chosen four evenly spaced "collocation points" or "nodes".

[5]A system like (5.1) can be written in matrix form as:

$$\begin{bmatrix} 1 & 0 & 0 & 0 \\ 1 & 2.09440 & 4.38649 & 9.18704 \\ 1 & 4.18879 & 17.54596 & 73.49636 \\ 1 & 6.28319 & 39.47842 & 248.05021 \end{bmatrix} \begin{bmatrix} a_0 \\ a_1 \\ a_2 \\ a_3 \end{bmatrix} = \begin{bmatrix} 0 \\ 0.86603 \\ -0.86603 \\ 0 \end{bmatrix}.$$

It is then easy to solve it using a matrix inversion routine. Using a larger system does not significantly increase the computation time.

[6]This on an Intel Core Ultra 7 155H, 1.40 GHz CPU computer.

[7]Specifically, we would have large errors for the time subintervals between 0 and the first collocation point, and between the second collocation point and 4. In these parts, the stick (our second-order polynomial in t) would retain its shape.

[8]It can be important to specify a formal criterion to evaluate the behavior of the residuals. However, at this introductory level of the analysis, we omit a discussion of this point. Nevertheless, be prepared to handle this issue when dealing with formal research.

[9]In this exercise, the eight collocation points are equally spaced between 0 and 4.

[10]If you do not know what a nonlinear equation solver is, imagine that–having forgotten the standard formula–you need to solve a second-order equation.

In this contingency, you may draw a second-order polynomial on a plane, so that the solution(s) you are looking for are the intersection points $f(x) = 0$. To be specific, draw the polynomial oriented upwards. This function, $y = f(x)$, intersects the x-axis twice, once, or never. If there are no intersection points, there are no real solutions for the equation $f(x) = 0$. (In this case, you would be better drawing another second-order polynomial that intersects the x-axis.)

Now, pick a value for x and call it x_0; this is the initial condition for the procedure. Evaluate the function at x_0, obtaining $y_0 = f(x_0)$.

We can now sketch a naive and oversimplified numerical equation-solving procedure. This is made up of a set of instructions like the following:

If $f(x_0) > 0$, and $f'(x_0) > 0$, then decrease x_0 by a small amount.
If $f(x_0) > 0$, and $f'(x_0) < 0$, then increase x_0 by a small amount.
If $f(x_0) < 0$, and $f'(x_0) > 0$, then increase x_0 by a small amount.
If $f(x_0) < 0$, and $f'(x_0) < 0$, then decrease x_0 by a small amount.

Note that, following the instructions above, one moves toward a solution for the second-order polynomial. One should apply the above set of instructions over and over again, until a solution $f(x) = 0$ is reached.

Also note that–whenever the nonlinear equation admits more than one solution, which can well happen in our case–the initial condition is crucial to determine which of the possible solutions is selected. Finally, note that the initial condition is relevant to determine the time needed to converge to the solution. Miranda and Fackler (2002) and Judd (1998) provide compact treatments of techniques used in computational economics to find the solution of a system of nonlinear equations.

[11]Although it is possible to solve a system like (5.5), one often needs to provide the nonlinear equation solver with a very precise initial condition, and this can be unpleasant.

[12]The residuals were obtained by building a grid of 200 equally spaced points for capital in the interval $[0.5\hat{k}, \hat{k}]$. For each point on the grid, we obtained the corresponding next-period value using the second equation in (5.6), and then computed the difference, for each point, between the right- and the left-hand side of the first equation in (5.6).

[13]The problem with standard polynomials is similar to the multicollinarity issue in regression: the similarity in behavior among the x^i terms reduces the precision of the result.

[14]Pafnutij L'vovič Čebyšëv was a Russian mathematician whose surname is spelled as Tschebyscheff in German, which is why the symbol $T(.)$ is used in his honor.

[15]This point is explained in more detail in Heer and Maussner (2005, Chapter 8). Chapter 6 in Judd (1998) contains a more technical discussion.

[16]This experience led John P. Boyd –a mathematician at the University of Michigan, who devoted many of his over 250 publications to computational issues–to state what he dubbed "Moral Principle I":

1. When in doubt, use Chebyshev polynomials unless the solution is spatially periodic, in which case an ordinary Fourier series is better.

2. Unless you are sure another set of basis functions is better, use Chebyshev polynomials.

3. Unless you are really, really sure another set of basis functions is better, use Chebyshev polynomials. (Boyd, J.P., 2001: Chebyshev and Fourier Spectral Methods, Dover, New York–quoted in Fernandez-Villaverde *et al.*, 2016).

[17]One can check that by exploiting the steady-state condition one can obtain slightly smaller Euler equation errors.

[18]In Figure 2.1 a negative $\varphi_k(\hat{k})$ is captured by the paths starting from the steady state E and moving to the north-west, or by the one pointing to the south-east. These paths do not satisfy the transversality condition.

6

A Lagrangian approach to stochastic growth

ABSTRACT In our lives, very few things (if any!) can be held as completely certain. Accordingly, this chapter discusses a simple version of the Ramsey model in which productivity varies stochastically over time. The analysis is conducted using the Lagrangian approach.

6.1 The infinite-horizon problem

We focus on a Cobb-Douglas production function, $A_t k_t^\alpha$, in which the productivity parameter A_t is stochastic.[1] In particular, we assume that A_t can take two values, A_t^H and A_t^L, which occur with probabilities p^H and p^L $(\equiv 1 - p^H)$, respectively. The superscript H stands for "high", while L stands for "low", so $A_t^H > A_t^L$. We also assume that the probability for each realization is time independent, and that the two values, A_t^H and A_t^L, are constant. This means that the random variable A_t is identically distributed and independent over time. Note, in passing, that although we could take the subscript t as understood, we prefer *not* to simplify the notation, in the attempt to be clearer. Note also that we assume full depreciation.

In short, output is obtained by means of the stochastic production function:

$$y_t = A_t k_t^\alpha = \begin{cases} A_t^H k_t^\alpha, \text{ with probability } p^H, \\ A_t^L k_t^\alpha, \text{ with probability } 1 - p^H. \end{cases}$$

DOI: 10.4324/9781003774051-6

It is important to remark that the representative agent is assumed to know period t productivity when she decides on her period t consumption.

Preferences are logarithmic and do not vary over time. Labeling the present as period 0, our consumer's preferences can be summarized by our standard intertemporal utility function:

$$W_0 = \sum_{t=0}^{\infty} \beta^t \ln(c_t). \tag{6.1}$$

The representative agent's objective is to maximize the expected value of (6.1), namely:

$$E_0 [W_0] = E_0 \left[\sum_{t=0}^{\infty} \beta^t \ln c_t \right],$$

where $E_0 [.]$ denotes the expectation conditional on the time 0 information set. Note that–even in this simple case–unfolding the objective function is challenging. Its first term is simply $\ln c_0$ (which depends on period-0 productivity). For period 1 we have: $\beta \left(p^H \ln c_1^H + p^L \ln c_1^L \right)$, where c_1^H and c_1^L are the consumption levels that will be set in the next period, conditional on the period-1 productivity. At time 2, writing the pertinent term of the intertemporal utility function is more complex. Period-2 consumption levels will depend not only on that period's realization of productivity, but also on the productivity level that occurred at time 1. The latter influences period-1 consumption and, in turn, period-2 level of capital. Consequently, we should distinguish four cases. Following this line of reasoning, one would quickly get lost: the number of cases to be taken into account grows exponentially with the time period![2] Indeed, this effort would not only be huge, but also useless. Our representative agent's problem is to choose the c_t in a "sequential" way: that is, she chooses c_t knowing k_t, and having observed the time t realization for productivity. Hence, in every period t, what matters is only the next-period technological risk (which is limited to the random occurrence of the two states A_{t+1}^H, and A_{t+1}^L).[3]

Accordingly, we can express the representative consumer's problem by forming the present value stochastic Lagrangian in a way that emphasizes the "sequential" nature of our problem.

$$\begin{aligned}\mathcal{L}_0^i &= \ln c_0^i - \lambda_0^i \left(k_1 - A_0^i k_0^\alpha + c_0^i\right) + \\ &+E_0 \left[\beta \left(\ln c_1^j - \lambda_1^j (k_2 - A_1^j k_1^\alpha + c_1^j)\right) + \right. \\ &+E_1 \left[\beta^2 \left(\ln c_2^j - \lambda_2^j (k_3 - A_2^j k_2^\alpha + c_2^j)\right) + \right. \\ &\left.\left.+E_2 \left[\beta^3 (\ln c_3^j - \lambda_3^j (k_4 - A_3^j k_3^\alpha + c_3^j) + [...]\right]\right]\right].\end{aligned} \tag{6.2}$$

Some remarks are in order.

First, at time 0 the representative agent decides upon her consumption level and therefore upon her period-1 resources (k_1), knowing the level of available resources (k_0) and the current state of productivity. Hence, the Lagrangian depends on current productivity: one should write a Lagrangian for every productivity level. This is why we have denoted the Lagrangian with the superscript i, where $i \in \{H, L\}$.[4]

Second, at time 1, our representative agent decides on her period-1 consumption and on k_2, knowing the period-1 productivity and k_1. Specifically, the agent maximizes, for $j \in \{H, L\}$:

$$\beta \ln c_1^j - \beta\lambda_1^j (k_2 - A_1^j k_1^\alpha + c_1^j) + \\ + E_1 \left[\beta^2 \ln c_2^j - \beta^2 \lambda_2^j (k_3 - A_2^j k_2^\alpha + c_2^j) + E_2 \left[\ldots \right]\right].$$

Note that, at time 0 the representative agent is aware of the fact that–in period 1–she will be able to choose a consumption level contingent on the future realization of productivity (and, of course, on k_1). Accordingly, we shall first consider the optimality conditions for period 1 *from the perspective of that period*, and then we shall consider the implications of these first-order conditions from the vantage point of period 0. Of course, this line of reasoning can also be applied to the subsequent periods.

Third, note that from period 1 onward, the Lagrange multipliers become stochastic variables: they represent the marginal evaluations of consumptions, which are themselves stochastic, depending on the realization of productivity. Capital is stochastic from period 2, depending on productivity past realizations. Note that such dependence is taken as understood.

Finally, bear in mind that the we also need

$$\lim_{t \to \infty} E_0 \left[\beta^t \lambda_t^j k_{t+1}\right]$$

which is the stochastic version of the tvc (compare with Eq. (1.22)).[5]

Owing to the sequential nature of our problem, we first examine the period-1 first-order conditions from the perspective of that period. Next, we obtain the period-0 optimality conditions. Finally, we consider the implications of the period-1 optimality conditions from the perspective of the initial period.

The variables decided on in period 1 are: c_1^j, k_2, and λ_1^j. The first-order conditions are, respectively:

$$\frac{1}{c_1^j} - \lambda_1^j = 0 \tag{6.3a}$$

$$\lambda_1^j - \alpha\beta\left(p^H \lambda_2^H A_2^H + p^L \lambda_2^L A_2^L\right) k_2^{(\alpha-1)} = 0 \tag{6.3b}$$

$$k_2 - A_1^j k_1^\alpha + c_1^j = 0, \tag{6.3c}$$

for $j \in \{H, L\}$. Note, that, in period 1, the realization for productivity is known, so the representative agent should compute just the set of first-order conditions conditional on the realized productivity. Nonetheless, in period 1 we need to take into account the first-order conditions for $j = \{H, L\}$. This is because we need to consider the implications of these conditions from the vantage point of time 0, when the realization of productivity is still unknown.

The period-0 first-order conditions are:

$$\frac{1}{c_0^i} - \lambda_0^i = 0 \tag{6.4a}$$

$$\lambda_0^i - \alpha\beta\left(p^H \lambda_1^H A_1^H + p^L \lambda_1^L A_1^L\right) k_1^{(\alpha-1)} = 0 \tag{6.4b}$$

$$k_1 - A_0^i k_0^\alpha + c_0^i = 0. \tag{6.4c}$$

In period 0, the realization for productivity is known, so the representative agent computes just *one* set of first-order conditions like (6.4), that is, she computes them for $i = H$ *or* for $i = L$.

Let us now consider that, in period 0, the representative agent is aware that in period 1 she will choose her consumption knowing the realization of productivity. Moreover, she is also aware that these consumption levels will be decided upon with the same information (apart from productivity) that is available at time 0. In fact, besides being contingent on productivity, the period 1 consumption levels depend on k_1, which is decided upon at time 0. Accordingly, in period 0, the only element of risk faced by the representative agent when she decides on her consumption is time-1 productivity.

Substituting (6.3a) into (6.4b), and then taking advantage of (6.4a) gives:

$$\frac{1}{c_0^i} = \alpha\beta \left(p^H \frac{1}{c_1^H} A_1^H + p^L \frac{1}{c_1^L} A_1^L \right) k_1^{\alpha-1},$$

which can be compactly written as:

$$\frac{1}{c_0^i} = \alpha\beta E_0 \left[\frac{1}{c_1} A_1 \right] k_1^{\alpha-1}. \tag{6.5}$$

This is the period-0 version of the Euler equation, which relates the current marginal utility of consumption to the next-period marginal utility, which is stochastic, as it depends upon productivity.

The stochastic Euler equation is sometimes stated as:

$$E_0 \left[\frac{1}{c_t} \right] = \alpha\beta E_0 \left[\frac{1}{c_{t+1}} A_{t+1} k_{t+1}^{\alpha-1} \right]. \tag{6.6}$$

To check that this formulation is consistent with (6.5), keep in mind that the first-order conditions (6.3a-6.3c) are written from the vantage point of time 1. At the initial time 0, our representative consumer considers that, given the available information, it must be true that:

$$E_0 \left[\frac{1}{c_1^j} - \lambda_1^j \right] = 0 \tag{6.7a}$$

$$E_0 \left[\lambda_1^j - \alpha\beta \left(p^H \lambda_2^H A_2^H + p^L \lambda_2^L A_2^L \right) k_2^{\alpha-1} \right] = 0 \tag{6.7b}$$

$$E_0 \left[k_2 - A_1^j k_1^\alpha + c_1^j \right] = 0. \tag{6.7c}$$

In fact, each of the conditions (6.3a-6.3c) must be satisfied for every realization of productivity, and thus *a fortiori*, they must hold in expected value.

We can now eliminate the Lagrange multipliers λ_2^H and λ_2^L from Eq. (6.7b), using the time-2 version of Eq. (6.3a). This yields the stochastic counterpart of Eq. (1.10) for period 1, which is:

$$E_0 \left[\frac{1}{c_1} \right] = \alpha\beta E_0 \left[\frac{1}{c_2} A_2 k_2^{\alpha-1} \right].$$

Using this type of reasoning, one obtains that, in general, the Euler equation is given by (6.6), which tells us that the period t expected marginal utility of consumption must be equal to the discounted expectation of the product between period $t+1$ marginal utility of consumption and the marginal return of capital. The fact that this product matters in expectations makes economic sense. Indeed, suppose for a moment that the period $t+1$ capital is fixed. When its marginal productivity is high, the corresponding high level of output leads to a low marginal utility of consumption. Conversely, a low future marginal productivity of capital reduces future consumption, thereby increasing its marginal utility. The representative agent must take these co-movements into account when she decides upon her current consumption and hence her savings, which affect the period $t+1$ capital stock.

It is easy to see that it must also be true that:

$$E_0\left[k_{t+1}\right] = E_0\left[A_t k_t^{\alpha}\right] - E_0\left[c_t\right]. \tag{6.8}$$

To obtain the above equation, simply consider the appropriate version of Eq. (6.7c).

We will now work out the details of the explicit solution to the present example.

To determine the consumption levels, it is necessary to guess the consumption function. Our tentative solution is $c_0^i = \chi A_0^i k_0^{\alpha}$ where χ is an undetermined parameter. Note that Eq. (6.5) must pin down the *same* χ for any i. This is precisely because χ–being assumed to be a constant–must be independent of the realization for A_t and therefore of the initial state we pick. Hence, the same χ must be obtained from Eq. (6.5) when conditioned on any productivity level.

Choosing, for example, $i = H$, we obtain:

$$\frac{1}{\chi A_0^H k_0^{\alpha}} = \alpha\beta\left(\frac{p^H A_1^H}{\chi A_1^H k_1^{\alpha}} + \frac{p^L A_1^L}{\chi A_1^L k_1^{\alpha}}\right) k_1^{\alpha-1}.$$

Hence, simplifying where possible,

$$\frac{1}{A_0^H k_0^{\alpha}} = \alpha\beta\left(p^H + p^L\right) k_1^{-1}.$$

Note that, if $c_0^H = \chi A_0^H k_0^{\alpha}$, then $k_1 = (1-\chi) A_0^H k_0^{\alpha}$; therefore, the above equation reduces to:

$$\frac{1}{A_0^H k_0^{\alpha}} = \alpha\beta\frac{1}{(1-\chi) A_0^H k_0^{\alpha}},$$

since $p^H + p^L = 1$. The latter equation is satisfied for $\chi = (1 - \alpha\beta)$. Thus, the explicit formulation for the consumption function is:

$$c_t^{i*} = (1 - \alpha\beta)A_t^i k_t^\alpha. \tag{6.9}$$

The policy function above makes it clear that the optimal consumption level is chosen conditionally on the value of the state variables (capital and productivity).[6]

For completeness, we now check that our solution satisfies the stochastic Euler equation (6.6). Suppose that in period t state $i \in \{H, L\}$ realizes. Along an optimal path, substituting Eq. (6.9) into the pertinent version of Eq. (6.5), we obtain:

$$\frac{1}{c_t^{i*}} = \alpha\beta \left[p^H \frac{A_{t+1}^H}{(1-\alpha\beta)A_{t+1}^H k_{t+1}^{*\alpha}} + p^L \frac{A_{t+1}^L}{(1-\alpha\beta)A_{t+1}^L k_{t+1}^{*\alpha}} \right] k_{t+1}^{*(\alpha-1)}.$$

Simplifying where possible, this results in:

$$\frac{1}{c_t^{i*}} = \alpha\beta \left[\frac{p^H}{(1-\alpha\beta)k_{t+1}^*} + \frac{p^L}{(1-\alpha\beta)k_{t+1}^*} \right] = \frac{\alpha\beta}{(1-\alpha\beta)k_{t+1}^*}.$$

Note that this holds in both states. Taking the period-0 expectations of both sides of the equation above verifies that Eq. (6.6) is satisfied, which is consistent with the fact that, in any state i, $k_{t+1}^* = \alpha\beta A_t^i k_t^\alpha$, and $c_t^{i*} = (1-\alpha\beta)A_t^i k_t^\alpha$.

In general, Eq. (6.6) can be seen as a consequence of the law of iterated expectations.

In sum, we have illustrated the steps that allow us to derive the consumption function within a simple stochastic environment.

Exercise 16 *Modify the example in the present chapter, assuming that*

$$W_0 = \sum_{t=0}^{3} \beta^t \ln c_t,$$

and find the consumption function.

Exercise 17 *Modify the example in the present chapter, assuming that the time $t+1$ realization for productivity depends upon its time t realization. In particular, assume that $\Pr(A_{t+1}^H | A_t^H) = \Pr(A_{t+1}^L | A_t^L) = p$, and that $\Pr(A_{t+1}^H | A_t^L) = \Pr(A_{t+1}^L | A_t^H) = 1 - p$. Find the consumption function.*

Exercise 18 *In the example in the present chapter, use the guess* $c_t^i = \Psi(A_t^i)k_t^\alpha$ *(where the functional relation* $\Psi(A_t^i)$ *between consumption and productivity is assumed to be unknown) and find the consumption function (i.e,. show that* $\Psi(A_t^i)$ *is linear).*

Exercise 19 *Assume that: i) the return function is:* $c_t^{1-\gamma}/(1-\gamma)$, *where* $\gamma \in [0,1) \cup (1,\infty)$; *ii) the dynamic constraint is* $k_{t+1} = A_t^i k_t - c_t$, *where the structure for the productivity shocks is the one described in the present chapter. Find the consumption function.*

Notes

[1] We will stick to the standard definition, dating back to the works by Frank Knight in the 1920s, according to which risk is present when the realizations for the random variables have measurable (and known) probabilities, whereas uncertainty implies that the possible outcomes have no measurable probability.

[2] Bear in mind that we are considering the simplest possible case: typically, one deals with random variables with more than two realizations per period. Moreover, productivity is usually not time-independent, but rather highly persistent. Taking these relevant aspects into account would make the exposition much more intricate.

[3] In the jargon, our problem is of the "closed-loop" type, rather than of the "open-loop" kind, as it would be if the values for the entire sequence(s) of the control variable(s) were decided upon at time 0. For some details, see Chow (1997), Chapter 2.

[4] While i represents the state at time 0, the index j is used for all subsequent periods to label the possible productivity realizations in those periods.

[5] In writing Problem (6.2), we have used the Law of Iterated Expectations. This states that $E_t[E_{t+n}[X_T]] = E_t[X_T]$, where X_T is a random variable, $n \geqslant 1$, and $T > t+n$. In plain English, the law of iterated expectations tells you that what you expect today about the day after tomorrow must be equal to what you think today that you are going to expect tomorrow about the day after tomorrow (Otherwise, you should change your current expectation!).

Suppose the day you graduate, you decide to accept a job because you expect that your gross yearly income will be € 70,000 in four years time. Clearly, it is not sensible that, the very day of your graduation, you believe that the following year you will expect to earn, say, € 50,000 in three years' time.

[6] By choosing $i = L$, you can easily verify that Eq. (6.5) gives the same value for χ.

7

Stochastic growth: Bellman formulation and closed-form solutions

ABSTRACT This chapter briefly illustrates how to apply the dynamic programming approach to a simple stochastic growth model. Some closed-form examples will follow.

7.1 The Bellman formulation

We discuss a simple version of the Ramsey model where productivity varies stochastically over time; however, our reasoning applies to any form of risk that preserves the additive separability of the objective function.[1]

Assuming that productivity is stochastic, we formulate the consumer's intertemporal problem as:

$$\begin{aligned} V(k_0, A_0) = \max_{c_0} & \left\{ U(c_0) + \beta E_0 \left[V(k_1, \tilde{A}_1) \right] \right\}, \\ s.t.\ k_1 = & A_0 f(k_0) + (1-\delta)k_0 - c_0, \\ & A_0,\ k_0 \text{ given}, \end{aligned} \tag{7.1}$$

in which a tilde ($\sim$) over a random variable underscores that its realization is yet to be determined.

To fully specify Problem (7.1), we should discuss how productivity evolves over time, characterizing the stochastic process governing it. However, we

DOI: 10.4324/9781003774051-7

will postpone this discussion for a while. If you wish, for now you can imagine that the productivity process is independent over time (i.e. that A_{t+1} is independent of A_t for any t).

Importantly, note that the maximum value function in (7.1) depends on the states of the system: specifically, capital and productivity are its arguments. In the deterministic case, productivity was fixed and thus omitted from the arguments of the maximum value function.

The Bellman equation in (7.1) tells us that, to obtain the period-0 value function $V(k_0, A_0)$, it is necessary to maximize the expression $U(c_0) + \beta E_0 \left[V(k_1, \tilde{A}_1)\right]$ with respect to c_0. Accordingly, a necessary condition for a maximum is obtained by differentiation with respect to current consumption:

$$U_c(c_0^*) + \beta E_0 \left[V_k(k_1^*, \tilde{A}_1)\right] \frac{\partial k_1}{\partial c_0} = 0, \tag{7.2}$$

in which $\partial k_1 / \partial c_0 = -1$ from the capital accumulation equation. We can exploit the transition equation, the Bellman equation, and the first-order condition (7.2) to form the system:[2]

$$\begin{cases} V(k_0, A_0) = U(c_0^*) + \beta E_0 \left[V(k_1^*, \tilde{A}_1)\right] \\ k_1^* = A_0 f(k_0) + (1-\delta)k_0 - c_0^* \\ U_c(c_0^*) = \beta E_0 \left[V_k(k_1^*, \tilde{A}_1)\right] \\ A_0,\ k_0 \ \textit{given}. \end{cases}$$

Our task is to find the solution to the problem above. As in the deterministic case, there are two ways to proceed: we can either (try to) solve the problem by "guessing" the solution, or we can use numerical techniques. Whenever useful, we can exploit the Envelope Theorem to find a solution, which in this context implies:

$$V_k(k_0, A_0) = \beta E_0 \left[V_k(k_1^*, \tilde{A}_1)\right] \frac{\partial k_1}{\partial k_0}.$$

This result can be obtained trivially, so we will leave its derivation to the reader, who can also work out how to apply the Benveniste and Scheinkman formula.

Before proceeding to find a solution for Problem (7.1), we should specify the conditions under which its solution exists and is unique. In stochastic settings, this proves to be very difficult. In practice, what people often do (in addition to verifying that the conditions outlined in Theorem 1 or in

Theorem 2 are fulfilled) is to check whether the stochastic process playing a role in their model enjoys the Markov property.[3]

Here, we first review the definition of a Markov process and then explain why it is important to restrict our attention to dynamic optimization problems in which the stochastic disturbances belong to this class.

Definition 2 *(Markov process). A stochastic process x_t is Markov if for every $\bar{x}$ and for every period* $0, 1, 2, ..., t, ...$ *we have*

$$\Pr\{x_{t+1} \leq \bar{x} | x_t, x_{t-1}, \ ..., \ x_0\} = \Pr\{x_{t+1} \leq \bar{x} | x_t\}.$$

Simply put, a Markov process is a random process where future probabilities depend only on its most recent realization. In fact, this definition tells us that the probability that the next-period value for the process is below a given threshold (i.e., that $x_{t+1} \leq \bar{x}$) depends solely on the current state of the process, x_t. Therefore, past realizations $(x_{t-1}, ..., x_0)$ are irrelevant for determining $\Pr\{x_{t+1} \leq \bar{x}\}$. Sometimes it is said that with Markov processes, "history does not matter" because the current value, x_t, is all that is needed to compute future probabilities; how x arrived at that point is not relevant. Alternatively, we can think of a Markov process as a sequence of random variables for which "memory does not matter:" all we need to know is just x_t, the current state of the process, and we do not need to remember the past realizations.

The fact that random disturbances follow Markov processes greatly simplifies a dynamic optimization problem. This is because the maximum value and the policy function depend–in addition to the state variables found in the non-stochastic version of the problem–only on the most recent realization of the random variables. In other words, the most recent known realizations of the random variables are the *only* additional states of the system. The random variables considered in the examples and exercises in the previous chapter belong to a Markov process.[4]

7.2 Guess and verify, in two dimensions

7.2.1 Logarithmic preferences and stochastic Cobb-Douglas production

In this subsection, we incorporate a persistent productivity shock into the version of the traditional growth model considered in Chapter 6, and we show how to obtain its closed form solution.

The production function is Cobb-Douglas, characterized by complete capital depreciation, while the stochastic productivity A_t evolves according to:

$$\ln A_{t+1} = \rho \ln A_t + \epsilon_{t+1}, \tag{7.3}$$

where $\rho \in [0, 1]$ is the "autoregressive parameter," and ϵ_{t+1} is a random variable that is time-independent and identically distributed over time. This means that ϵ_{t+1} is not influenced by ϵ_t, ϵ_{t-1}, and so on, and that the distribution of ϵ_{t+1} does not change over time. Note that ϵ_{t+1} represents the innovation in the stochastic process (7.3); if you wish, you can think of ϵ_{t+1} as a normal random variable with mean 0 and variance σ_ϵ^2. Applying Definition 2 to $\ln A_{t+1}$, we immediately see that such process is Markov. While some autocorrelation in productivity is highly realistic, the structure for A_t postulated in (7.3) may seem rather *ad hoc*. It requires that it is the logarithm of productivity that depends on its past realization. However, note that this particular structure ensures that productivity remains positive, regardless of the realization of the innovation, which is sensible. Additionally, this structure is an essential ingredient for obtaining a closed form solution, so we have to live with it.[5]

The consumer's side of the problem is unchanged, so her preferences are given by (3.1).

As before, we assume that the representative agent knows the period t productivity when making her period t decision.

Our problem is then to solve:

$$\begin{aligned} V(k_0, A_0) &= \max_{c_0} \left\{ \ln c_0 + \beta E_0 \left[V(k_1, \tilde{A}_1) \right] \right\}, \\ s.t.\ k_1 &= A_0 k_0^\alpha - c_0, \\ \ln \tilde{A}_1 &= \rho \ln A_0 + \tilde{\epsilon}_1, \\ &A_0,\ k_0 \text{ given.} \end{aligned}$$

We now posit the tentative solution:

$$V(k_t, A_t) = F + G \ln k_t + H \ln A_t. \tag{7.4}$$

It is worth emphasizing that since the value function depends on two state variables, it is necessary to specify a solution involving both of them. This simple but important fact remains true for numerical solutions.

The first-order condition is $1/c_0 = \beta E_0 \left[V_k(k_1, \tilde{A}_1) \right]$, which rapidly gives: $k_1 = \beta G c_0$. This expression is used to obtain c_0 from the dynamic constraint:

$$c_0 = \frac{1}{1+\beta G} A_0 k_0^\alpha. \tag{7.5}$$

This equation implies that the period-1 capital stock is:

$$k_1 = \frac{\beta G}{1+\beta G} A_0 k_0^\alpha.$$

The above equation, Eq. (7.5), and the tentative solution (7.4) must be substituted into the Bellman equation, which gives:

$$F + G\ln k_0 + H\ln A_0 =$$
$$= \ln\left(\frac{1}{1+\beta G} A_0 k_0^\alpha\right) + \beta E_0\left[F + G\ln\left(\frac{\beta G}{1+\beta G} A_0 k_0^\alpha\right) + H\ln \tilde{A}_1\right].$$

Exploiting the properties of logarithmic functions, we obtain:

$$F + G\ln k_0 + H\ln A_0 = -\ln(1+\beta G) + \ln A_0 + \alpha\ln k_0$$
$$+\beta F + \beta G\ln(\beta G) - \beta G\ln(1+\beta G) + \beta G\ln A_0 + \alpha\beta G\ln k_0 + \beta H E_0\left[\ln \tilde{A}_1\right].$$

Note that we have taken advantage of the assumption that the period-0 realization for A_t is known when choosing period-0 consumption. We now exploit (7.3) to substitute $\beta H\rho\ln A_0$ for $\beta H E_0\left[\ln \tilde{A}_1\right]$ in the equation above. Recall that the resulting equation must be satisfied for *any* k_0, *any* A_0, and *any* admissible value of the parameters β and α. Therefore, it must be that:

$$\begin{cases} G = \alpha + \alpha\beta G \\ H = 1 + \beta G + \beta H\rho \\ F = -\ln(1+\beta G) + \beta F + \beta G\ln(\beta G) - \beta G\ln(1+\beta G). \end{cases} \tag{7.6}$$

From the first equation in the system above, we obtain:

$$G = \frac{\alpha}{1-\alpha\beta}.$$

Exploiting this result in the second equation of the system, we get:

$$H = \frac{1}{(1-\rho\beta)(1-\alpha\beta)}.$$

Note that $G, H > 0$, because $\alpha, \beta \in (0,1)$ and $\rho \in [0,1]$. This implies that $V_k(k_t, A_t) > 0$ and $V_A(k_t, A_t) > 0$. A wealthier consumer enjoys a higher overall utility, as does a consumer who lives in a more productive economy. Note also that the higher ρ, the larger $V_A(k_t, A_t)$ becomes. When productivity is more persistent, its increase has a larger positive impact on the overall utility simply because its influence extends over a longer period.

Substituting G in the third equation in (7.6) gives:

$$F = \frac{1}{1-\beta}\left(\frac{\alpha\beta}{1-\alpha\beta}\ln(\alpha\beta) + \ln(1-\alpha\beta)\right).$$

Because F, G, and H are independent of capital and productivity, our guess (7.4) is verified, and the maximum value function is:

$$V(k_t, A_t) = \frac{1}{1-\beta}\left(\frac{\alpha\beta}{1-\alpha\beta}\ln(\alpha\beta) + \ln(1-\alpha\beta)\right) + \\ + \frac{\alpha}{1-\alpha\beta}\ln k_t + \frac{1}{(1-\rho\beta)(1-\alpha\beta)}\ln A_t.$$

The value function above is strikingly similar to the one we obtained in Section 3.1. This is an effect of the functional forms we have chosen to describe preferences, production, and the evolution of productivity.[6]

It is now easy to obtain the consumption function. Exploiting G in equation (7.5), we obtain $c_0^* = (1-\alpha\beta)A_0k_0^\alpha$, as in the non-stochastic case; this gives us $k_1^* = \alpha\beta A_0 k_0^\alpha$. This is a neat but slightly disappointing result, because optimal consumption is, once again, a linear function of output.

Exercise 20 *Find the value function and the consumption function for the two-states i.i.d. example in Chapter 6.*

In the next exercises, take as given that $\beta \in (0,1)$.

Exercise 21 *Assume that: i) the return function is:* $\ln c_t$; *ii) the dynamic constraint is* $k_{t+1} = A_t^i k_t^\alpha - c_t$; *iii) there are two productivity levels,* A_t^H *and* A_t^L, *iv)* $\Pr(A_{t+1}^H \,|A_t^H) = \Pr(A_{t+1}^L \,|A_t^L) = p$, $\Pr(A_{t+1}^H \,|A_t^L) = \Pr(A_{t+1}^L \,|A_t^H)$ $= 1-p$. *Find the value and the consumption functions.*

Exercise 22 *Assume that: i) the return function is:* $c_t^{1-\gamma}/(1-\gamma)$, *where* $\gamma \in [0,1) \cup (1,\infty)$; *ii) the dynamic constraint is* $k_{t+1} = A_t^i k_t - c_t$; *the structure of the productivity is the one described in Chapter 6. Find the value and the consumption functions.*

Exercise 23 *(Based on Brock and Mirman 1972.) Assume that i) the single period utility function is:* $\ln c_t + \gamma\ln(1-l_t)$, *where* l_t *is labor time and* $\gamma > 0$; *ii) the dynamic constraint is* $k_{t+1} = A_t k_t^\alpha l_t^{1-\alpha} - c_t$, *where* $0 < \alpha < 1$, *and*

A_t is described by Eq. (7.3). Find the value function, and the related policy functions.

Exercise 24 *Assume that i) the single period utility function is: $\ln(c_t - \phi l_t^{\psi})$, where l_t is labor time and $\phi > 0$, $\psi > 1$; ii) the dynamic constraint is $k_{t+1} = A_t k_t^{\alpha} l_t^{1-\alpha} - c_t$, where $0 < \alpha < 1$, and A_t is described by Eq. (7.3). Find the value function and the related policy functions.*

Exercise 25 *(Cake eating with taste shocks.[7]) Assume that i) the return function is: $\ln(z_t c_t)$, where z_t is a random variable that can assume two values, z^H and z^L with probabilities p^H and $1-p^H$; ii) the dynamic constraint is $y_{t+1} = y_t - c_t$. Find the value and the consumption functions.*

7.2.2 Quadratic preferences with a linear constraint

When the time horizon is infinite, the return function is quadratic, and the transition function is linear and affected by additive shocks, a closed form solution for the maximum value function exists.

To be specific, assume that preferences are given by Equation (3.8), and that the intertemporal constraint, which is linear in the state variable k_t, is given by:

$$k_{t+1} = (1+r)k_t - c_t + \epsilon_t, \tag{7.7}$$

with ϵ_t representing a random variable that is independent and identically distributed over time.

The logic of the solution method is the same as we have experienced in Subsections 3.2 and 7.2.1: the tentative solution takes the same functional form as the return function. Since it is quadratic, our tentative solution is a second-order polynomial in the state variables (k_t and ϵ_t), namely:

$$V(k_t, \epsilon_t) = F + Gk_t + Hk_t^2 + I\epsilon_t + L\epsilon_t^2 + Mk_t\epsilon_t,$$

where F, G, H, I, L, and M are undetermined coefficients. The equation above suggests that our standard procedure requires solving a system of six equations. Therefore, this problem is usually handled using numerical techniques based on matrix manipulations. For this, the standard (and very good) references are Chow (1997) and Ljungqvist and Sargent (2018).

Exercise 26 *A firm obtains its output according to the production function $y_t = \varepsilon_t k_t$, where ε_t is an i.i.d. shock with mean μ and standard deviation σ. Output is sold at price p. An investment, gross of depreciation, of size i_t costs to the firm $c/2i_t^2$ (c being constant). Capital depreciation is captured* *by* $\delta \in (0,1)$. *Future profits are discounted at the constant factor* $1+r>1$ *(so that* $\beta \equiv 1/(1+r) < 1$*). Obtain the firm's maximum value function.*

Exercise 27 *Consider a Central Bank which can control output (by means of the nominal interest rate) and aims to minimize:*

$$W_0 = E_0\left[\sum_{t=0}^{\infty} \beta^t \left(y_t^2 + \delta\pi_t^2\right)\right],$$

where π_t *is inflation and* y_t *the deviation of output from its target value;* $\beta \in (0,1)$. *The dynamic constraint the Central Bank faces is a traditional Phillips curve:* $\pi_t = \pi_{t-1} + \gamma y_t + \epsilon_t$, *where* ϵ_t *is an i. i. d. random variable. Find the value function and the policy function.*

Notes

[1] For example, one can deal with stochastic preferences of the type: $W_0 = \sum_{t=0}^{\infty} \beta^t U(c_t, \epsilon_t)$, where ϵ_t is a sequence of random variables. In fact, we may write $W_0 = U(c_0, \epsilon_0) + \beta \sum_{t=1}^{\infty} \beta^t U(c_t, \epsilon_t)$, which is the basis for the Bellman formulation.

[2] An alternative formulation exploits the transition equation and the first-order condition to substitute out c_0^*.

[3] A rigorous discussion is provided by Stokey, Lucas, and Prescott (1989).

[4] Let us introduce a little technical jargon. When the random variables in a Markov process can take only a finite number of values, the process is called a Markov chain. When the random variables in a Markov process are continuous, the process is known as a Markov sequence. A dynamic optimization problem in which the stochastic variables belong to Markov processes and the payoff enters additively is known as a Markov decision process.

[5] An often-used alternative formulation for the autoregressive process is

$$A_{t+1} = \hat{A}^{1-\rho} A_t^{\rho} \exp(\epsilon_{t+1}).$$

This slightly more general formulation implies that the non-stochastic steady state for the process is $\hat{A}$, whereas in (7.3) the steady state is normalized to one.

[6] When the productivity process is specified as in Footnote 5, the constant in the value function becomes:

$$F = \frac{1}{1-\beta}\left(\frac{\alpha\beta}{1-\alpha\beta}\ln(\alpha\beta) + \ln(1-\alpha\beta) + \frac{\beta(1-\rho)}{(1-\alpha\beta)(1-\rho\beta)}\ln(\hat{A})\right).$$

[7] Interpret y_t as the remaining share of a cake, and c_t as the slice of the cake the consumer decides to cut out at time t. The implicit assumption is that the consumer has free access to a very efficient fridge.

8

Solving the stochastic growth model: a brief tour of the techniques

ABSTRACT This chapter extends the value function iteration method–introduced in Section 4.1–to the case of stochastic productivity. Section 8.1 proceeds in steps, dealing first with a time-independent process and then discussing the case of autoregressive shocks. Since the iteration methods bitterly suffer from the curse of dimensionality, the collocation method is discussed in Section 8.2. However, the curse of dimensionality never sleeps: implementing this technique in a multidimensional setting requires a considerable coding effort. Hence, Section 8.3 illustrates how to handle productivity shocks using the perturbation method. Finally, Section 8.4 outlines an alternative approach that suffers only mildly from the curse of dimensionality: the Parameterized Expectation Algorithm.

8.1 Value function iteration and the curse of dimensionality

In this section we illustrate a stochastic version of the Ramsey model using the Bellman equation, and we solve it using value-function iteration methods. First, we consider a time-independent process; then we illustrate how to handle a two-state Markov chain. Finally we discuss how to incorporate an autoregressive productivity process in the growth model.

DOI: 10.4324/9781003774051-8

8.1.1 *The first step: a time-independent disturbance*

For ease of comparison, we present the value function iteration method by extending the example presented in Section 4.1. Specifically, we modify that example to include the simplest possible stochastic process for productivity. We assume that A_t is independent and identically distributed (i.i.d.) over time and that it can take two values, $A_t^L = 3.367698$ and $A_t^H = 3.505155$, each with a probability of 0.5. Note that $E_{t-1}[\tilde{A}_t]$ is equal to the productivity value used in the non-stochastic example; thus we are considering a mean-preserving spread in productivity. When productivity is unknown due to its randomness, it is denoted by a tilde.[1] Furthermore, since A_t is i.i.d. we will drop the time subscript. As before, α is 0.3, β is 0.97, and δ is 1 so that the non-stochastic steady state for capital is normalized to unity.

Accordingly, our problem is to solve:

$$\begin{aligned} V(k_0, A) = \max_{c_0} &\left\{\ln(c_0) + 0.97E_0\left[V(k_1, \tilde{A})\right]\right\}, \\ s.t.\ k_1 &= Ak_0^{0.3} - c_0, \\ A &\in \{3.367698,\ 3.505155\}, \\ &k_0 \text{ given.} \end{aligned} \tag{8.1}$$

As in Section 4.1, we are interested in solving the problem for values of capital that are around the non-stochastic steady state. We will only consider five possible levels for capital: $\{0.98, 0.99, 1, 1.01, 1.02\}$. Therefore, our state space is composed of ten points, as the five capital levels must be coupled with the two possible productivity values.

The strategy to obtain the maximum value function is not significantly different from the one we described for the deterministic case. We proceed as follows:

- (Step 1) Specify $E_0[V(k_1, \tilde{A})]$ as a set of five arbitrary values, one for each capital level, and denote this set of initial values as $E_0[V_0(k_1, \tilde{A})]$.
- (Step 2a) Solve Problem (8.1) for each state (k_0, A), finding a new (and therefore different) maximum value function. (In our case this step results in a set of ten values, which we will denote by $V_1(k_0, A)$).
- (Step 2b) For each capital level on the grid, and for each productivity level, let $V_1(k_1, A) = V_1(k_0, A)$, then compute the expected maximum value function $E_0[V_1(k_1, \tilde{A})]$ using the probability distribution of $\tilde{A}$.[2]
- (Step 3) Using $E_0[V_1(k_1, \tilde{A})]$ as a new initial guess for the expected maximum value function, obtain $E_0[V_2(k_1, \tilde{A})]$.

- (Step 4) Iterate the steps above until $E_0[V_n(k_1, \tilde{A})]$ and $E_0[V_{n+1}(k_1, \tilde{A})]$ are sufficiently close.

The convergence criterion for the set of values representing $E_0[V(k_1, \tilde{A})]$ will be analogous to the one in the non-stochastic case.

We will now illustrate the above procedure using an extremely simplified example analogous to that used in Section 4.1.

We start by choosing the set of values for $E_0[V_0(k_1, \tilde{A})]$. Note that the i.i.d. assumption about productivity implies that the expected maximum value function, $E_0[V(k_1, \tilde{A})]$, is the same for all period-0 productivity realizations. This is because the expected maximum value function conditional on a realization for productivity is identical to the unconditional one. In the example in the following subsection, where we drop the i.i.d. assumption, we will specify the expected value function for each possible productivity realization.

In the present example, we choose: $E_0[V_0(k_1, \tilde{A})] = 0$ for any k_1 (Step 1).

As for Step 2a, note that the choice above implies we face the following types of problems:

$$V_1(k_0, A) = \max_{c_0} \{\ln(c_0)\},$$
$$s.t.\ k_1 = Ak_0^{0.3} - c_0,$$
$$A \in \{3.367698,\ 3.505155\},$$
$$k_0 \text{ given.}$$

We first consider the case $A = A^L$. Note that, as before, both k_0 and k_1 must take one of the possible values for capital (i.e., {0.98, 0.99, 1, 1.01, 1.02}). This restricts the set of feasible consumption levels. For example, if $k_0 = 0.98$, for $k_1 = \{0.98, 0.99, 1, 1.01, 1.02\}$, we compute the following consumption levels $c_0 = \{2.367349,\ 2.357349,\ 2.347349,\ 2.337349,\ 2.327349\}$. The corresponding utilities are {0.861771, 0.857536, 0.853286, 0.849017, 0.844730}. The highest utility level is obtained with $c_0 = 2.367349$, which is the consumption level that results in a next-period capital level of $k_1 = 0.98$.

Thus, the solution for this specific problem is $V_1(k_0 = 0.98, A = A^L) = 0.861771$.

Repeating this process, we obtain: $V_1(k_0 = 0.99, A = A^L) = 0.866074$, $V_1(k_0 = 1, A = A^L) = 0.870330$, $V_1(k_0 = 1.01, A = A^L) = 0.874537$, $V_1(k_0 = 1.02, A = A^L) = 0.878699$. As expected, in every problem, the solution corresponds to the maximum feasible consumption level, which is the one that leads to $k_1 = 0.98$.

We then consider the case where $A = A^H$. For example, if $k_0 = 0.98$, for $k_1 = \{0.98, 0.99, 1, 1.01, 1.02\}$, we compute the following consumption levels: $c_0 = \{2.503975, 2.493975, 2.483975, 2.473975, 2.463975\}$. The corresponding utilities are $\{0.917880, 0.913878, 0.909860, 0.905826, 0.901776\}$. The highest utility level is obtained with $c_0 = 2.50397$, which is, once again, the consumption level consistent with a next-period capital level of $k_1 = 0.98$. The solution for this problem is $V_1(k_0 = 0.98, A = A^H) = 0.91788$.

As for the other capital levels, we obtain: $V_1(k_0 = 0.99, A = A^H) = 0.922115$, $V_1(k_0 = 1, A = A^H) = 0.926302$, $V_1(k_0 = 1.01, A = A^H) = 0.930444$, $V_1(k_0 = 1.02, A = A^H) = 0.934539$. This completes Step 2a of the procedure.

The second part of Step 2 in the procedure is easily executed: given that $p^H = p^L = 0.5$, $E_0[V_1(k_0, A)] = [0.889825,\ 0.894094, 0.898316, 0.902490, 0.906619]$. We use this set of values as a new starting point for the maximum value function (Step 3); accordingly, we assume $E_0[V_1(k_1, \tilde{A})] = E_0[V_1(k_0, \tilde{A})]$, and we move to the second iteration, just as we did in Section 4.1.

We let our numerical routine perform Step 4. The results of the routine are reported in Table 3; the last line provides the exact solution as a reference point.

TABLE 3: results for $E[V_n(k,\tilde{A})]$

iter. #	k = 0.98	k = 0.99	k = 1.00	k = 1.01	k = 1.02
0	0	0	0	0	0
1	0.889825	0.894094	0.898316	0.902490	0.906619
2	1.753071	1.757366	1.761613	1.765815	1.769976
3	2.590458	2.594755	2.599010	2.603218	2.607381
4	3.402731	3.407029	3.411284	3.415492	3.419656
5	4.190637	4.194935	4.199190	4.203398	4.207563
10	7.789475	7.793774	7.798029	7.802236	7.806402
50	23.197025	23.201323	23.205579	23.209786	23.213952
100	28.255542	28.259841	28.264096	28.268304	28.272469
200	29.599175	29.603474	29.607729	29.611937	29.616102
300	29.663068	29.667367	29.671622	29.675830	29.679995
375	29.665933	29.670232	29.674487	29.678695	29.682860
376	29.665943	29.670242	29.674497	29.678705	29.682870
true	29.666455	29.670751	29.675004	29.679214	29.683383

Note that the uncertainty about future productivity has an interesting impact on the value function: an increase in the variance of $\tilde{A}$ reduces the overall utility. (Compare the last line in Table 3 with the last one in Table 2.) This is because the utility function (3.1) describes a risk-averse representative consumer.

To provide a more challenging example, we use the Matlab program written for the problem above to study what happens for $k \in [0.7, 1.1]$ with 800 grid points and five equiprobable productivity levels (evenly spaced in the interval $A \in \{3.367698,\ 3.505155\}$). Figure 8.1a plots the expected maximum value function, while Figure 8.1b shows the differences between the true expected value function and the approximated one; it takes around 165 seconds to achieve convergence.[3] Let me draw your attention to the fact that, even in this simple example, the required computer time is (relatively) high.

Exercise 28 *Check that the values for* $E\left[V(k,\tilde{A})\right]$ *in the last line of Table 3 are correct.*

8.1.2 Persistent shocks

Simulating a stochastic model with time-independent shocks is certainly instructive, but the real interest lies in the capacity to handle persistence. When it comes to productivity, both common sense and empirical evidence suggest that current levels are highly correlated to past values.

A two-state Markov chain

A simple way to handle persistence–possibly the simplest one–is to consider productivity as being governed by a two-state Markov chain. This means we assume that productivity can take two levels, A^L and A^H, with the following transition probabilities: $\Pr(A_{t+1}^H \,|A_t^H) = p$, $\Pr(A_{t+1}^L \,|A_t^L) = q$, which implies that $\Pr(A_{t+1}^L \,|A_t^H) = 1-p$, and $\Pr(A_{t+1}^H \,|A_t^L) = 1-q$.

Note that our stochastic process enjoys the Markov property (as introduced in Section 7.1). Also, we can summarize the transition probabilities by means of the matrix,

$$P = \begin{bmatrix} q & 1-p \\ 1-q & p \end{bmatrix}.$$

In this matrix, element P_{11} represents the probability that next-period productivity will be low given that productivity is low in the current period; P_{21} is the probability that productivity will be high next period given that it is low today, and so on. Finally, note that the higher p and q are, the stronger the persistence in the productivity level.

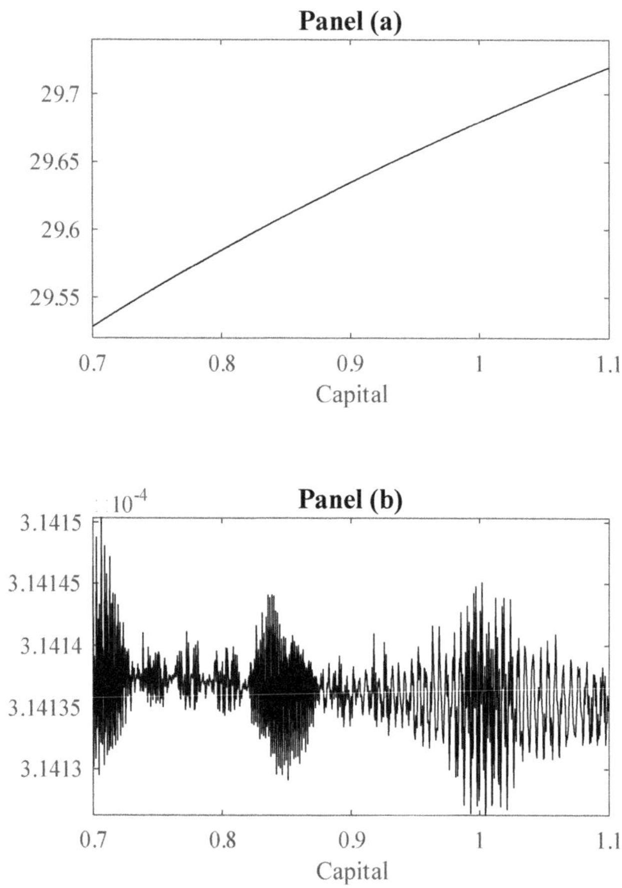

FIGURE 8.1. Expected maximum value function with time-independent shocks (Panel a) and approximation errors (Panel b)

We now consider $p = q = 0.8$ and, as above, $A^L = 3.367698$ and $A^H = 3.505155$. We will again cover the steps of the procedure we briefly discussed earlier, highlighting the required changes.

For Step 1, note that the expected value of the period-1 maximum value function depends on the period-0 productivity realization. Accordingly, we need to specify a set of values for *each* possible productivity realization. We will again choose 0 for all k_1 and for both $E\left[V_0(k_1,\tilde{A})\middle| A^L\right]$ and $E\left[V_0(k_1,\tilde{A})\middle| A^H\right]$.

Then, Step 2a goes exactly as before. We readily compute (rounded to the fifth decimal):

	$k_0 = 0.98$	$k_0 = 0.99$	$k_0 = 1.00$	$k_0 = 1.01$	$k_0 = 1.02$
$A = A^L$	0.86177	0.86608	0.87033	0.87454	0.87870
$A = A^H$	0.91788	0.92211	0.92630	0.93044	0.93454

Step 2b requires a minor modification. Given that the probability distribution of future realizations depends on the current productivity, the expected maximum value function is state-contingent and must be computed using the transition probability matrix P, which captures all the conditional probability distributions. Accordingly, we obtain:

$$\begin{bmatrix} E_0[V_1(k_1,\tilde{A})\middle| A = A^L] \\ E_0[V_1(k_1,\tilde{A})\middle| A = A^H] \end{bmatrix} =$$

$$= \begin{bmatrix} 0.8 & 0.2 \\ 0.2 & 0.8 \end{bmatrix} \begin{bmatrix} 0.86177 & 0.86608 & 0.87033 & 0.87454 & 0.87870 \\ 0.91788 & 0.92211 & 0.92630 & 0.93044 & 0.93454 \end{bmatrix} =$$

$$= \begin{bmatrix} 0.87299 & 0.87728 & 0.88152 & 0.88572 & 0.88987 \\ 0.90666 & 0.91091 & 0.91511 & 0.91926 & 0.92337 \end{bmatrix}.$$

We now use this set of values as a starting point for a new maximum value function (Step 3), and we iterate the procedure until convergence. The choice of modeling the evolution of productivity as a Markov chain is convenient because, when combined with a logarithmic utility function, a Cobb–Douglas production function, and complete capital depreciation, we can analytically solve the simple growth model. Note, in fact, that we are solving a version of the economy described in Exercise 21. Once we have the analytic solution for the model, we can compute the approximation errors, defined as the differences between the true value functions (conditional on each state) and the approximated ones.

In the numerical exercise, the Markov chain takes the values specified above, and we set $k \in [0.5, 1.3]$ with 800 equally spaced grid points. Our routine takes approximately 65 seconds to achieve convergence. Panel (a) of Figure 8.2 shows the maximum value function for the two states, Panels (b) and (c) show the approximation errors for the low and the high productivity levels, respectively.

8.1.3 Approximating an autoregressive process

It is common practice to assume that the logarithm of productivity follows a first-order autoregressive process, and therefore we will follow suit. So, we will begin by approximating the simple specification introduced in Subsection 7.2.1 with a two-state Markov chain, and subsequently we will generalize this approach. We will then consider a slightly more elaborate formulation for the first-order autoregressive process, and finally we will present an alternative method for its approximation.

A two-state Markov process as an approximation of an AR(1)

Denoting the autoregressive parameter by $\rho \in [0, 1)$, and defining ϵ_{t+1} an i.i.d. shock with mean zero and variance σ_ϵ^2, we have:

$$A_{t+1} = A_t^\rho \exp(\epsilon_{t+1}), \tag{8.2}$$

which becomes, with $a_t = \log A_t$,

$$a_{t+1} = \rho a_t + \epsilon_{t+1}. \tag{8.3}$$

The goal of this subsection is to approximate the continuous Process (8.3) with a two-state Markov chain that mimics the true process as closely as possible. To do this, we need to appropriately choose two points on the state space and determine the transition probabilities among them. Note that we assume that the distribution for ϵ_{t+1} is normal.[4]

With this idea in mind, we first consider what happens to log-productivity in the long run.

From (8.3) it is easy to obtain, by iterated substitution:

$$\begin{aligned} a_{t+n} &= \rho a_{t+n-1} + \epsilon_{t+n} = \rho^2 a_{t+n-2} + \rho\epsilon_{t+n-1} + \epsilon_{t+n} = \\ &= \rho^n a_t + \rho^{n-1}\epsilon_{t+1} + \rho^{n-2}\epsilon_{t+2} + \dots + \rho\epsilon_{t+n-1} + \epsilon_{t+n}, \end{aligned} \tag{8.4}$$

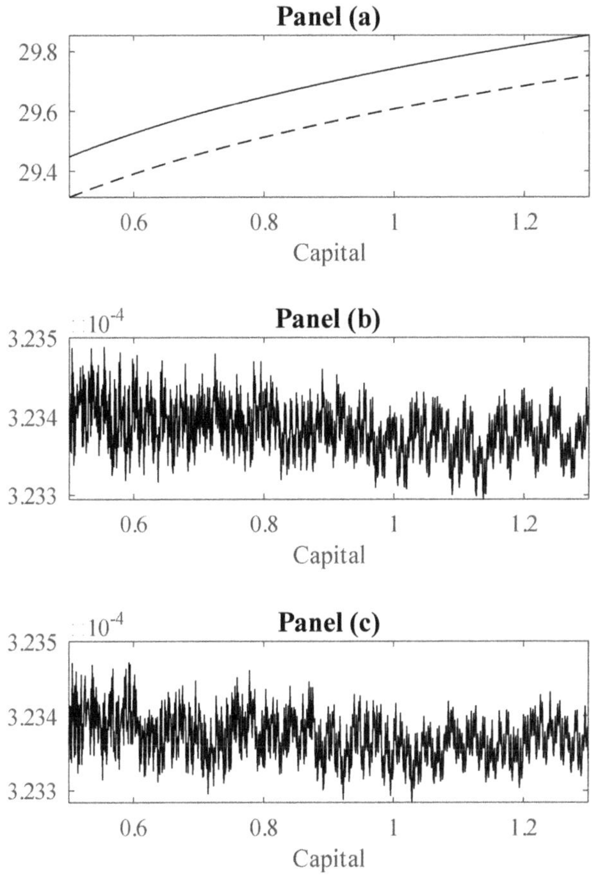

FIGURE 8.2. Panel (a): maximum value function; Panels (b) and (c): approximation errors for the two-state Markov chain model

so that $E\left[\left.\tilde{a}_{t+n}\right| a_t\right] = \rho^n a_t$. Since $\rho \in [0,1)$, we have that:

$$\lim_{n\to\infty} E\left[\left.\tilde{a}_{t+n}\right| a_t\right] = 0.$$

Exploiting the fact that $E\left[\left.\tilde{a}_{t+n}\right| a_t\right] = \rho^n a_t$, from (8.4) we easily obtain:

$$Var\left[\left.\tilde{a}_{t+n}\right| a_t\right] = \left(\rho^{2n-2} + \rho^{2n-4} + ... + \rho^2 + 1\right)\sigma_\epsilon^2 = \sigma_\epsilon^2 \sum_{i=0}^{n-1}\left(\rho^2\right)^i,$$

and therefore:

$$\lim_{n\to\infty} Var\left[\left.\tilde{a}_{t+n}\right| a_t\right] = \frac{\sigma_\epsilon^2}{1-\rho^2}.$$

In words, the long-run expected value of log-productivity is 0, and its variance is $\sigma_\epsilon^2/\left(1-\rho^2\right)$.

Since we are approximating the long-run distribution with a two-state distribution, we need to match the mean and the variance of the latter with the ones we have just computed. Let us call the approximating process a', and let its two states be a^L and a^H, with $a^L < a^H$. Taking into account the symmetry of the normal distribution, to match the long-run average, it must be true that $a^L = -a^H$. Moreover, again by symmetry, it must be that $\Pr(a^L) = \Pr(a^H) = 1/2$. The variance for the long-run approximated distribution must then be equal to:

$$\frac{1}{2}\left(a^L\right)^2 + \frac{1}{2}\left(a^H\right)^2 = \frac{\sigma_\epsilon^2}{1-\rho^2},$$

so that, exploiting $a^L = -a^H$, we have:

$$a^L = -\frac{\sigma_\epsilon}{\sqrt{1-\rho^2}}, \quad a^H = \frac{\sigma_\epsilon}{\sqrt{1-\rho^2}}. \tag{8.5}$$

Note that we have characterized the approximated *long run* distribution for the random variable of interest, but we still need to determine how it behaves in the *short run*. In other words, we need to pin down the transition probabilities for log-productivity. As for the two-state process, we assume the Markov chain is characterized by the following probability matrix, which reflects symmetry:

$$P = \begin{bmatrix} p & 1-p \\ 1-p & p \end{bmatrix}.$$

Therefore we have:

$$E[\tilde{a}'|\, a^L] = pa^L + (1-p)a^H = (2p-1)a^L$$

(by using the fact that $a^L = -a^H$). Going back to the true Process (8.3), we note that $E[\tilde{a}_{t+1}|\, a_t] = \rho a_t$. Therefore, when the true process takes the value $a_t = a^L$ to guarantee $E[\tilde{a}_{t+1}|\, a_t = a^L] = E[\tilde{a}'|\, a^L]$, we must have that $2p - 1 = \rho$. Accordingly, we obtain $p = (1+\rho)/2$. In this way, we have approximated the autoregressive log-productivity process with a two-state Markov chain. The states are given by (8.5), and the transition probability is the one we have just determined. We obtain the same result by considering state $a_t = a^H$.

Tauchen's approach

The generalization of the reasoning in the previous subsection is due to Tauchen (1986). He suggests choosing a set of values for $a = \{a_1, a_2, ..., a_j, ..., a_M\}$ with M being odd. To select the values for a_j Tauchen proposes letting a_M be a multiple μ of the unconditional standard deviation $\sigma_\epsilon/\sqrt{1-\rho^2}$. Then, one sets $a_1 = -a_M$ and lets the remaining states be evenly spaced over the interval $[a_1, a_M]$. Note that the distance between two consecutive nodes is $d = \frac{2\mu}{M-1}\sigma_\epsilon/\sqrt{1-\rho^2}$, so that

$$a_j = a_1 + (j-1)\,d = \left(\frac{2}{M-1}j - \frac{M+1}{M-1}\right)\mu\frac{\sigma_\epsilon}{\sqrt{1-\rho^2}}.$$

For example, if $\mu = 2$ and $M = 5$, we have:

$$a = \left\{-2\frac{\sigma_\epsilon}{\sqrt{1-\rho^2}}, -\frac{\sigma_\epsilon}{\sqrt{1-\rho^2}}, 0, +\frac{\sigma_\epsilon}{\sqrt{1-\rho^2}}, +2\frac{\sigma_\epsilon}{\sqrt{1-\rho^2}}\right\}.$$

Having discretized the state space, we now need to compute the probability that log-productivity moves from state i to state j. When $j \neq 1, M$, this probability, p_{ij}, is:

$$p_{ij} = Pr\left\{a_t = a_j \middle|\, a_{t-1} = a_i\right\} \approx$$
$$\approx Pr\left\{a_j - d/2 < \rho a_i + \epsilon_t < a_j + d/2\right\}; \quad (8.6)$$

denoting by $\Phi(.)$ the cumulative distribution function of a standard normal random variable, we have that[5]

$$p_{ij} = \Phi\left(\frac{a_j + d/2 - \rho a_i}{\sigma_\epsilon}\right) - \Phi\left(\frac{a_j - d/2 - \rho a_i}{\sigma_\epsilon}\right).$$

Note that the "arrival" state j has been assumed to be different from 1 and M. In these cases, we have a boundary problem (the existence of a state

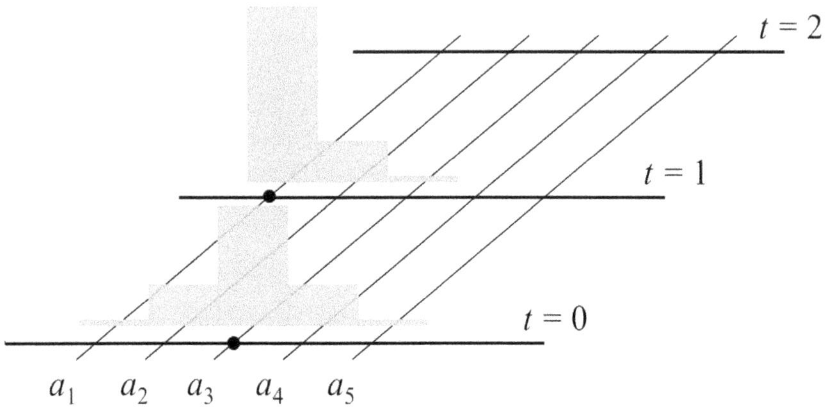

FIGURE 8.3. Probabilities of transition at $t = 0$ (conditional on a_3) and at $t = 1$ (conditional on a_1)

lower than a_1 or higher than a_M has been ruled out, since the probability of its occurrence in the long-run is judged negligible), so that we have:

$$p_{i1} = \Phi\left(\frac{a_1 + d/2 - \rho a_i}{\sigma_\epsilon}\right),$$

and

$$p_{iM} = 1 - \Phi\left(\frac{a_M - d/2 - \rho a_i}{\sigma_\epsilon}\right).$$

In Figure 8.3, we illustrate how the conditional probabilities (represented by the shaded rectangles) for log-productivity change when log-productivity jumps, in period 0, from state $a_3(= 0)$ to state a_1 (despite the low conditional probability assigned to this event, a value represented in the figure by the first rectangle on the left in the first row). In period 1, since the process has moved to the boundary state a_1, the conditional probability of remaining there becomes high.

Fernández-Villaverde *et al.* (2016) underscore that Tauchen's procedure can be extended to vector autoregressive processes instead of a simple univariate process. This is convenient because any p-th order vector autoregressive process scan be rewritten as a first-order process by properly redefining the state variables.[6]

A more general AR(1) process

In (8.3) the mean of the log-process is constrained to be zero. To remove this limitation, it is sufficient to generalize (8.2) by assuming:

$$A_{t+1} = \hat{A}^{1-\rho} A_t^{\rho} \exp\left(\epsilon_{t+1}\right).$$

To see that this formulation allows for a long-run log-productivity level different from 0, note that:

$$\log A_{t+1} \equiv a_{t+1} = (1-\rho)\log \hat{A} + \rho a_t + \epsilon_{t+1},$$

and hence, by iterated substitution,

$$\begin{aligned} a_{t+n} = {} & (1-\rho)\left(1+\rho+\rho^2+...+\rho^{n-1}\right)\log \hat{A} + \\ & + \rho^n a_t + \rho^{n-1}\epsilon_{t+1} + \rho^{n-2}\epsilon_{t+2} + ... + \rho\epsilon_{t+n-1} + \epsilon_{t+n}, \end{aligned}$$

so that $E\left[\tilde{a}_{t+n} | a_t\right] = (1-\rho^n)\log \hat{A} + \rho^n a_t$ and, because $\rho \in [0,1)$,

$$\lim_{n\to\infty} E\left[\tilde{a}_{t+n} | a_t\right] = \log \hat{A}.$$

Accordingly, $\log \hat{A}$ is the long-run average of a_t.[7] The computations based on Tauchen's method (or on Rouwenhorst's, which we will explain in the next subsection) need to be modified to account for the constant $\hat{A}$. In this respect, note not only that the support for log-productivity shifts due to the presence of the mean, but also that the probabilities for log-productivity to transition from state a_i to state a_j are given by:

$$\begin{aligned} p_{ij} = {} & Pr\left\{a_t = a_j \middle| a_{t-1} = a_i\right\} \approx \\ & \approx Pr\left\{a_j - d/2 < (1-\rho)\log(\hat{A}) + \rho a_i + \epsilon_t < a_j + d/2\right\}. \end{aligned}$$

(Compare the last expression with Eq. 8.6).

An alternative for highly autocorrelated processes: Rouwenhorst's method

Kopecky and Suen (2010) argue that Tauchen's (1986) approach and its variants are very accurate when the persistence of the autoregressive process is low, but that their performance severely deteriorates when the serial correlation is close to 1. They show that the method proposed by Rouwenhorst (1995) is more reliable in approximating highly persistent processes.

This method obtains the transition probabilities recursively. It starts with the probabilities that approximate the process using a two-state Markov chain, and then expands the dimension of the transition matrix up to the desired size, M.

As mentioned, the starting point is the two-state Markov chain with $a^L = -a^H = -\sigma_\epsilon/\sqrt{1-\rho^2}$; the matrix of the transition probabilities is therefore:

$$P_2 = \begin{bmatrix} p & 1-p \\ 1-p & p \end{bmatrix},$$

with $p = (1+\rho)/2$.

For $M > 2$, the matrix of probabilities P_M is obtained recursively. For $n = 3, 4, ..., M$, we first compute the matrix:

$$P_n' = p\begin{bmatrix} P_{n-1} & \mathbf{0} \\ \mathbf{0}' & 0 \end{bmatrix} + (1-p)\begin{bmatrix} \mathbf{0} & P_{n-1} \\ 0 & \mathbf{0}' \end{bmatrix} + \\ + (1-p)\begin{bmatrix} \mathbf{0}' & 0 \\ P_{n-1} & \mathbf{0} \end{bmatrix} + p\begin{bmatrix} 0 & \mathbf{0}' \\ \mathbf{0} & P_{n-1} \end{bmatrix},$$

where $\mathbf{0}$, the column vector of zeros, is understood to be of dimensions $(n-1) \times 1$. To obtain P_n from P_n' it is then necessary to divide all rows, but for the top and bottom ones, by 2 (so that the sum of the elements of each row equals 1).

Obtaining the productivity grid is simple: with M states, we choose the lower bound as $a_1 = -\left(\sqrt{M-1}\right)\sigma_\epsilon/\sqrt{1-\rho^2}$ and the upper bound as $a_M = +\left(\sqrt{M-1}\right)\sigma_\epsilon/\sqrt{1-\rho^2}$. The other $M-2$ states are equally spaced. The following subsection shows that the Kopecky and Suen variant performs better than Tauchen's method when simulating a Ramsey economy driven by an autoregressive productivity process characterized by high autocorrelation.

Currently, some attention is being devoted to the approximation of non-stationary processes, where the persistence parameter and the variance of the shocks may vary over time. Fella *et al.* (2019) represent a good starting point to explore this issue. They generalize both Tauchen's and Rouwenhorst's discretization methods and evaluate their performance in the context of a life-cycle, income-fluctuation problem. Farmer and Toda (2017) provide a method for accurately discretizing non-Gaussian Markov processes by matching low order moments of the conditional distributions.

8.1.4 The Ramsey model with AR(1) disturbances

We now present the results for some alternative numerical exercises using the Ramsey model. We chose 800 nodes for $k \in [0.7\hat{k}, 1.1\hat{k}]$, and we adopt our "standard" values $\alpha = 0.3$, $\beta = 0.97$, and $\hat{A} = 3.43643$ (so that $\hat{k} = 1$ and $\hat{c} = 2.43643$). The depreciation parameter δ is set to 1 to allow for comparison with the exact solution; the productivity autocorrelation parameter ρ is 0.9, and the innovation ϵ_t has a mean of 0 and a standard deviation of 0.01.

First, we take advantage of our basic value function iteration routine, modeling the autoregressive process using, in turn, the Tauchen method as detailed in Fernández-Villaverde *et al.* (2016) and the method by Kopecky and Suen (2010).

Next, we obtain the policy function using a routine based on the endogenous gridpoint method.

In all cases, the grid for productivity is composed of 17 points. We assume that convergence is reached when the maximum (absolute) difference between two successive iterations of the value function is below 10^{-7}.

Using the value function iteration with the Tauchen method, convergence is reached at the 793rd iteration, after around 860 seconds. Figure 8.4 shows the results.

The approximation errors reported in Panel (b) are far from being exciting, although they concentrate at high and low productivity values. Therefore, one could argue that the simulation decently captures the behavior of the economy "in normal times."

The variant by Kopecky and Suen (2010) uses the same amount of time (saving around one second), but it yields approximation errors that are, on average, smaller by around 125 times. The highest absolute error is reduced by about 40 times. Figure 8.5 shows the results.

Finally, we turn to the endogenous grid method.

The routine for the stochastic version of our model is very similar to the one we built in Subsection 4.2.3. Since we will discretize the stochastic process, let $\{A(j)\}$ denote the points on the grid we will use for productivity, and let $\bar{k}_1$ be a point on the grid for capital. For each period-1 realization $A(j)$, we let the representative agent consume a fraction μ of output:

$$\bar{c}_1^{(0)}(j) = \mu A(j)\bar{k}_1^{\alpha}. \tag{8.7}$$

where the superscript (0) highlights that this is the initial guess. In period 0, the representative agent is assumed to act optimally, satisfying the

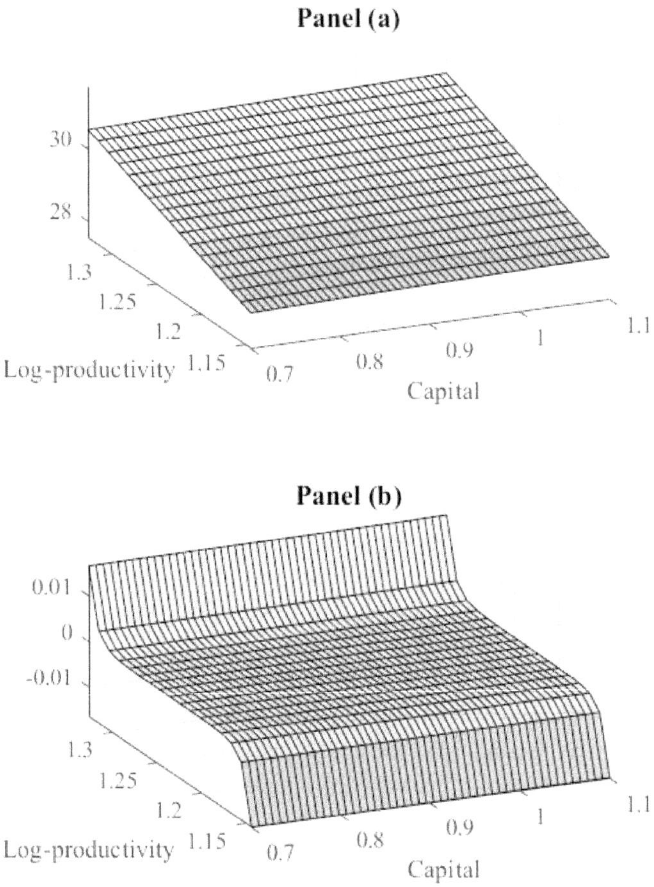

FIGURE 8.4. Panel (a): maximum value function; Panel (b): approximation errors using the Tauchen method

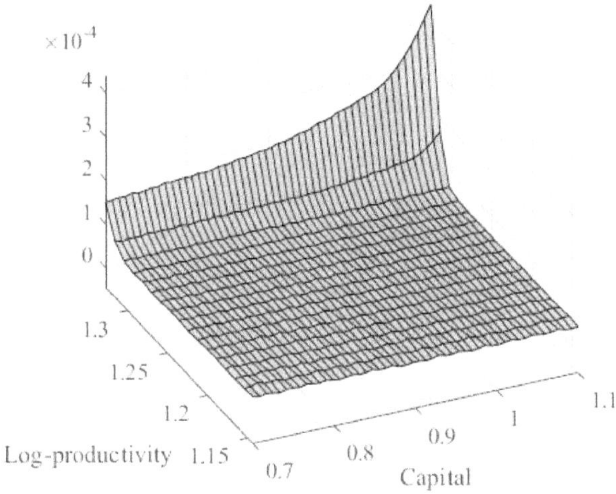

FIGURE 8.5. Approximation errors using value function iteration with the Kopecky and Suen method

stochastic Euler equation. Hence we have:

$$\bar{c}_0^{(0)}(h) = \left(\sum_j p_{hj} \frac{1}{\bar{c}_1^{(0)}(j)} \beta \left(\alpha A(j) \bar{k}_1^{\alpha-1} + 1 - \delta \right) \right)^{-1}, \tag{8.8}$$

where the p_{hj} are the transition probabilities from state h in period 0 to state j in period 1 (with productivity realization $A(j)$). These probabilities are obtained using the Kopecky and Suen method.

In the simple case with full capital depreciation, we can explicitly compute the endogenous gridpoint for period 0 given the productivity state h, $\bar{k}_0^{(0)}(h)$, which corresponds to $\bar{k}_1$. This is obtained by substituting $\bar{c}_1^{(0)}(j)$ from Eq. (8.7) into Eq. (8.8) and then taking advantage of the intertemporal budget constraint

$$A(h) \left(\bar{k}_0^{(0)}(h) \right)^{\alpha} - \bar{c}_0^{(0)}(h) = \bar{k}_1.$$

The next candidate for the period-1 consumption function is obtained by interpolation, by exploiting–for each productivity level–the relationship between the endogenous grid and the period-0 policy function; we then iterate until convergence.

The outcome for this numerical exercise is quite satisfactory. Figure 8.6 shows the approximation errors which are around 100 times lower than those previously obtained. Notably, the routine converges in a blink of an eye.

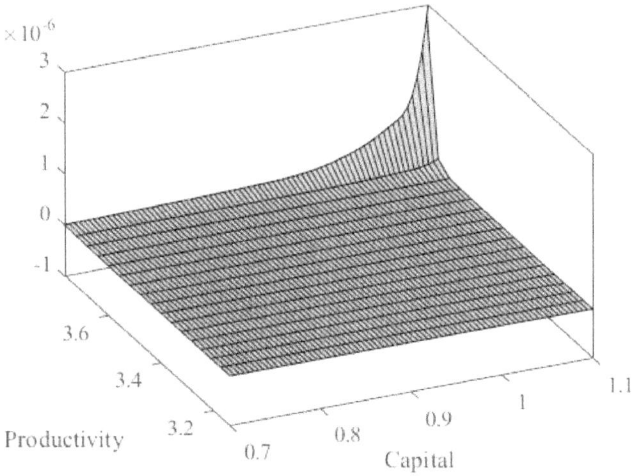

FIGURE 8.6. Approximating the policy function with the endogenous grid method: errors using the Kopecky and Suen method

As in the deterministic case, when depreciation is not complete, the budget constraint cannot be solved explicitly for $\bar{k}_0^{(0)}(h)$, meaning we must resort to a numerical equation solver, though this inevitably slows down the process. Nonetheless, the use of the endogenous grid routine is convenient: in this case it requires 150 seconds. Indeed, the endogenous gridpoint method involves the evaluation of expected values only when computing a refinement of period-0 consumption via the Euler equation (8.8). In contrast, value function iteration methods require such computations every time a possible choice for period-0 consumption is considered.

This makes the endogenous grid method worth considering whenever obtaining the period-0 grid is not too demanding.

This justifies the attention this method has received. Barillas and Fernández-Villaverde (2007) show how to mix the endogenous grid method with standard value function iteration to achieve higher efficiency, and explain how to handle the presence of multiple control variables. White (2015) develops an interpolation technique that facilitates the use of endogenous grid methods in high-dimensional models. Iskhakov *et al.* (2017) extend the endogenous grid method to solve dynamic models where discrete and continuous choices coexist, as it happens when (continuous) consumption decisions are intertwined for example with a (discrete) retirement choice.

8.2 Collocation in two dimensions using Chebyshev polynomials

Suppose we want to approximate a two-dimensional function using a polynomial. In particular, suppose we want to approximate a function $f(x, y)$ using a standard polynomial of second degree in x and of third degree in y. Let $\mathbf{d}$ be a matrix of constants, so that our approximating polynomial is:

$$\begin{aligned} p_{2,3}(x, y, \mathbf{d}) &= d_{0,0} + d_{0,1}y + d_{0,2}y^2 + d_{0,3}y^3 + \\ &\quad + d_{1,0}x + d_{1,1}xy + d_{1,2}xy^2 + d_{1,3}xy^3 + \\ &\quad + d_{2,0}x^2 + d_{2,1}x^2y + d_{2,2}x^2y^2 + d_{2,3}x^2y^3. \end{aligned}$$

Note in passing that we see the curse of dimensionality in action: the number of coefficients to be determined is now 12. Our polynomial is composed of three polynomials of degree three, each with its four coefficients.

The polynomial above can be written in compact form as:

$$p_{2,3}(x, y, \mathbf{d}) = \sum_{i=0}^{2} \sum_{j=0}^{3} d_{i,j} x^i y^j.$$

The use of a Chebyshev polynomials leads us to essentially the same formulation. Consider two state variables, x and y. Let n and r denote the degree of the polynomial in x and y, respectively. In this case, the combination of Chebyshev polynomials is defined as:

$$P_{n,r}(x, y, \mathbf{d}) = \sum_{i=0}^{n} \sum_{j=0}^{r} d_{i,j} T_i(x) T_j(y),$$

where of course $T_i(x) = \cos(i \arccos(x))$ and $T_j(y) = \cos(j \arccos(y))$. If, for example, we decide to use polynomials up to the second degree in the first variable and the third degree in the second, we have:

$$\begin{aligned} P_{2,3}(x, y, \mathbf{d}) &= d_{0,0} + d_{0,1}T_1(y) + d_{0,2}T_2(y) + d_{0,3}T_3(y) + \\ &\quad + d_{1,0}T_1(x) + d_{1,1}T_1(x)T_1(y) + d_{1,2}T_1(x)T_2(y) + d_{1,3}T_1(x)T_3(y) + \\ &\quad + d_{2,0}T_2(x) + d_{2,1}T_2(x)T_1(y) + d_{2,2}T_2(x)T_2(y) + d_{2,3}T_2(x)T_3(y). \end{aligned}$$

This is conceptually analogous to what we would have written using standard monomials.

Note again that the curse of dimensionality is at play: the number of coefficients to be determined is $(n + 1) \times (r + 1)$.

We can now numerically solve the stochastic version of the Ramsey model. Conceptually, this is similar to solving the deterministic version. However, the differences prove to be significant in practice,[8] so we provide details on how to handle some of the intricacies of the two-dimensional case.

Using collocation routines based on Chebyshev polynomials, we can solve the Ramsey model in several alternative ways. Here, we approximate the policy function by discretizing the productivity process with a variant of the Tauchen method. We choose this approach simply because the precision we obtain is superior to many alternatives, and in our experience, the computing time is quite low.

Productivity is assumed to follow the process:

$$A_{t+1} = \hat{A}^{1-\rho} A_t^{\rho} \exp\left(\epsilon_{t+1}\right).$$

To implement our collocation routine, we need to choose the interval for the state variables and determine the collocation points. The state variable are now k and A; let the intervals of interest for the state variables be $\left[\underline{k}, \overline{k}\right]$, and $\left[\underline{A}, \overline{A}\right]$. We define two auxiliary variables on the interval $[-1, +1]$, x and y, which are related to k and A, respectively. We choose $n+1$ collocation nodes for x, and $r+1$ (r can be equal to n) for y, so that the degree of the Chebyshev approximation is $n+r$. The collocation nodes for x and y are obtained via (5.9). Note that (5.11) then gives us the relationship between each node $\left(x_i, y_j\right)$, and the corresponding levels for capital and productivity:

$$k_0\left(x_i\right) = \underline{k} + \frac{\overline{k} - \underline{k}}{2}\left(x_i + 1\right), \; A_0\left(y_j\right) = \underline{A} + \frac{\overline{A} - \underline{A}}{2}\left(y_j + 1\right).$$

Second, as in the unidimensional case (Subsection 5.1.4), we use a Chebyshev approximation for aggregate consumption. Accordingly, at each node, we have:

$$c_0(k_0(x_i), A_0\left(y_j\right)) \approx P_{n,r}(x_i, y_j, \mathbf{d}). \tag{8.9}$$

Third, we address the evolution of productivity and capital. For productivity, we follow the same logic employed in Subsection 8.1.3. Note, however, that when computing the conditional probability matrix, we must account for the fact that the grid points are not equally spaced (for details, refer directly to the routine in the Appendix). The evolution for capital is governed by the intertemporal constraint, so that, for each Chebyshev node (x_i, y_j), the capital stock at time 1 is:

$$k_1(x_i, y_j) = A_0(y_j) k_0(x_i)^{\alpha} + (1-\delta) k_0(x_i) - P_{n,r}(x_i, y_j, \mathbf{d}). \quad (8.10)$$

Fourth, from Eq. (8.9) and the Euler equation, we consider period-1 consumption to be a function of $A_1(y_h)$ and $k_1(x_i, y_j)$. While the grid for productivity is time-invariant, period-1 capital does not necessarily coincide with the values used for period 0. Taking into account that the period-1 capital is also influenced by period-0 productivity, to compute period-1 consumption, we transform capital into a variable with a scale comparable to that of x. We do this by using the inverse of (5.11), as detailed in Subsection 5.1.4:

$$x'_{i,j} = \frac{2}{\overline{k} - \underline{k}} \left(k_1(x_i, y_j) - \underline{k}\right) - 1.$$

The grid for productivity is time-invariant (see Subsection 8.1.3) so that the period-0 nodes remain valid.

We are now ready to take a crucial step: we consider the building blocks of the system that allows us to determine the matrix $\mathbf{d}$. Every optimal intertemporal consumption decision must satisfy the pertinent version of the Euler equation, given by Eq. (6.6), reproduced here for convenience.

$$\frac{1}{c_0} = \beta E_0 \left[\frac{1}{\tilde{c}_1} \left(\alpha \tilde{A}_1 k_1^{\alpha-1} + 1 - \delta \right) \right].$$

For each node (x_i, y_j), the expectation operator $E[.]$ is computed using the probabilities provided by discretization. Recall that each element of the matrix obtained via the Tauchen method represents the probability of transitioning from node j to node h. The stochastic Euler equation is the first dynamic equation we must consider; the second is the evolution of capital, which is given by Eq. (8.10). Period 1 capital–via consumption–depends on, and therefore allows for, the computation of $\mathbf{d}$. For each node (x_i, y_j) we have the system:

$$\begin{cases} \left(P_{n,r}(x_i, y_j, \mathbf{d})\right)^{-1} = \\ = \beta E \left[\left(P_{n,r}\left(x'_{i,j}, y_h, \mathbf{d}\right)\right)^{-1} \left(\alpha A_1(y_h) k_1(x_i, y_j)^{\alpha-1} + 1 - \delta \right) \right] \\ k_1(x_i, y_j) = \\ = A_0(y_j) k_0(x_i)^{\alpha} + (1-\delta) k_0(x_i) - P_{n,r}(x_i, y_j, \mathbf{d}). \end{cases} \quad (8.11)$$

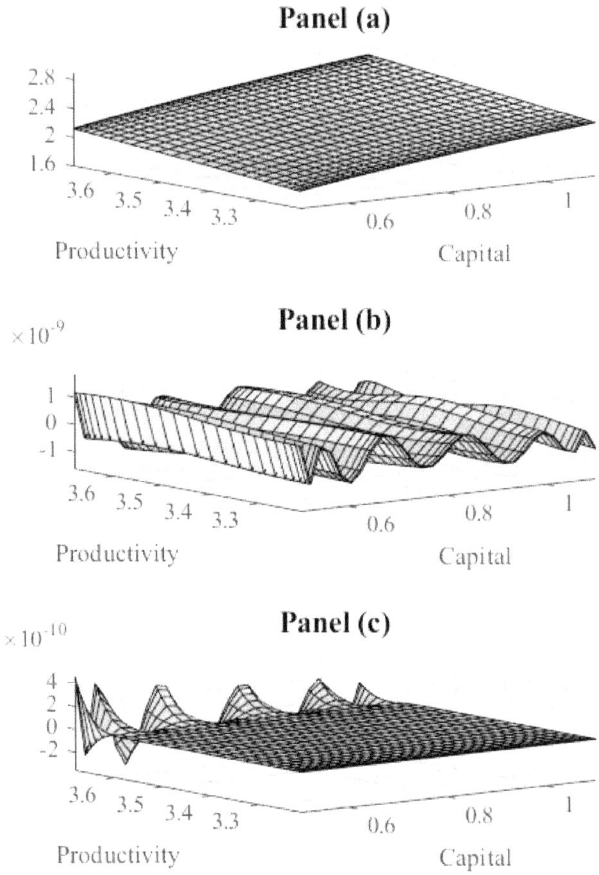

FIGURE 8.7. Panel (a): consumption function; Panel (b): approximation errors; Panel (c): Euler equation residuals

To better understand how to exploit System (8.11), first consider that each period-1 capital level $k_1(x'_{i,j})$ depends on both dimensions of the time-0 node, (x_i, y_j), so that there are $(n+1)\times(r+1)$ levels for k_1. The parameters in $\mathbf{d}$ are, of course, $(n+1)\times(r+1)$. Thus, System (8.11), which is composed of two equations, involves $2\times(n+1)\times(r+1)$ unknowns. Accordingly, System (8.11)–when replicated for all the $(n+1)\times(r+1)$ nodes–suffices to determine the parameters in $\mathbf{d}$ and the period-1 capital levels.

In the numerical exercise, the depreciation parameter δ is set to 1 to allow for an exact solution. As usual, we let $\alpha = 0.3$, $\beta = 0.97$, and $\hat{A} = 3.43643$ (so that $\hat{k} = 1$ and $\hat{c} = 2.43643$). The productivity autocorrelation parameter ρ is 0.9, while the disturbance ϵ_{t+1} has a mean of 0 and a standard deviation, σ_ϵ, of 0.01. The interval for k is $\left[0.5\hat{k}, 1.2\hat{k}\right]$; for productivity we set the interval as $A \in \left[\hat{A}\exp\left(-3\sigma_\epsilon/\sqrt{1-\rho^2}\right),\ \hat{A}\exp\left(3\sigma_\epsilon/\sqrt{1-\rho^2}\right)\right]$. By setting $n = 7$ and $r = 12$, the routines in the Appendix achieve good precision, with approximation errors on the order of 10^{-7}, in about 20 seconds. This is a significant increase from the tenths of a second recorded when we considered only one state variable in Subsection 5.1.4, but the computation time is still reasonable. With $n = 12$ and $r = 24$ we can achieve the remarkable precision shown in Figure 8.7, but note that the computation time rises to around four minutes.

In a nutshell, this simple exercise illustrates the pros and the cons of using collocation techniques. On the bright side, solutions can be very precise, but on the dark side, computation and coding times increase at a very unpleasant rate.

8.3 Perturbation of the stochastic growth model

We now turn to the local approximation of the stochastic optimal growth model. While the underlying logic closely follows the deterministic version, the increased number of state variables makes the details far more intricate. This complexity often suggests, or better yet, necessitates, the use of existing numerical packages. Despite this demotivating statement, we believe that understanding the details of this approach can be beneficial.

We will consider a version of our standard model where randomness stems from productivity, as in our previous examples. We could also assume that the variance of productivity changes over time. This would result in a model with three state variables, pushing us, once again, to the brink of what can be solved with pencil and paper. Instead, we will consider the standard deviation of productivity as a perturbation parameter (like ϵ in Subsection 5.2.1) without introducing a law of motion for it.

As in Section 5.2, we begin with the Euler equation, which is the starting point for the perturbation. To save on notation, we let $h(k_t, a_t) \equiv e^{a_t} f(k_t) + (1-\delta) k_t$. This gives us:

$$U_c(c_t) = E_t \left[\beta U_c(c_{t+1}) h_k(k_{t+1}, \tilde{a}_{t+1})\right]. \tag{8.12}$$

The reference point for which we have a solution is the steady state for the non-stochastic version of the model.

Productivity evolves according to the autoregressive process:

$$a_{t+1} = (1-\rho)\log \hat{A} + \rho a_t + \sigma \epsilon_{t+1}, \tag{8.13}$$

where the productivity innovation ϵ_{t+1} is a standard normal. As usual, our formulation accounts for the persistence in productivity shocks through ρ. Moreover, when matched with convenient choices for the utility and production function, it allows for a comparison of the approximate and exact solutions, as discussed in Subsection 7.2.1.

The policy function, which is the function we will obtain, is denoted by:

$$c_t = \varphi(k_t, a_t, \sigma).$$

Thus, Eq. (8.12) can be written as:

$$U_c(\varphi(k_t, a_t, \sigma)) = E_t \left[\beta U_c(\varphi(k_{t+1}, \tilde{a}_{t+1}, \sigma)) h_k(k_{t+1}, \tilde{a}_{t+1})\right],$$

so that the Euler equation residual is given by:

$$R(k_t, a_t, \sigma) = U_c(\varphi(k_t, a_t, \sigma)) - E_t \left[\beta U_c(\varphi(k_{t+1}, \tilde{a}_{t+1}, \sigma)) h_k(k_{t+1}, \tilde{a}_{t+1})\right]. \tag{8.14}$$

It is easy to obtain the level for capital that satisfies the Euler equation in the non-stochastic steady state. Following the logic of perturbation theory, we then set the total differential of the Euler equation residual (with respect to σ and the state variables k_t and a_t) to zero:

$$R_k(k_t, a_t, \sigma) dk_t + R_a(k_t, a_t, \sigma) da_t + R_\sigma(k_t, a_t, \sigma) d\sigma = 0.$$

This requires calculating and then equating to 0 the partial derivatives $R_k(k_t, a_t, \sigma)$, $R_a(k_t, a_t, \sigma)$, and $R_\sigma(k_t, a_t, \sigma)$.

The fact that period $t+1$ consumption depends on time $t+1$ capital suggests that it is convenient, before "perturbing" Eq. (8.14), to express the next-period state, k_{t+1}, as:

$$k_{t+1} = h(k_t, a_t) - \varphi(k_t, a_t, \sigma),$$

so that, exploiting also Eq. (8.13), we obtain:

$$\begin{aligned}
\frac{dk_{t+1}}{dk_t} &= h_k(k_t, a_t) - \varphi_k(k_t, a_t, \sigma), \\
\frac{dk_{t+1}}{da_t} &= h_a(k_t, a_t) - \varphi_a(k_t, a_t, \sigma), \\
\frac{dk_{t+1}}{d\sigma} &= -\varphi_\sigma(k_t, a_t, \sigma), \\
\frac{da_{t+1}}{da_t} &= \rho, \\
\frac{da_{t+1}}{dk_t} &= 0, \\
\frac{da_{t+1}}{d\sigma} &= \epsilon_{t+1}.
\end{aligned}$$

Note that the last derivative implies:

$$E_t\left[\frac{d\tilde{a}_{t+1}}{d\sigma}\right] = 0.$$

With all these preliminaries in mind, we proceed to computing the first-order perturbation of the Euler equation (8.14). To save space, and avoid seasickness for readers looking at the equations, we will now omit the arguments of the functions $\varphi(k_t, a_t, \sigma)$ and $h(k_t, a_t)$ and of their derivatives as well. Moreover, we will abuse notation, replacing the arguments with the pertinent time index. The evaluation of a function at the steady state will be denoted by a "hat" (e.g., $\hat{\varphi} = \varphi(\hat{k}, \hat{a}, 0)$).

First, we consider $R_k(k_t, a_t, \sigma) = 0$, which is:

$$\begin{aligned}
&R_k(t) = 0 = \\
&= U_{cc}(\varphi(t))\varphi_k(t) - E_t\left[\beta U_{cc}(\varphi(t+1))\varphi_k(t+1)\left[h_k(t) - \varphi_k(t)\right]h_k(t+1) + \right. \\
&\qquad\qquad \left. + \beta U_c(\varphi(t+1))h_{kk}(t+1)\left[h_k(t) - \varphi_k(t)\right]\right].
\end{aligned}$$

Evaluating the above equation at the deterministic steady state allows us to do away with the expectation operator (since $\sigma = 0$), and to exploit the fact that $\beta\hat{h}_k = 1$. Thus, we obtain the following steady-state condition:

$$U_{cc}(\hat{\varphi})\hat{\varphi}_k - U_{cc}(\hat{\varphi})\hat{\varphi}_k\left[\hat{h}_k - \hat{\varphi}_k\right] - U_c(\hat{\varphi})\hat{h}_{kk}\left[1 - \beta\hat{\varphi}_k\right] = 0, \tag{8.15}$$

which is an equation in $\hat{\varphi}_k$, identical to the one obtained in Section 5.2, the solution to which is provided by (5.23).

The first-order effect of the stochastic disturbance is computed from $R_a(k_t, a_t, \sigma) = 0$, which yields:

$$\begin{aligned} R_a(t) = 0 = {} & U_{cc}(\varphi(t))\varphi_a(t) + \\ & - E_t\left[\beta U_{cc}(\varphi(t+1))\varphi_k(t+1)\left(h_a(t) - \varphi_a(t)\right)h_k(t+1)\right] + \\ & - E_t\left[\beta U_{cc}(\varphi(t+1))\varphi_a(t+1)\rho h_k(t+1)\right] + \\ & - E_t\left[\beta U_c(\varphi(t+1))\left(h_{kk}(t+1)\left(h_a(t) - \varphi_a(t)\right) + h_{ka}(t+1)\rho\right)\right]. \end{aligned}$$

In the steady state:

$$\hat{\varphi}_a = \beta\left[\hat{\varphi}_k\left(\hat{h}_a - \hat{\varphi}_a\right) + \rho\hat{\varphi}_a\right]\hat{h}_k + \beta\frac{U_c(\hat{\varphi})}{U_{cc}(\hat{\varphi})}\left(\hat{h}_{kk}\left(\hat{h}_a - \hat{\varphi}_a\right) + \rho\hat{h}_{ka}\right).$$

Given that $\hat{\varphi}_k$ has already been computed, we have a linear equation in $\hat{\varphi}_a$. By again using $\beta\hat{h}_k = 1$, we get:

$$\hat{\varphi}_a = \frac{\hat{\varphi}_k\hat{h}_a + \beta\frac{U_c(\hat{\varphi})}{U_{cc}(\hat{\varphi})}\left(\hat{h}_{kk}\hat{h}_a + \hat{h}_{ka}\rho\right)}{1 + \hat{\varphi}_k - \rho + \beta\frac{U_c(\hat{\varphi})}{U_{cc}(\hat{\varphi})}\hat{h}_{kk}}. \tag{8.16}$$

Finally, we consider the first-order effects of a change in σ by setting $R_\sigma(k_t, a_t, \sigma) = 0$. When computing $R_\sigma(k_t, a_t, \sigma)$ we take advantage of the fact that $h(k_t, a_t)$ does not depend on σ. This yields:

$$\begin{aligned} & R_\sigma(t) = 0 = U_{cc}(\varphi(t))\varphi_\sigma(t) + \\ & + E_t\left[\beta U_{cc}(\varphi(t+1))\left[\varphi_k(t+1)\varphi_\sigma(t) - \varphi_a(t+1)\epsilon_{t+1} - \varphi_\sigma(t+1)\right]h_k(t+1)\right] \\ & \qquad + E_t\left[\beta U_c(\varphi(t+1))\left[h_{kk}(t+1)\varphi_\sigma(t) - h_{ka}(t+1)\epsilon_{t+1}\right]\right]. \end{aligned}$$

In the steady state, the equation above gives:

$$\hat{\varphi}_\sigma = -\hat{\varphi}_k\hat{\varphi}_\sigma + \hat{\varphi}_\sigma - \beta\frac{U_c(\hat{\varphi})}{U_{cc}(\hat{\varphi})}\hat{h}_{kk}\hat{\varphi}_\sigma.$$

Note that the properties of the utility and production functions guarantee that this equation is satisfied only for $\hat{\varphi}_\sigma = 0$. This tells us that the variance of the disturbance has no first-order effect, which is not surprising. Indeed, to capture the effect of the variance, at least a second-order approximation is required. We will, however, stop our analysis here, since we feel that we are at the verge of what can be done "with paper and pencil."

Accordingly, our (first-order) approximation of the policy function is:

$$\overline{\varphi}(k_t, a_t, \sigma) = \varphi(\hat{k}, \hat{a}, 0) + \varphi_k(\hat{k}, \hat{a}, 0)\left(k_t - \hat{k}\right) + \varphi_a(\hat{k}, \hat{a}, 0)\left(a_t - \hat{a}\right),$$

where the pertinent derivatives of $\hat{\varphi}$ are provided by Eqs. (8.15-8.16).

We provide a quantitative assessment of the first-order perturbation, considering the traditional growth model with $U(c_t) = \ln(c_t)$ and $y_t = A_t k_t^{\alpha}$. We adopt the same parameter values as in the previous section; in particular, $\sigma = 0.01$ is used to compute approximation errors and Euler equation residuals. From Eq. (8.13), the steady-state value for $a_t (= \ln(A_t))$ is 1.234432. Accordingly, the first-order approximation for the policy function is:

$$\overline{\varphi}(k_t, a_t, \sigma) = 2.436426 + 0.730928\,(k_t - 1) + 2.436426\,(a_t - 1.234432). \tag{8.17}$$

Panel (a) of Figure 8.8 plots $\overline{\varphi}(k_t, a_t, \sigma)$. The interval for a_t is centered on the steady state $\ln(\hat{A}) = 1.234432$, while its width (0.2) has been chosen arbitrarily.

Our version of the Ramsey model admits the closed-form solution presented in Subsection 7.2.1, which allows us to obtain the approximation errors. These errors, computed as the difference between the true consumption function and $\overline{\varphi}(k_t, a_t, \sigma)$, are depicted in Panel (b) of Figure 8.8. We conclude our exercise by substituting our first-order approximation $\overline{\varphi}(k_t, a_t, \sigma)$ for the true policy function $\varphi(k_t, a_t, \sigma)$ in Eq. (8.14), thereby obtaining the Euler equation errors shown in Panel (c).

The errors reported in Panel (b) of Figure 8.8 may seem rather large; keep in mind, however, that ours is a first-order approximation. To obtain higher-order approximations, it is convenient to use Dynare: writing a "model file" containing the model description is a matter of minutes. As for our exercise, Dynare provides a first-order approximation for the policy function that is indistinguishable (up to the sixth decimal) from (8.17), given by:

$$c_t' = 2.436426 + 0.730928\,(k_t - 1) + 2.436426\,(a_t - 1.234432).$$

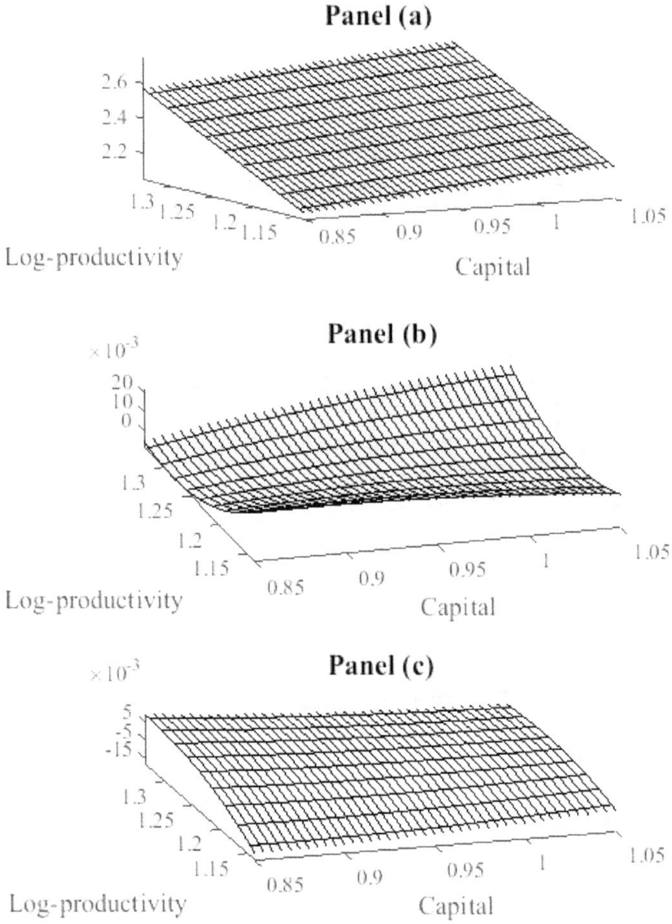

FIGURE 8.8. Panel (a): consumption function; Panel (b): approximation errors; Panel (c): Euler equation residuals

The second-order approximation is instead:

$$\begin{aligned} c_t^{''} = 2.436426 + 0.730928\,(k_t - 1) + 2.436426\,(a_t - 1.234432) + \\ - 0.255825\,(k_t - 1)^2 + 0.730928\,(k_t - 1)\,(a_t - 1.234432) + \\ + 1.218213\,(a_t - 1.234432)^2 \,. \end{aligned}$$

Note that the first-order terms of $c_t^{''}$ are identical to those for $c_t^{'}$.[9] Denoting the exact solution for consumption by c_t^*, one can show that the mean absolute error based on $c_t^{''} - c_t^*$ is approximately 95% lower than that computed for $c_t^{'} - c_t^*$ in the interval $a_t \in [1.134432, 1.334432]$.

When the true solution is unknown, which means of course in all the interesting cases, the accuracy analysis becomes challenging. Collard and Juillard (2001) provide accuracy criteria for higher-order perturbation, using an asset pricing model as a working example.

When dealing with time-varying volatility for the shocks, at least a third-order approximation is required. Caldara *et al.* (2012) use a model with recursive preferences and highlight that a third order approximation is required to achieve a precision comparable to that guaranteed by value function iteration in a large interval around the deterministic steady state. Furthermore, one might be interested in the possibility of "rare disasters"–that is, situations in which one or more state variables may undergo a sudden reduction. In our set-up, a "disaster" could amount to a simultaneous and significant damage to both the capital stock and technology. Levintal (2017) argues that the presence of disaster risk in a model means that it cannot be accurately dealt with using second- or third-order approximations, requiring instead a fifth-order one.[10] Increasing the order of approximation at almost no additional cost in terms of coding time is possible thanks to Dynare for Matlab (and Octave), which can now approximate models up to an arbitrary order. Computation time, unsurprisingly, increases almost exponentially, but it remains low. Nonetheless, higher-order perturbations raise some relevant issues. Fernández-Villaverde *et al.* (2016) underscore that the consumption function for the stochastic growth model, when approximated with a fifth-order perturbation, is not concave, which is at odds with the theory.[11]

An interesting issue that can arise in a stochastic model is that of "occasionally binding" constraints. Consider a version of our basic setup in which the depreciation rate is very low, and imagine that the economy is hit by a large negative technology shock. If the economy is close to its steady state, our representative agent may find it optimal to consume some of her capital stock. This would be impossible (temporarily abandoning the fiction of a one-good economy). This calls for imposing a non-negativity constraint on investment (gross of depreciation). This type of constraint is an occasionally binding constraint, and binding constraints prevent the differentiability of the model's equations. Nonetheless, Dynare allows for the simulation of models with up to two occasionally binding constraints by relying on a piecewise linear solution originally proposed by Guerrieri and Iacoviello (2015).

If you need to implement your own routine, consider that reformulating the model through a change of variables (e.g., from linear to log-linear) can make the equations composing it "less nonlinear." This can improve the accuracy of perturbation approximations. Judd (2003) exploits this idea and shows how changes of variables can be implemented efficiently. Fernández-Villaverde *et al.* (2016) discuss how to find a higher-order perturbation solution for stochastic general equilibrium models, following much of the structure and notation of Schmitt-Grohé and Uribe (2004).

While Dynare offers several advantages in terms of ease of use and flexibility, the caveats discussed in Subsection 5.2.1 also apply to stochastic models. Therefore, before succumbing to its allure (or to that of other algorithms), you should assess whether perturbation methods are suitable for the problem at hand.

8.4 The Parameterized Expectations Approach

This method approximates the conditional expectation in the Euler equation using a function of the state variables. It finds the parameters that minimize the distance between the expectation, as simulated within the model, and the chosen approximating function. The advantages of this approach include its straightforward coding and the fact that a low-degree polynomial often provides a sufficiently accurate approximation. Consequently, computing time remains low, even for models with many state variables.

As usual, we introduce this new approach with an example.

We consider a version of the Ramsey model identical to the one discussed in Subsection 8.1.3, except that capital does not depreciate entirely within one period, thus $\delta \in (0,1)$.[12] Accordingly, in our example, the stochastic Euler equation is given by (6.6), though modified to account for the partial capital depreciation. From the perspective of period t, (i.e., when the expectation is conditioned upon the time t information), the Euler equation is:

$$\frac{1}{c_t} = \beta E_t \left[\frac{1}{\tilde{c}_{t+1}} (\alpha \tilde{A}_{t+1} k_{t+1}^{\alpha-1} + 1 - \delta) \right]. \tag{8.18}$$

The set of relevant equations is completed by the standard transition function:

$$k_{t+1} = A_t k_t^{\alpha} + (1 - \delta) k_t - c_t,$$

with:

$$A_{t+1} = \hat{A}^{1-\rho} A_t^{\rho} \exp(\epsilon_{t+1}).$$

The right hand side of Eq. (8.18) is an expectation (discounted by β) conditional on the period t information set. The information available at time t is condensed into the state variables, k_t and A_t. Hence, the expectation is a function of capital and productivity. Also note that the discounted value of the expectation must be equal to the marginal utility of period t consumption, which is itself a function of k_t and A_t.[13]

The fact that the expectation $E_t \left[1/\tilde{c}_{t+1} (\alpha \tilde{A}_{t+1} k_{t+1}^{\alpha-1} + 1 - \delta) \right]$ is a function of the state variables allows us to approximate it by a polynomial in these variables. As with any polynomial, this approximation is characterized by its parameters. Therefore, once the polynomial's degree and its parameter values are chosen, we have parameterized the expectation.

The approximating function is denoted by $F(\Psi, A_t, k_t)$, where Ψ represents the set of coefficients of the polynomial. Following Marcet and Lorenzoni (1999), we opt for an exponentiated polynomial of low order–actually, of order one–to represent $F(\Psi, A_t, k_t)$:

$$F(\Psi, A_t, k_t) = e^{\psi_1} k_t^{\psi_2} A_t^{\psi_3} \left(= \exp(\psi_1 + \psi_2 \ln k_t + \psi_3 \ln A_t)\right). \tag{8.19}$$

In this example, Ψ is composed of ψ_1, ψ_2, and ψ_3. We usually approximate the conditional expectation with better and better accuracy by increasing the degree of the exponentiated polynomial.[14]

To obtain the vector of parameters, we start with an arbitrary choice Ψ_0 (as we will shortly see, Ψ_0 cannot be *too* arbitrary, but for now we leave aside this issue). We can simulate the model given the initial values for the state variables, A_t, and k_t, and a given sequence of random numbers representing the future innovations in the productivity process. This simulation yields "artificial" time series for consumption and next-period capital. Indeed, for any period $\tau = \{t, t+1, t+2, ...\}$, we have:

$$c_\tau(\Psi_0) = [\beta F(\Psi_0, A_\tau, k_\tau)]^{-1} \tag{8.20a}$$

$$k_{\tau+1}(\Psi_0) = A_\tau k_\tau^\alpha + (1-\delta)k_\tau - c_\tau(\Psi_0). \tag{8.20b}$$

Starting in the initial period t, we compute $c_t(\Psi_0)$ using the known values A_t and k_t. The period t consumption, along with A_t and k_t, is used to determine $k_{t+1}(\Psi_0)$. For period $t+1$, we consider the first random draw provided by our software, ϵ_{t+1}, which determines A_{t+1}; we then couple A_{t+1}, with $k_{t+1}(\Psi_0)$, obtaining $c_{t+1}(\Psi_0)$ and subsequently $k_{t+2}(\Psi_0)$. This process can be iterated as desired (e.g., 10,000 times).

Note that the dependence of c_τ and $k_{\tau+1}$ on k_τ and A_τ is taken as understood. We prefer to emphasize the fact that the values for consumption and capital, obtained from (8.20a) and (8.20b), depend on the vector of parameters; hence the notation $c_\tau(\Psi_0)$, and $k_{\tau+1}(\Psi_0)$.

System (8.20a-8.20b) highlights a key reason why standard polynomials are seldom used to approximate the expectation on the right-hand side of Eq. (8.18). A standard polynomial can be problematic because, in searching for the solution, it can generate a negative value for the approximated expectation $F(\Psi, A_\tau, k_\tau)$. Consumption would then become negative, leading to implausible capital accumulation decisions that can preclude the attainment of a fixed point. In the case of a constant intertemporal elasticity of substitution utility, the marginal utility of consumption on the left-hand side of Eq. (8.18) would be $c_\tau^{-\gamma}$; this, with $\gamma \in [0,1)$, can also induce numerical errors.

The artificial time series for A_τ, k_τ, and c_τ allows us to construct a series for the auxiliary variable $w_{\tau+1}$, which is based on our arbitrary choice for the vector of parameters, Ψ_0:

$$w_{\tau+1}(\Psi_0) = \frac{1}{c_{\tau+1}(\Psi_0)}(\alpha A_{\tau+1}k_{\tau+1}(\Psi_0)^{\alpha-1} + 1 - \delta), \quad \tau = \{t, t+1, ...\}.$$

One can think of the time series for $w_{\tau+1}(\Psi_0)$ as being based on some "beliefs" about the optimal consumption decision, with those beliefs being "incorporated" into the parameter vector Ψ_0.

Our representative agent could ask herself if she could improve her knowledge about the relationship between optimal consumption and the state variables, thereby refining her beliefs. The relationship between c_τ, A_τ, and k_τ, is constrained to take the form posited in (8.19), hence "improve her knowledge," in this context, means minimizing the distance between $w_{\tau+1}(\Psi_0)$

and the function in (8.19). Since $F(\Psi_0, A_\tau, k_\tau)$ is an exponentiated polynomial, this is achieved by running the regression:

$$\ln w_{\tau+1} = \psi_{1,1} + \psi_{1,2} \ln k_\tau + \psi_{1,3} \ln A_\tau + \xi_{\tau+1},$$

where the ordinary least squares regression coefficients $\psi_{1,1}$, $\psi_{1,2}$, and $\psi_{1,3}$ compose the new set of parameters, Ψ_1, and $\xi_{\tau+1}$ is the error. Note for future use that–when the "forecast" is efficient–the least squares error is orthogonal to the regressors and uncorrelated over time (otherwise, such correlations could be exploited to improve the forecast).

If the parameter vector Ψ_0 were correct, the regression parameters that make up Ψ_1 would be identical to those in Ψ_0, and thus no "knowledge improvement" would take place.

Otherwise, the regression coefficients Ψ_1 are used to simulate the model again. Hence, we substitute the vector Ψ_1 for the initial arbitrary vector Ψ_0 to obtain new values for $c_\tau(\Psi_1)$, $k_\tau(\Psi_1)$, and thus for the related time series $w_{\tau+1}(\Psi_1)$. Proceeding in this manner, we obtain a new estimate Ψ_2.

The idea is to obtain the "correct" expectations $E_t\left[w_{\tau+1}\right]$–and therefore the optimal consumption c^*_τ series–by iterating this process.

Note the simplicity of the parameterized expectation algorithm, which consists of only the two steps we have described:

- (Step 1) Simulation of the economy based on a given parameter set (initially Ψ_0);

- (Step 2) Updating of the parameters–using a least squares projection–until convergence.

Note also that when updating the parameters, the first observations–for example, 1,000 out of a sample of 10,000–are discarded to eliminate the influence of the initial values for k_t and A_t.

We now provide the results of a simulation exercise. Its initialization, in addition to the values for the structural parameters, requires the definition of an initial condition for k_t and A_t, and an initial guess for the coefficients of the exponentiated polynomial.

As for the parameters characterizing our economy, we choose the values used in Section 8.2 with the exception of the depreciation parameter, which is set to $\delta = 0.15$. The other parameters are $\beta = 0.97$, $\alpha = 0.3$, $\hat{A} = 3.436426$ and $\rho = 0.9$; the disturbance ϵ_τ has a mean of 0, and a standard deviation of 0.01. These values imply a non-stochastic steady state for capital, $\hat{k}$, of 12.011690. The initial condition for the capital stock is $k_t = \hat{k}$. Similarly, the initial condition for productivity matches $\hat{A}$. Choosing an initial condition far from the steady state is pointless: discarding the first, say, 500 or 1,000 observations of the artificial time series eliminates its transitional part. Moreover, note that k_T takes a relatively small number of periods to move from its initial value to its long-run distribution. Therefore, the transitional part of the time series is significantly impacted by the limited number of actual realizations of the stochastic component of productivity and is thus of limited interest.

Finally, we need to provide the initial values for the parameters in Ψ_0. Although we have defined these values as "arbitrary," it is sensible to feed the routine with values that are as close as possible to the "true" solution: this speeds up the computation, and, most importantly, helps avoid convergence problems. Accordingly, for Ψ_0, we have chosen the values that can be computed when $\delta = 1$ (refer to Subsection 7.2.1). These values are: $\psi_{0,1} = 0.37436 (= \log 1.45406)$, $\psi_{0,2} = -0.3$, and $\psi_{0,3} = -1$.[15]

We simulate the model for 11,000 periods, discarding the first 1,000.[16] At the end of each iteration, for each parameter we compute the difference between its initial value and the estimated one. When the largest difference in absolute value is lower than 10^{-8}, we assume that convergence is attained. It turns out that this happens in 46 iterations, the required computer time being below half a second.

Panel (a) in Figure 8.9 shows the scatter plot for consumption as a function of capital and productivity. Panel (b) displays the evolution of the parameters values: the solid line represents $\psi_{j,1}$; the dotted line is $\psi_{j,2}$, and the dashed line is $\psi_{j,3}$.

Up to now, we have not dealt with the important issue of deciding whether the solution we obtained is sufficiently close to the (unknown) truth. Several tests have been developed to assess the validity of the parameterized expectation solution. Den Haan and Marcet (1994) proposed to exploit a property of the rational expectation equilibrium. As already remarked, the forecast errors agents commit have to be uncorrelated with past realizations of the relevant variables, otherwise agents could exploit this correlation to obtain a better forecast. Den Haan and Marcet suggest regressing the residuals from the simulated Euler equation on past values of the relevant variables, and then testing whether the regression coefficients are all equal to zero. We increased the number of observations to one hundred thousand, and then regressed the residuals on the lagged values for capital and productivity

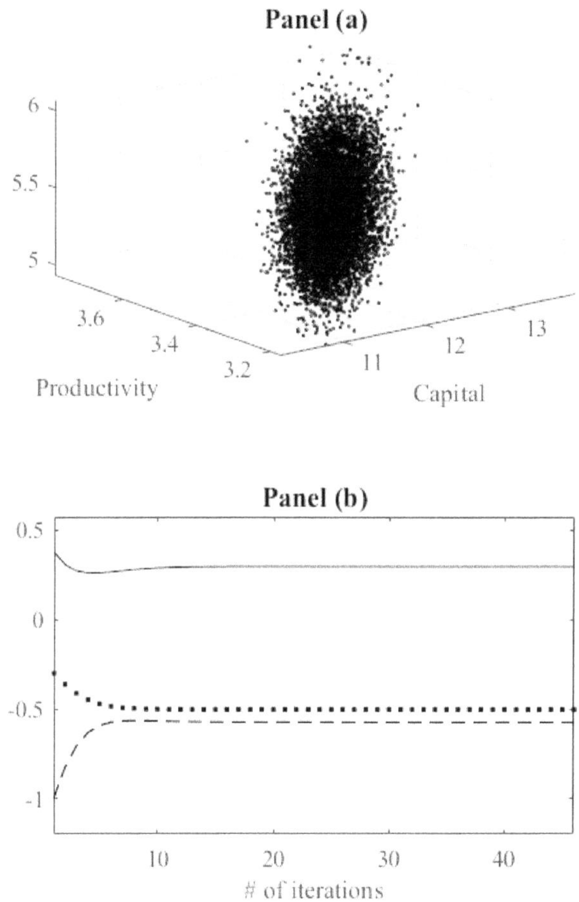

FIGURE 8.9. Panel (a): consumption scatterplot; Panel (b): evolution of the parameters

(plus a constant). We found that the coefficients obtained are very low, on the order of 10^{-4} for the constant and for k_T, and of 10^{-5} for A_T.[17]

The upside of what we have done is that we were able to compute a good approximation in a very short time: the Parameterized Expectations Approach only mildly suffers from the "curse of dimensionality" because the polynomial used to approximate the expectation is a low-degree one.

The main drawback of the PEA is that it does not rely on the contraction mapping theorem, and therefore there is no guarantee that a solution can be found (although convergence has been proven for several economic models; for more details on early results refer to Marcet and Lorenzoni (1999) and to the literature cited therein). This fact has some practical implications: it is advisable to provide "sensible" initial values for the parameters characterizing the approximating function. It is also often necessary to dampen the updating of the parameters in each iteration.

In this respect, we offer a simple but hopefully interesting exercise: we run a parameterization of the Ramsey model for which the exact solution is known, which is the same parameterization as above, but with $\delta = 1$. We feed the routine with an initial guess that is 40% lower than the correct one, and we find that a convergence problem emerges. Accordingly, we modify our algorithm, considering a "slow" update of the parameter vector. Let $\bar{\Psi}$ denote the parameter vector estimated in the least squares section of the procedure from an artificial time series based on the vector Ψ_{n-1}. Instead of choosing $\Psi_n = \bar{\Psi}$, we considered the damped update $\Psi_n = \mu\bar{\Psi} + (1 - \mu)\Psi_{n-1}$, with $\mu = 0.6$. This achieves convergence (in this case required up to the fifth decimal) but, as shown in Figure 8.10, the convergence is not monotonic, a remnant of the explosive behavior we observe with higher values for μ. Maliar and Maliar (2005) suggest a simple alternative approach that improves the convergence properties of the algorithm. They propose to initially constrain the endogenous state variables to stay close to the steady state (they "bound" the variable and hence the series). Over the iterations, the bounds are gradually relaxed, so that their initial presence should not affect the final solution.

The PEA is a global solution method: once the parameters for the pertinent functions are obtained, we can determine the values of the endogenous variables across the entire range of interest for the state variables. However, as previously mentioned, these parameters are estimated using state variable values that are (relatively) close to the non-stochastic steady state. For certain (non-standard) utility and production functions, this can create a discrepancy between the true and computed functions for portions of the state space far from the steady state.

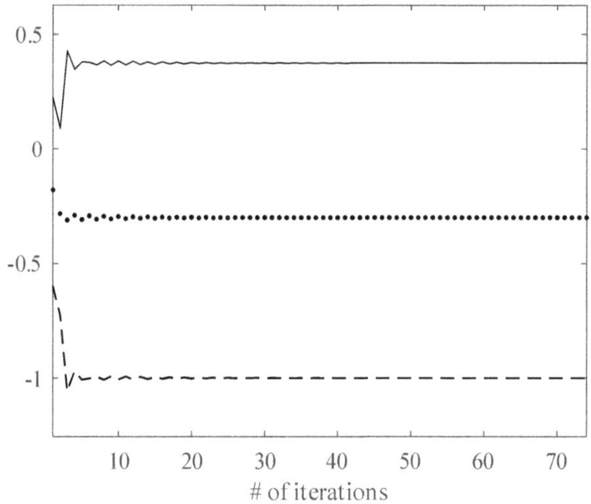

FIGURE 8.10. Parameter evolution with dampened updating

In general, the Parameterized Expectations Approach performs quite well, as it requires a limited coding effort and the resulting routines run fairly quickly. In addition, Christiano and Fisher (2000) point out that it can be easily adapted to solve models with stochastic constraints. Heer and Maussner (2009) make a similar point and provide two applications.

In summary, this is a method that is well worth considering when solving large stochastic models.

8.5 Appendix

8.5.1 Numerical routines for the stochastic growth model

valfun_iter2.m

This script executes the value function iteration procedure described in Subsection 8.1.1. There are 800 gridpoints for capital (ranging again from 0.7 to 1.1) and five equally-spaced and equiprobable productivity levels (going from 3.367697 to 3.505155). This routine yields Figure 8.1. Table 3 is obtained by changing the number of gridpoints for the capital stock and the number of productivity levels, specifically setting the number of states to 5, assuming 2 equiprobable productivity levels, and letting $kmin = 0.98$, $kmax = 1.02$.

```
clear;
format('long');

alpha=0.3;
beta=0.97;

A=1/(alpha*beta);
kstar=(alpha*beta*A)^(1/(1-alpha));

states=800; % Number of gridpoints.
kmin=0.7; % Lowest level for capital.
kmax=1.1; % Highest level for capital.

deltak = (kmax-kmin)/(states-1);
kvec=kmin:deltak:kmax;
% The last two lines compute the 'grid' for the state variable.

% The next three line describe the productivity process.
prods=5; % Number of possible productivity levels.
Amin=0.98*A;
Amax=2*A-Amin;
% Productivity differential between best and worst case is 4%.

deltaA=(Amax-Amin)/(prods-1);
Avec=Amin:deltaA:Amax;
% The last two lines create the 'grid' for productivity.

p_vec=1/prods*ones(prods,1);
% Identical probability for every productivity level.

vini=zeros(1,states);
% Initial guess for the expected maximum value function.
% Note that in the current version of Matlab it is not necessary to
% initialize the end-of cycle value function (vfin), the consumption
% choice matrix (consV) and the optimal choices matrix (opt_choice).

err=10;
% "err" is the variable used to substantiate the convergence crite-
% rion. When "err" is below a threshold (specified below), the rou-
% tine has converged.

z=0; % Counter for the # of iterations.

tic;

while err > 10^(-5) % Convergence criterion.
z=z+1;
```

```
for h=1:prods
  for i=1:states
    for j=1:states
      consV(h,j)=Avec(h)*kvec(i)^alpha-kvec(j);
      % For any given capital (i), and for any productivity (h), this
      % gives the consumption consistent with next period state (j).
    end
    opt_choice(h,i)=max((log(consV(h,:))+ beta*vini)');
    % This is the maximum value that is obtained choosing among con-
    % sumption level, taking into account the related next-period
    % capital stock (whose values are in vini). Note that i indexes
    % current capital and h indexes current productivity.
  end
end

vfin=p_vec'*opt_choice;
% This is the expected maximum value function: for every capital le-
% vel, we compute the expected value of the optimal choices.

delta=abs(vini-vfin);
% This computes the difference between the maximum value before and
% after the optimization cycle, in absolute value.

err=max(delta');
% Our convergenge criterion is based on the maximum absolute diffe-
% rence between the maximum value before and after the optimization
% cycle.

vini=vfin;
% The new cycle will start with this new guess.

% Table2(z,:)=[z vini]
% Uncommenting the line above and by properly modifying kvec, Avec,
% p_vec, and the pertinent # of states gives us the values displayed
% in Table 3.
end

toc

% "True" maximum value function   refer to Chapter 7
par=alpha*beta;
cost1=1/(1-beta)*( par/(1-par)*log(par)+log(1-par));
cost2=alpha/(1-par);
cost3=1/(1-par)*log(Avec)*p_vec*(1/(1-beta));
true_val=cost1+cost2*log(kvec)+cost3;

err_approx=true_val-vfin;
```

```
% Approximation errors (with respect to the true expected value
% function).

% =============== The lines below produce Figure 8.1 ===============
font=11; % size of font (in points)

% This builds Panel (a).
subplot1 = subplot(2,1,1,'FontSize',10,'FontName','Times␣New␣Roman');
plot(kvec',vfin');
xlim([0.7 1.1]);
ylim([29.52 29.74]);
xlabel('Capital','FontSize',font, 'FontName','Times␣New␣Roman');
ylabel('Maximum␣value','FontSize',font,'FontName','Times␣New␣Roman');
title('Panel␣(a):␣Expected␣maximum␣value␣function','FontSize',...
font+3,'FontName','Times␣New␣Roman')

% This builds Panel (b).
subplot2 = subplot(2,1,2,'FontName','Times␣New␣Roman');
plot(kvec',err_approx');
xlim([0.7 1.1]);
xlabel('Capital','FontSize',font,'FontName','Times␣New␣Roman');
ylabel('Approximation␣errors','FontSize',font,'FontName', ...
  'Times␣New␣Roman');
title('Panel␣(b):␣Approximation␣Errors','FontSize',font+3,...
 'FontName','Times␣New␣Roman')
```

valfun_iter3.m

This script solves the model with the two-states Markov process presented in Subsection 8.1.2, and produces Figure 8.2. Plain repetitions of the comments for the previous routine have been avoided.

```
% Value function iteration to simulate the two-states Markov case for
% the Ramsey model (Subsection 8.1.2).

clear;

format('long');

alpha=0.3;
beta=0.97;
A=1/(alpha*beta);

kstar=(alpha*beta*A)^(1/(1-alpha));

states=800;
```

```
kmin=0.5;
kmax=1.3;

deltak = (kmax-kmin)/(states-1);
kvec=kmin:deltak:kmax;

prods=2; % Number of states for productivity.
Amin=0.98*A;
Amax=2*A-Amin;
Avec=[Amin,Amax];
% Productivity differential between best and worst case is 4%.

p=.8;
PP=[p,1-p;1-p,p];
% Two-states (symmetric) Markov chain involving persistency.

vini=zeros(prods,states);
% Initial "guess" for the epected maximum value function.

% Note that in the current version of Matlab it is not necessary to
% initialize the end-of cycle value function (vfin), the consumption
% choice matrix (consV) and the optimal choices matrix (opt_choice).

err=10;
z=0;

tic;

while err > 10^(-5)

z=z+1;

for h=1:prods
  for i=1:states
  % i is the index for current capital, h for current productivity,
  % and j will be used for next period capital

     for j=1:states
         consV(h,j)=Avec(h)*kvec(i)^alpha-kvec(j);
         % Computes the consumption compatible with next period
         % capital (j), for given capital (i) and productivity (h).
     end

  opt_choice(h,i)=max((log(consV(h,:))+ beta*vini(h,:))');
  % This is the optimal choice among feasible consumption values, ta-
  % king into account the expected maximum value
  end
```

```
end

vfin=PP*opt_choice;
% Expected value function.
% Note that row h of PP is used to take into account that expected
% maximum value is conditional on state h

delta=abs(vini-vfin);
err=max(delta');

vini=vfin;
end

toc

% This computes the "true" maximum value function (see pertinent
% exercise in Chapter 7)
A_bar=log(Avec)*[0.5;0.5];
% Unconditional mean for log-productivity

cost1=1/(1-beta)*( alpha*beta/(1-alpha*beta)*log(alpha*beta)+...
    log(1-alpha*beta)+2*beta*(1-p)*A_bar/((1-alpha*beta)*(1+ ...
    beta*(1-2*p))));
cost2=alpha/(1-alpha*beta);
cost3=1/((1+beta*(1-2*p))*(1-alpha*beta));

true_val=cost1+cost2*ones(prods,1)*log(kvec)+cost3*log(Avec)'*...
    ones(1,states);

err_approx=true_val-opt_choice;

% ============== This gives the three-panel Figure 8.2 ==============
figure;
fontsize=11; % size of font (in points)
xLow=min(kvec);
xHigh=max(kvec);
yLow=min(min(opt_choice));
yHigh=max(max(opt_choice));

subplot1 = subplot(3,1,1,'FontSize',10,'FontName','Times␣New␣Roman');
plot(kvec',opt_choice');
xlim([xLow xHigh]);
ylim([yLow yHigh]);
xlabel('Capital','FontSize',fontsize,'FontName','Times␣New␣Roman');
ylabel('Maximum␣value','FontSize',fontsize,...
    'FontName','Times␣New␣Roman');
title({'Panel␣(a):','Expected␣maximum␣value␣function'},'FontSize',...
```

```
    fontsize+2,'FontName','Times␣New␣Roman')

subplot2 = subplot(3,1,2,'FontName','Times␣New␣Roman');
plot(kvec',err_approx(1,:)');
xlim([xLow xHigh]);
xlabel('Capital','FontSize',fontsize,'FontName','Times␣New␣Roman');
ylabel('Approximation␣errors','FontSize',fontsize,...
    'FontName','Times␣New␣Roman');
title({'Panel␣(b):␣Approximation␣Errors', '-␣Low␣Productivity'}, ...
    'FontSize',fontsize+2,'FontName','Times␣New␣Roman')

subplot3 = subplot(3,1,3,'FontName','Times␣New␣Roman');
plot(kvec',err_approx(2,:)');
xlim([xLow xHigh]);
xlabel('Capital','FontSize',fontsize,'FontName','Times␣New␣Roman');
ylabel('Approximation␣errors','FontSize',fontsize,...
    'FontName','Times␣New␣Roman');
title({'Panel␣(c):␣Approximation␣Errors','-␣High␣Productivity'},...
    'FontSize',fontsize+2,'FontName','Times␣New␣Roman')
```

tauchen_FV.m

The output of this function file is composed of a matrix of transition probabilities and of a vector of log-productivity levels. Inputs are: the standard deviation for log-productivity, the autocorrelation parameter, the number of log-productivity levels, the long-run non-stochastic productivity and a parameter capturing the width of the log-productivity support.

```
% This routine uses the Tauchen method as detailed in Fernandez-Vil-
% laverde et al. (2016);
% mu is width of the interval, n is number of points.

function [P,a]=tauchen_FV(s_eps,ro,n,A,mu)

width=2*mu*s_eps/(1-ro^2)^0.5;
% Total width of the support for log-productivity.
dist=width/(n-1);
% Distance between two contiguous realizations.
a=-width/2+log(A):dist:+width/2+log(A);
% Vector of (equally spaced) realizations for log-productivity.

for i=1:n
    P(i,1:n)=cdf('Normal',a+dist/2,(1-ro)*log(A)+ro*a(i),s_eps)- ...
        cdf('Normal',a-dist/2,(1-ro)*log(A)+ro*a(i),s_eps);
end
% The above cycle computes probabilities.
```

```

for i=1:n
    P(i,1)=cdf('Normal',a(1)+dist/2,(1-ro)*log(A)+ro*a(i),s_eps);
    P(i,n)=1-cdf('Normal',a(n)-dist/2,(1-ro)*log(A)+ro*a(i),s_eps);
    % corrections in the probabilities for highest and lowest states
end
```

rouwen.m

This function file gives a matrix of transition probabilities and a vector of log-productivity levels, computed as suggested by Kopecky and Suen (2010). Inputs are: the autocorrelation parameter, the standard deviation for log-productivity, the number of log-productivity nodes, and the long-run non-stochastic productivity level.

```
% This routine uses the Kopecki and Suen (2010) version of Rouwen-
% horst method.

function [P,zgrid] = rouwen(ro,s_eps,n,A)
% ro is the 1st order autocorrelation, s_eps the standard deviation
% of the error term, n the number of points in the grid for A.

width = 2*((n-1)/(1-ro^2))^(1/2) * s_eps;
% Total width of the support for log-productivity

zgrid = linspace(-width/2+log(A),width/2+log(A),n);
% Vector of (equally spaced) realizations for log-productivity

q = (1+ro)/2;
P = [q 1-q;1-q q];
for i=2:n-1
   P = q*[P zeros(i,1);zeros(1,i+1)] + (1-q)*[zeros(i,1) P; ...
       zeros(1,i+1)] + (1-q)*[zeros(1,i+1); P zeros(i,1)] + q*[ ...
       zeros(1,i+1); zeros(i,1) P];
   P(2:i,:) = P(2:i,:)/2;
   % This computes the probabilities.
end
```

valfun_iter4.m

This script solves the model for the auto-regressive process presented in Subsection 8.1.3, and delivers Figure 8.4 (alternatively, with the appropriate modification, Figure 8.5). Plain repetitions of the comments for the previous routine have been avoided.

```
% Value function iteration to simulate a Ramsey model with AR(1) pro-
% ductivity disturbances (Subsection 8.1.4),
clear;

format('long');

alpha=0.3;
beta=0.97;

A=1/(alpha*beta);
kstar=(alpha*beta*A)^(1/(1-alpha));

states=800;
kmin=0.5;
kmax=1.2;

deltak = (kmax-kmin)/(states-1);
kvec=kmin:deltak:kmax;


% This introduces the auto-regressive process for log-productivity.
prods=17; % Number of nodes for log-productivity, must be odd.
ro=0.9; % Autocorrelation parameter for log-productivity.
s_eps=0.01; % standard deviation for innovations.

mu=4;
[PP,a]=tauchen_FV(s_eps,ro,prods,A,mu);
% When prods=17, mu=4 makes the width of the log-productivity support
% equal using tauchen_FV.m or rouwen.m function files.
% [PP,a]=rouwen(ro,s_eps,prods,A);
% Uncommenting the line above uses rouwen.m.

Avec=exp(a);
% Generates the productivity vector from the log-productivity one.

vini=zeros(prods,states);

err=10;
z=0;

tic

while err > 10^(-7)

z=z+1;

for h=1:prods
```

```
    for i=1:states
       for j=1:states
          consV(h,j)=Avec(h)*kvec(i)^alpha-kvec(j);
       end
      [opt_choice(h,i),ind(i)]=max((log(consV(h,:))+ beta*vini(h,:))');
    end
end

vfin=PP*opt_choice;
% Expected value function.
% Note that row h of PP is used to take into account that expected
% maximum value is conditional on state h

delta=abs(vini-vfin);
err=max(delta');

vini=vfin;

end

toc

% This computes the 'true' value function (refer to Section 7.2).

cost1=1/(1-beta)*( alpha*beta/(1-alpha*beta)*log(alpha*beta)+...
    log(1-alpha*beta) +beta*(1-ro)*log(A)/((1-ro*beta)*(1- ...
    alpha*beta)) );
% This is F - note a modification due to a non-zero long-run
% log-productivity
cost2=alpha/(1-alpha*beta);
% This is G
cost3=1/((1-ro*beta)*(1-alpha*beta));
% This is H

true_val=cost1+cost2*ones(prods,1)*log(kvec)+cost3*a'*ones(1,states);

err_approx=true_val-opt_choice;
% Approximation errors (with respect to the true value function)

% ==================== this produces Figure 8.4 ===================
font=11;

figure;
subplot1 = subplot(2,1,1,'FontSize',10,'FontName','Times␣New␣Roman');
surf(kvec,a',opt_choice);
axis([kmin kmax min(a) max(a) min(min(opt_choice))-1 ...
    max(max(opt_choice))+1])
```

```
view([-24.4 38.8]);
xlabel('Capital','FontSize',font,'FontName','Times␣New␣Roman');
ylabel('Log-productivty','FontSize',font,...
    'FontName','Times␣New␣Roman');
zlabel('Maximum␣value','FontSize',font,'FontName','Times␣New␣Roman');
title('Panel␣(a):␣Maximum␣value␣function','FontSize',font+3,...
'FontName','Times␣New␣Roman')

subplot2 = subplot(2,1,2,'FontName','Times␣New␣Roman');
zh=max(max(err_approx));
zl=min(min(err_approx));
% Compute the max absolute approximation error to set limits
surf(kvec,a',err_approx)
axis([kmin kmax a(1) a(prods) zl zh])
view([-24.4 38.8]);
xlabel('Capital','FontSize',font,'FontName','Times␣New␣Roman');
ylabel('Log-productivity','FontSize',font,...
    'FontName','Times␣New␣Roman');
zlabel('Approximation␣Errors','FontSize',font,'FontName',...
    'Times␣New␣Roman');
title('Panel␣(b):␣Approximation␣Errors','FontSize',font+3,...
'FontName','Times␣New␣Roman');
```

endogrid_stoch.m

This script solves the model with the endogenous grid method, for the auto-regressive process presented in Subsection 8.1.3, and delivers Figure 8.6 (when δ is set to 1). Plain repetitions of previous comments have been avoided.

```
% The stochastic policy function is obtained with the endogenous grid
% method. Use of the non-linear eqtuation solver for the initial time
% grid is required.

clear;

options = optimoptions('fsolve','Display','none');

format('long');

alpha=0.3;
beta=0.97;
delta=1;

A=(1-beta*(1-delta))/(alpha*beta);
k_hat=1;
```

```
states=800;

kmin=.7*k_hat;
kmax=1.2*k_hat;

delta_k = (kmax-kmin)/(states-1);
kvec=kmin:delta_k:kmax;

% This considers the AR process for log-productivity.
prods=17; % Number of nodes, must be odd.
ro=0.9; % Autocorrelation parameter for log-productivity.
s_eps=0.01; % Standard deviation.

[PP,a]=rouwen(ro,s_eps,prods,A);
Avec=exp(a);

cons1=Avec'*kvec.^alpha; % Initial guess for consumption.

err=10;
z=0;

tic;

while err > 10^(-7)
z=z+1;

for h=1:prods

cons0(h,:)=PP(h,:)*(beta*( alpha*kron(Avec',kvec.^(alpha-1))+ ...
    1-delta )./cons1).^(-1);
% In period 0, for each productivity state h, consumption statisfies
% the stochastic version of the Euler equation.
% Usage of Kronecker's product speeds up the calculations.

if delta==1
    kvec0(h,:)=((delta*kvec+cons0(h,:))/Avec(h)).^(1/alpha);
else
    kvec0(h,:)=fsolve(@endo_k0,kvec,options,kvec,cons0(h,:), ...
        Avec(h),delta,alpha);
    % This obtains the numerical solution for period 0 (in vector
    % form). The initial condition is kvec, which is reasonably
    % efficient.
    kvec0=real(kvec0);
    % This helps the routine in case of some numerical instability.
end
```

```
cons1new(h,:)=interp1(kvec0(h,:),cons0(h,:),kvec,'pchip','extrap');
% This interpolates for consumption given the productivity level 'h'.
% Note that it allows for extrapolation, should the interval for kvec
% be too small; 'pchip' is a Matlab built-in cubic interpolation op-
% tion (refer to Matlab manual).

end % This closes the 'productivity' loop.

resid=cons1-cons1new;

err=max( max(abs(resid)) );
cons1=cons1new;
disp(z)
end

disp('used␣cpu␣time')
toc;

if delta == 1

% The lines below compute the "true" consumption function
true_cons=(1-alpha*beta)*( kron(Avec',ones(1,states)) .*kvec0...
    .^(alpha) );

err_approx=true_cons-cons0;
% Approximation error as difference between true values and those ap-
% proximated by "cons0".

% ==================== this produces Figure 8.6 ===================

fsz=10; % fontsize.

figure;

surf(kvec,Avec',err_approx);
axis([kmin kmax min(Avec) max(Avec) -0.5*10^(-7) +0.5*10^(-7)])
view([-24.4 38.8]);
xlabel('Capital','FontSize',fsz+1, 'FontName','Times␣New␣Roman');
ylabel('␣␣Productivity','FontSize',fsz+1,...
    'FontName','Times␣New␣Roman');
zlabel('Approximation␣errors','FontSize',fsz+1, ...
    'FontName','Times␣New␣Roman');

end
```

chebypoly_2.m

This function file generates a two-dimensional Chebyshev polynomial. Use has been made of the "Kronecker product" operator, so that, for example:

$$\text{kron}\left(\begin{bmatrix} T_0(k) \\ T_1(k) \\ T_2(k) \end{bmatrix}, [T_0(A), T_1(A), T_2(A), T_3(A)]\right) =$$

$$= \begin{bmatrix} T_0(k)T_0(A) & T_0(k)T_1(A) & T_0(k)T_2(A) & T_0(k)T_3(A) \\ T_1(k)T_0(A) & T_1(k)T_1(A) & T_1(k)T_2(A) & T_1(k)T_3(A) \\ T_2(k)T_0(A) & T_2(k)T_1(A) & T_2(k)T_2(A) & T_2(k)T_3(A) \end{bmatrix}.$$

```
% This function produces two-dymensional Chebychev basis using the
% Kronecker product.
function M=chebypoly_2(x,y,n,r)
d1=chebypoly_1(x,n);
d2=chebypoly_1(y,r);
M=kron(d1,d2');
```

Tauchen_FV_T.m

The output of this function file is composed of an $r \times r$ matrix of transition probabilities, and by two vectors of r elements each, representing the grid for productivity and the corresponding Chebyshev nodes. Refer also to the function file Tauchen_FV.m.

```
function [P,Acheby,Avec]=tauchen_FV_T(s_eps,ro,rdim,A)

w=3;
width=2*w*s_eps/(1-ro^2)^0.5;
% Total width of the support for log-productivity.

Acheby=chebynodes(rdim);
Amax=A*exp(width/2);
Amin=A*exp(-width/2);
Avec=(Amax-Amin)/2*Acheby+(Amax+Amin)/2;
a=log(Avec); % Vector of realizations for log-productivity

for i=1:rdim
for j=2:rdim-1
    P(i,j)=cdf('Normal',(a(j)+a(j+1))/2,(1-ro)*log(A)+ro*a(i),...
    s_eps)-cdf('Normal',(a(j-1)+a(j))/2,(1-ro)*log(A)+ro*a(i),s_eps);
end
```

```
end
% The cycle above computes the transition probabilities. Since the
% nodes for log-productivity are not equally spaced, instead of defi-
% ning a distance between them I use their average. More sophistica-
% ted method can be adopted, but the precision obtained is comparable
% with that of Tauchen's method for evenly spaced nodes.

for i=1:rdim
P(i,1)=cdf('Normal',(a(1)+a(2))/2,(1-ro)*log(A)+ro*a(i),s_eps);
P(i,rdim)=1-cdf('Normal',(a(rdim-1)+a(rdim))/2,(1-ro)*log(A) ...
    +ro*a(i),s_eps);
end
% The above corrects for highest and lowest states probabilities.

end
```

colloc_4.m

This file solves System (8.11); as before the Matlab built-in nonlinear equation solver is exploited. Figure 8.7 represents the output for this script.

```
% Collocation routine to approximate a Ramsey model with AR(1) pro-
% ductivity disturbances using Chebychev polynomials (Subsect. 8.2).
clear;

tic;
options = optimset('display','final','MaxFunEvals',500);
% These options display the final output of the non-linear solution
% process.

al=0.3;
de=1;
be=0.97;
s_eps=0.01;
ro=0.9;
A=1/(al*be);

kss=(al*be*A/(1+be*(de-1)) )^(1/(1-al)); % Steady state capital.

kmin=0.5*kss;
kmax=1.1*kss;

css=A*kss^al-de*kss; % Steady state consumption.

ndim=3; % Initial number of coefficients for the polynomial for k.

rdim=5; % Initial number of coefficients for the polynomial for A.
```

```
MC=[ css, css/10, -css/100;
       css/10, 0, 0;
    - css/100, 0, 0];
ZM=zeros(rdim-ndim,ndim);
MC=[MC;ZM];
% Initial guess for the matrix of coefficients for the consumption
% function (MC is the initial guess for matrix 'd' in the text).

z=fsolve(@sys_cheby_2dim,MC,options,ndim,rdim,A,al,be,de, ...
    kmin,kmax,s_eps,ro);
% This solves the nonlinear system; z is d in the main text.
z=real(z);
% This avoids considering the imaginary part (should any be produced
% by the nonlinear equation solver)

for ndim=4:13

n=2;
% This gradually increases the degree of the Chebycheff polynomial
% both for capital and for A (n is size of the increase in the num-
% ber of nodes).

MC=[z,zeros(rdim,1);zeros(n,ndim-1),zeros(n,1)];

rdim=rdim+n;

z0=fsolve(@sys_cheby_2dim,MC,options,ndim,rdim,A,al,be,de,kmin, ...
    kmax,s_eps,ro);
z=real(z0);

end

toc;

% The following lines are useful to build the Figure.
% The grid for A is not changed, the probabilities of 'transition'
% are those of the main routine. The grid for k is finer.

[P,T_A,Avec]=tauchen_FV_T(s_eps,ro,rdim,A);

bignum=30; % Number of nodes in the grid for capital .

T_kap=linspace(-1,1,bignum);
% This creates nodes for capital consistent with support of Tcheby
% nodes.
chk_kap=(kmax-kmin)/2*T_kap+(kmax+kmin)/2;
```

```
% Translates the Chebychev nodes in (kmin,kmax).

for i=1:bignum
for j=1:rdim

true_cons(i,j)=(1-al*be)*Avec(j)*chk_kap(i)^al;
% Exact solution for consumption.

approx_cons(i,j)=sum(sum(chebypoly_2(T_kap(i),T_A(j),ndim,rdim).*z));
% Approximation for consumption.

chk_k1(i,j)=Avec(j)*chk_kap(i)^al+(1-de)*chk_kap(i)-...
    sum(sum( chebypoly_2(T_kap(i),T_A(j),ndim,rdim).*z ));
% Capital consistent with the next-period nodes.

Tk1(i,j)=2*(chk_k1(i,j)-kmin)/(kmax-kmin)-1;
% Translates the Chebychev nodes in (-1,1).

for h=1:rdim

err_add(h)=(sum(sum( chebypoly_2(T_kap(i),T_A(j),ndim,rdim).*z ))*...
    be*( al*Avec(h)*chk_k1(i,j)^(al-1)+ 1-de )/...
    sum(sum( chebypoly_2(Tk1(i,j),T_A(h),ndim,rdim).*z)) - 1)*P(j,h);
% This computes the Euler equation residual for any given time 1 pro-
% ductivity node.

end

error(i,j)=real(sum(err_add));

end
end

figure;

% =========== This produces the three-panels Figure 8.7 ===========
sizefont=10; % Size of font (in points).

subplot1 = subplot(3,1,1,'FontSize',10,'FontName','Times␣New␣Roman');

surf(chk_kap,Avec,approx_cons');
xlim([kmin kmax]);
ylim([Avec(1) Avec(rdim)]);
zlim([min(min(approx_cons))-0.1 max(max(approx_cons))+0.1]);
set(subplot1,'FontName','Times␣New␣Roman','FontSize',10);
xlabel('Capital','FontSize',sizefont+1,...
    'FontName','Times␣New␣Roman');
```

```
ylabel('Productivity','FontSize',sizefont+1,...
    'FontName','Times␣New␣Roman');
title('Panel␣(a)','FontSize',sizefont+3,...
    'FontName','Times␣New␣Roman')

subplot2 = subplot(3,1,2,'FontSize',10,'FontName','Times␣New␣Roman');

surf(chk_kap,Avec,(approx_cons-true_cons)');
xlim([kmin kmax]);
ylim([Avec(1) Avec(rdim)]);
zlim([min(min(approx_cons-true_cons)) ...
    max(max(approx_cons-true_cons))])
set(subplot2,'FontName','Times␣New␣Roman','FontSize',10);
xlabel('Capital','FontSize',sizefont+1,...
    'FontName','Times␣New␣Roman');
ylabel('Productivity','FontSize',sizefont+1,...
    'FontName','Times␣New␣Roman');
 title('Panel␣(b)','FontSize',sizefont+3,...
    'FontName','Times␣New␣Roman')

subplot3 = subplot(3,1,3,'FontName','Times␣New␣Roman');

surf(chk_kap,Avec,real(error)');
xlim([kmin kmax]);
ylim([Avec(1) Avec(rdim)])
zlim([min(min(error)) max(max(error))])
set(subplot3,'FontName','Times␣New␣Roman','FontSize',10);
xlabel('Capital','FontSize',sizefont+1,...
    'FontName','Times␣New␣Roman');
ylabel('Productivity','FontSize',sizefont+1,...
    'FontName','Times␣New␣Roman');
title('Panel␣(c)','FontSize',sizefont+3,...
  'FontName','Times␣New␣Roman')
```

sys_cheby_2dim.m
This file stores System (8.11).

```
function F=sys_cheby_2dim(MC,kdim,Adim,A,al,be,de,kmin,kmax,s_eps,ro)

[Q,Acheby,Avec]=tauchen_FV_T(s_eps,ro,Adim,A);
% This creates the Chebychev nodes for A, translates the nodes in
% (Amin, Amax) and computes the matrix of probabilities Q; q(j,h) is
% the probability of moving from state j to state h.

Tk=chebynodes(kdim);
Ta=Acheby;
```

```
% Chebychev nodes in (-1,1) for capital (Tk) and productivity (Ta).

k0=(kmax-kmin)/2*Tk+(kmax+kmin)/2;
% Translates the Chebychev nodes in (kmin,kmax)

for i=1:kdim
for j=1:Adim

  for h=1:Adim

   kap(i,j)= Avec(j)*k0(i)^al+(1-de)*k0(i)-sum(sum( chebypoly_2 ...
       (Tk(i),Ta(j),kdim,Adim).*MC ));
       % Second equation of System 8.11.

   Tk1(i,j)=2*(kap(i,j)-kmin)/(kmax-kmin)-1;
       % Creates the time-1 nodes in (-1,1), note that time 1 capital
       % depends upon both time 0 capital and productivity.

   Dummy(h)= ( 1- sum(sum( chebypoly_2(Tk(i),Ta(j),kdim,Adim).*MC ...
          ) )*be*( al*Avec(h)*kap(i,j)^(al-1)+ 1-de )/sum(sum(...
          chebypoly_2(Tk1(i,j),Ta(h),kdim,Adim).*MC )) )*Q(j,h);

       % 'Dummy' is a single addendum of the expected value in the
       % first equation of System 8.11.

  end

Dummy=real(sum(Dummy));
% This sums up all the addenda, creating the first equation of the
% pertinent system in Section 8.2.

  F(i,j)=Dummy;

end
end
```

pea_rmsy.m

This builds the script for the Parameterized Expectations Approach described in Section 8.4; its output is Figure 8.9.

```
% Approximation of the policy function for the Ramsey model with
% AR(1) disturbances using the PEA.

clear;
rng('shuffle')
% Seeds the random number generator based on the current time.
```

```
alfa=0.3;
beta=0.97;
Ass=1/(alfa*beta);

delta=.15;

ro=0.9;
k0=((1/beta + delta - 1)/(alfa*Ass))^(1/(alfa-1));
% Initial capital is at the non stochastic steady-state.

n=10000;
% This is number of "observations" for the artificial time series.
init=1000; % This sets the 'initialization period'

eps=randn(n+init+1,1);
% Vector of productivity shocks, obtained from a standard normal; its
% lenght takes into account the final period;

std_dev=0.01;

vecA(1)=Ass; % The initial At is at its 'steady-state' value.

for i=2:n+init+1
    vecA(i)=Ass^(1-ro)*vecA(i-1)^ro*exp(std_dev*eps(i));
end
% This generates the realizations for At, which remain the same in
% all the iterations.

psi1=log((beta*(1-alfa*beta))^(-1));
psi2=-alfa;
psi3=-1;
% Initial values for parameters in the approximating polynomial;
% They are the correct ones for delta = 1.

% Iterations.
maxj=200;
% Max number of iteration (after maxj iteration routine stops even if
% convergence has failed).

new_psi=zeros(3,1); % parameter vector.

err=10;

j=0; % This tracks the number of iterations.

tic;
```

```

while err>10^(-8) & j <= maxj
% Convergence criterion and exit condition.

j=j+1;

% The next four variables are used to trace the parameters' evolution
% (gives Figure 8.10, Panel (b)).
track_psi(j,1)=j;
track_psi(j,2)=psi1;
track_psi(j,3)=psi2;
track_psi(j,4)=psi3;

Kap(1)=k0;
funct(1)=exp(psi1+psi2*log(Kap(1))+psi3*log(vecA(1)) );
% funct(i) is the functional form F(.), see eq. 8.19
cons(1) = (beta*funct(1))^(-1);
% Consumption as a function of parameter vector psi.

for i=2:init+n+1 % This cycle generates the "artificial" time series
   Kap(i)=vecA(i-1)*Kap(i-1)^alfa-cons(i-1)+(1-delta)*Kap(i-1);
   funct(i)=exp(psi1+psi2*log(Kap(i))+psi3*log(vecA(i)) );
   cons(i)= (beta*funct(i))^(-1);
   W_regr(i-1)=cons(i)^(-1)*(alfa*vecA(i)*Kap(i)^(alfa-1)+(1-delta));
   % This corresponds to variable wt in Section 8.4.
end

% The following lines transform the variables to run ols and cuts the
% first 'init' observation to initialize the process and the last
% 'observation' (for which W_regr is missing).
ln_W=log(W_regr(init+1:init+n)');
ln_K=log(Kap(init+1:init+n)');
ln_A=log(vecA(init+1:init+n)');

XMATR = [ones(size(ln_K)) ln_K ln_A];
% This builds the matrix of independent variables.
new_psi = XMATR\ln_W; % Least squares fit.

change_fi=[abs(new_psi(1)-psi1); abs(new_psi(2)-psi2); ...
    abs(new_psi(3)-psi3)]; % Vector of changes in psi

err=max(change_fi); % Allows to check convergence.

mu=1; % Reduce this updating parameter in case of instability.

 psi1=mu*new_psi(1)+(1-mu)*psi1;
 psi2=mu*new_psi(2)+(1-mu)*psi2;
```

```
 psi3=mu*new_psi(3)+(1-mu)*psi3;
end
toc;
figure;
% ============================ Figure 8.9 ============================
font=10;
subplot1 = subplot(2,1,1,'FontName','Times␣New␣Roman');
scatter3(Kap,vecA',cons,1.5,'red');
xlim([k0*.85 k0*1.15]);
ylim([min(vecA) max(vecA)]);
zlim([min(cons) max(cons)]);
set(subplot1,'FontName','Times␣New␣Roman','FontSize',10);
xlabel('Capital','FontSize',font+1,...
    'FontName','Times␣New␣Roman');
ylabel('Productivity','FontSize',font+1,...
    'FontName','Times␣New␣Roman');
zlabel('Consumption','FontSize',font+1,...
    'FontName','Times␣New␣Roman');
title('Panel␣(a)','FontSize',font+2,...
    'FontName','Times␣New␣Roman')

subplot2 = subplot(2,1,2,'FontName','Times␣New␣Roman');
p2=plot(track_psi(:,1),track_psi(:,2),'-',track_psi(:,1),...
    track_psi(:,3),'.',track_psi(:,1),track_psi(:,4),'--');
xlim([1 size(track_psi,1)]);
ylim([min(min(track_psi(:,2:4)))-0.2 max(max(track_psi(:,2:4)))+0.2]);
xlabel('#␣of␣iterations','FontSize',font+1,...
    'FontName','Times␣New␣Roman');
ylabel('Values␣of␣parameters','FontSize',font+1,...
    'FontName','Times␣New␣Roman');
title('Panel␣(b)','FontSize',font+2,...
    'FontName','Times␣New␣Roman')
```

8.5.2 *Your coding exercises*

In all the exercises, let $\alpha = 0.30$ and $\beta = 0.98$.

Consider the Ramsey model with return function $U(c_t) = \ln c_t$ and dynamic constraint $k_{t+1} = k_t + A_t k_t^{\alpha} - c_t$, where $A_{t+1} = \hat{A}^{1-\rho} A_t^{\rho} \exp(\epsilon_{t+1})$. Let $\hat{A} = 10$, $\rho = 0.9$, $E[\epsilon_{t+1}] = 0$ and $E\left[\epsilon_{t+1}^2\right] = (0.015)^2$ (note that $\delta = 0$).

Assume that the irreversibility constraint $k_{t+1} \geq k_t$ applies. Find the value function by means of a value function iteration routine, and compare your results with those you obtain in the absence of the irreversibility constraint.

Consider a modified version of the Brock and Mirman model with return function $U(c_t, l_t) = \ln c_t + \gamma \ln(1 - l_t)$ and dynamic constraint $k_{t+1} = (1 - \delta) k_t + A_t k_t^{\alpha} l_t^{1-\alpha} - c_t$, where $A_{t+1} = \hat{A}^{1-\rho} A_t^{\rho} \exp(\epsilon_{t+1})$. The parameter values are $\delta = 0.15$, $\gamma = 2.5$, $\hat{A} = 1$, $\rho = 0.9$, $E[\epsilon_{t+1}] = 0$ and $E\left[\epsilon_{t+1}^2\right] = (0.02)^2$. Find the value and the policy functions by means of a value function iteration routine.

Consider a modified version of the Brock and Mirman model with return function $U(c_t, l_t) = \ln c_t + \gamma \ln(1 - l_t)$ and dynamic constraint $k_{t+1} = (1 - \delta) k_t + A_t k_t^{\alpha} l_t^{1-\alpha} - c_t$, where $A_{t+1} = \hat{A}^{1-\rho} A_t^{\rho} \exp(\epsilon_{t+1})$. Let $\delta = 0.15$, $\gamma = 2.5$, $\hat{A} = 1$, $\rho = 0.9$, $E[\epsilon_{t+1}] = 0$ and $E\left[\epsilon_{t+1}^2\right] = (0.02)^2$. Find the policy functions using the endogenous gridpoint method.

Consider a simple growth model with return function $U(c_t) = \ln c_t$ and dynamic constraint $k_{t+1} = (1 - \delta) k_t + A_t k_t^{\alpha} - c_t$, where $A_{t+1} = \hat{A}^{1-\rho} A_t^{\rho} \times$ $\times \exp(\epsilon_{t+1})$. Let $\delta = 0.15$, $\hat{A} = 10$, $\rho = 0.9$, $E[\epsilon_{t+1}] = 0$ and $E\left[\epsilon_{t+1}^2\right] = (0.015)^2$. Find the value function by means of a collocation routine based on Chebyshev polynomials.

Consider a modified version of the Brock and Mirman model with return function $U(c_t, l_t) = \ln c_t + \gamma \ln(1 - l_t)$, $\gamma > 0$, and dynamic constraint $k_{t+1} = (1 - \delta) k_t + A_t k_t^{\alpha} l_t^{1-\alpha} - c_t$, where $A_{t+1} = \hat{A}^{1-\rho} A_t^{\rho} \exp(\epsilon_{t+1})$. Let $\delta = 0.15$, $\gamma = 2.5$, $\hat{A} = 1$, $\rho = 0.9$, $E[\epsilon_{t+1}] = 0$ and $E\left[\epsilon_{t+1}^2\right] = (0.02)^2$. Find the policy functions using the parameterized expectations approach.

Notes

[1] Accordingly, the absence of the tilde indicates that productivity has been realized (i.e. it has taken one of its possible values).

[2] Note that Step 2 in Section 4.1 has been split into Step 2a and 2b.

[3] This is, again, exploiting an Intel Core Ultra 7 155H CPU @ 1.40 Ghz.

[4] Normality is not a crucial assumption for our exercise. What we do need to assume is a specific distribution for ϵ_{t+1} and while normality is reasonable, it is also computationally convenient.

[5]If you feel confused by the equation that follows this footnote in the main text, consider that ρa_i is the conditional mean $E\left[a_{t+1}\right|a_t = a_i]$.

[6]An alternative to Tauchen's method is provided by Tauchen and Hussey (1991), who applied a quadrature-based method to an autoregressive process like (8.3). Flodén (2008) compares the standard Tauchen's approach with the Gaussian quadrature method proposed by Tauchen and Hussey. Flodén finds that the latter delivers better approximations when the persistence of the process is low, but the converse holds for high values of the autocorrelation parameter.

[7]Note that the above argument does *not* allow us to conclude that:

$$\lim_{n\to\infty} E\left[\tilde{A}_{t+n}\middle| A_t\right] = \hat{A}.$$

To see why, refer to the properties of log-normal distributions, which you can find summarized at `https://en.wikipedia.org/wiki/Log-normal_distribution.`

[8]"In theory, there is no difference between theory and practice. In practice, there is." (A remark heard at a computer science conference. This quote is sometimes attributed to Lawrence Peter 'Yogi' Berra, a very successful American professional baseball catcher.)

[9]If you find this fact surprising, you may want to have another look at Subsection 5.2.1.

[10]Levintal (2017) also proposes a method to derive high-order perturbation solutions, which significantly reduces the computational costs of the algorithm.

[11]Fernández-Villaverde *et al.* (2016) also briefly discuss the "pruning" approach, which consists in eliminating all the terms in the recursive formulation for the policy functions that are of a higher order than that of the solution.

[12]The case $\delta = 1$ gives the parameterized expectation algorithm an unfair advantage, as the expectation takes the precise form assumed in Eq. (8.19), as can be seen from the results in Subsection 7.2.1.

[13]You may be thinking that k_{t+1} belongs to period t information set. While this is true, remember that k_{t+1} depends on c_t. Because consumption is the variable we want to determine, it is inconvenient to condition the expectation on the right-hand side of (8.18) on k_{t+1}.

[14]The word "usually" is important here. Unfortunately, there is no guarantee that increasing the degree of the polynomial will monotonically improve the approximation. The same issue arises when dealing with collocation methods (see Section 5.1).

[15]The difference between $\delta = 1$ and $\delta = 0.15$ is large. Thus, our starting values for the parameters may actually be far from the "true" ones. Consequently, the initial values may induce instability. Should this happen (which is not the present case), a sensible approach is as follows. First, run the routine for a δ close to 1, say $\delta = 0.9$, obtaining the "true" values for this case. Second, reduce δ, for example to 0.8, using the "true" values obtained in the first step as a starting point for Ψ. This should allow for the computation of a new set of "true" values for Ψ. One can proceed this way until the desired value ($\delta = 0.15$) is reached.

[16]This relatively short time series is chosen to avoid problems with its graphical representation, increasing its length tenfold does not significantly change our results.

[17]Although these low coefficients could, in principle, be statistically significant, we can be reasonably satisfied with the magnitude of the residual correlation in our simple exercise.

Conclusion

Starting with an exposition of the traditional growth model, we have acquired a fair amount of knowledge of many relevant numerical techniques: value function iteration (with some relevant variants), collocation based on Chebyshev polynomials, perturbation, and parameterized expectations.

The question that naturally arises is: What to use and when?

The answer is not obvious. It ultimately depends upon the nature of the problem, the coding time, the speed of execution, and the required accuracy.

Function iteration methods require a reasonable coding effort–in the presence of a limited number of state variables, say three or four–but they suffer severely from the "curse of dimensionality." Furthermore, increasing the number of nodes for the states only slowly improves the accuracy. For models similar to the one we have considered, it is often necessary to use a grid for capital with over 100,000 nodes to achieve a precision comparable to that obtained using Chebyshev polynomials. Needless to say, the computation time increases rapidly. Value function iteration, however, can be appealing when one or more state variables are naturally discrete (e.g., regarding the decision to retire or to remain at work, or the choice of the degree level) and also in the presence of occasionally binding constrains, which can be handled seamlessly. The endogenous grid version of the function iteration method allows for relevant savings in computing time at almost no addi-

DOI: 10.4324/9781003774051-9

tional coding costs and is therefore worth considering whenever obtaining the period-0 grid is not too demanding.

The collocation approach, based on Chebyshev polynomials, provides fast and accurate solutions, but its implementation in a multidimensional setting becomes quite challenging when the number of state variables exceeds three. Furthermore, Chebyshev polynomials like smooth functions: in the presence of kinks in the value function, such as those generated by binding constraints, the accuracy can be compromised. The flip side is that this method, being "global," is suited for analyzing economies that are far from the steady state. When this aspect is relevant, accuracy is prized, and the dimensionality of the state space is not too high, the use of Chebyshev polynomials is worth considering.

Second- and higher-order perturbations perform remarkably well in terms of accuracy for simple growth models, being competitive with function iteration and with Chebyshev polynomials. Unlike the latter two methods, perturbation can feasibly solve medium-scale dynamic stochastic general equilibrium models with many state variables. The availability of toolboxes (the best known being Dynare) and the striking speed of execution make it a valuable contender. Perturbation is probably the natural choice whenever limiting the analysis to a neighborhood of the steady state is not a problem.

If that is an issue, though, the parameterized expectation approach is worth considering. Compared to perturbation, the coding is more demanding (when using Dynare or similar tools for perturbation) but not prohibitive, and execution is fast (though not as fast as perturbation). However, accuracy–especially when we move outside the neighborhood of the steady state–is higher. The parameterized expectations approach does not rely on the contraction mapping theorem, and therefore there is no guarantee that a solution can be found. Thus, it is often necessary to provide "sensible" initial values for the parameters that characterize the approximating function. The results of a perturbation-based solution can be used as a starting condition for a parameterized expectations routine. Dealing with occasionally binding constraints is possible, but rather demanding.

In conclusion, the availability of fast and reliable methods for solving stochastic models, combined with the ever-increasing speed of computers, paves the way to research that explores, and to applications that use, complex, interesting and hopefully realistic dynamic frameworks. I sincerely hope that this introductory textbook will prove to be a valuable gateway into the use of these tools.

Appendix: solutions of the exercises

Exercise 1 The Lagrangian for this problem is:

$$\begin{aligned}\mathcal{L}_0 &= \ln c_0 + \beta \ln c_1 + ... + \beta^T \ln c_T + \\ &-\lambda_0[k_1 - Ak_0^\alpha + c_0] + \\ &-\beta\lambda_1[k_2 - Ak_1^\alpha + c_1] - ... + \\ &-\beta^T\lambda_T[k_{T+1} - Ak_T^\alpha + c_T] + \\ &+\beta^T \mu k_{T+1}.\end{aligned}$$

The first-order conditions allow us to quickly obtain the Euler equation, which, for $t \in \{0, 1, \ ..., \ T-1\}$ is:

$$c_{t+1} = \beta\alpha A k_{t+1}^{\alpha-1} c_t.$$

In period $T+1$, the capital stock is useless for our agent, which implies $k_{T+1} = 0$, so that the dynamic constraint for period T yields:

$$c_T^* = Ak_T^\alpha,$$

which, together with the period $T-1$ Euler equation, implies:

$$c_T^* = Ak_T^\alpha = \beta\alpha A k_T^{\alpha-1} c_{T-1}.$$

In turn, this equation gives:

$$k_T = \beta \alpha c_{T-1},$$

a relationship that, together with the dynamic constraint of period $T-1$, allows us to obtain the consumption function of period $T-1$:

$$c^*_{T-1} = \frac{1}{1+\alpha\beta} A k^\alpha_{T-1}.$$

Following the same steps, the period $T-1$ consumption function along with the period $T-2$ Euler equation allows us to relate k_{T-1} to c_{T-2}. The consumption of period $T-2$ is then obtained through the dynamic constraint of period $T-2$. The solution for the exercise then proceeds recursively.

Exercise 2 The Lagrangian for this problem is:

$$\begin{aligned} \mathcal{L}_0 \quad = \quad & \ln c_0 + \beta \ln c_1 + \beta^2 \ln c_2 + \\ & -\lambda_0 [k_1 - A k_0^\alpha - (1-\delta) k_0 + c_0] + \\ & -\beta\lambda_1 [k_2 - A k_1^\alpha - (1-\delta) k_1 + c_1] + \\ & -\beta^2\lambda_2 [k_3 - A k_2^\alpha - (1-\delta) k_2 + c_2] + \\ & +\beta^2 \mu k_3. \end{aligned}$$

The first-order conditions allow us to quickly obtain the Euler equation, which, for $t \in \{0, 1\}$ is:

$$c_{t+1} = \beta \left(\alpha A k_{t+1}^{\alpha-1} + 1 - \delta \right) c_t.$$

In period 3, the capital stock is useless to our agent (who is alive in periods 0, 1 and 2), which implies $k_3 = 0$, so that the dynamic constraint for period 2 allows us to obtain:

$$c_2^* = A k_2^\alpha + (1-\delta) k_2.$$

Together with the period 1 Euler equation, this implies:

$$c_2^* = A k_2^\alpha + (1-\delta) k_2 = \beta \left(\alpha A k_2^{\alpha-1} + 1 - \delta \right) c_1.$$

Exploiting the dynamic constraint $k_2 = Ak_1^\alpha + (1-\delta)\,k_1 - c_1$, we obtain:

$$A\left(Ak_1^\alpha + (1-\delta)\,k_1 - c_1\right)^\alpha + (1-\delta)\left(Ak_1^\alpha + (1-\delta)\,k_1 - c_1\right) = \\ = \beta\left(\alpha A\left(Ak_1^\alpha + (1-\delta)\,k_1 - c_1\right)^{\alpha-1} + 1 - \delta\right)c_1, \quad (A.1)$$

which, in general, has no explicit solution for c_1. Note, however, that:
$l.h.s.(A.1)|_{c_1=0} = A\left(Ak_1^\alpha + (1-\delta)\,k_1\right)^\alpha + (1-\delta)\left(Ak_1^\alpha + (1-\delta)\,k_1\right) > 0$;
$l.h.s.(A.1)|_{c_1=Ak_1^\alpha+(1-\delta)k_1} = 0$;
$\partial l.h.s.(A.1)/\partial c_1 < 0$.

Focusing on the right-hand-side of Eq. (A.1) we see that:
$r.h.s.(A.1)|_{c_1=0} = 0$;
$\lim_{c_1 \to (Ak_1^\alpha+(1-\delta)k_1)^-} r.h.s.(A.1) = +\infty$;
$\partial r.h.s.(A.1)/\partial c_1 > 0$.

Hence, the solution $c_1^*(k_1)$ of Eq. (A.1) is unique. It is then simple to show that a higher k_1 shifts up the left-hand side of Eq. (A.1), while it shifts the right-hand side down. Thus, a higher k_1 implies a larger $c_1^*(k_1)$. A similar argument allows us to show that $c_0^*(k_0)$ is also unique (exploit the Euler equation relating c_1 to c_0, and therefore also to k_0).

Exercise 3 Follow the main steps in Section 1.2. Even in this simple case, a closed-form solution for the saddlepath does not exist. The steady-state levels for capital and consumption are:

$$\hat{k} = \left(\alpha A \frac{\beta}{1-\beta(1-\delta)}\right)^{\frac{1}{1-\alpha}},$$
$$\hat{c} = \hat{k}\left(\frac{1-\beta+\beta\delta(1-\alpha)}{\alpha\beta}\right).$$

Note that the steady state does not depend upon γ (why?).

Exercise 4 The first order conditions of the Lagrangian allow us to obtain the Euler equation, which is:

$$c_t^{-\gamma} = \beta\,(1+\bar{r})\,c_{t+1}^{-\gamma},$$

so that:

$$c_{t+1} = (\beta(1+\bar{r}))^{\frac{1}{\gamma}} c_t. \tag{A.2}$$

Write the period 0 intertemporal constraint as:

$$k_0 = \frac{c_0 - \bar{y}}{1+\bar{r}} + \frac{k_1}{1+\bar{r}}.$$

A similar formulation applies for period 1, so that by substituting the latter into the former, we obtain:

$$k_0 = \frac{c_0 - \bar{y}}{1+\bar{r}} + \frac{c_1 - \bar{y}}{(1+\bar{r})^2} + \frac{k_2}{(1+\bar{r})^2}.$$

Iterating this reasoning we obtain:

$$k_0 = \sum_{t=0}^{T} \frac{c_t - \bar{y}}{(1+\bar{r})^{t+1}} + \frac{k_{T+1}}{(1+\bar{r})^{T+1}}.$$

To satisfy the transversality condition, a solution must preclude paths involving an infinite accumulation of capital (and also of "debt" when k is interpreted as assets). When $T \to \infty$, since $\bar{r} > 0$, we then have:

$$k_0 = \lim_{T\to\infty} \sum_{t=0}^{T} \frac{c_t - \bar{y}}{(1+\bar{r})^{t+1}}.$$

Eq. (A.2) allows us to express all the future consumption levels in terms of the initial one, which in turn allows us to reformulate the above equation as:

$$k_0 = \lim_{T\to\infty} \sum_{t=0}^{T} \frac{c_0 (\beta(1+\bar{r}))^{\frac{t}{\gamma}} - \bar{y}}{(1+\bar{r})^{t+1}} =$$

$$= \frac{1}{1+\bar{r}} \lim_{T\to\infty} \left(\sum_{t=0}^{T} c_0 \beta^{\frac{t}{\gamma}} (1+\bar{r})^{\frac{1-\gamma}{\gamma}t} - \sum_{t=0}^{T} \frac{\bar{y}}{(1+\bar{r})^t} \right).$$

Let, for convenience, $\varphi = \beta^{1/\gamma}(1+\bar{r})^{(1-\gamma)/\gamma}$; note that, when $\beta(1+\bar{r}) < 1$ and $\gamma > 1$, then $\varphi < 1$. Taking advantage of the properties of convergent series, we obtain:

$$k_0 = \frac{1}{1+\bar{r}} \frac{c_0}{1-\varphi} - \frac{\bar{y}}{\bar{r}}.$$

Note that the above argument holds for any period t, so we obtain the consumption function:

$$c_t^* = (1+\bar{r})(1-\varphi)\left(k_t + \frac{\bar{y}}{\bar{r}}\right), \tag{A.3}$$

which tells us that in any period our agent consumes a constant fraction of her wealth, which is composed of assets and the discounted value of future incomes. The consumption function (A.3) implies that the asset accumulation equation is:

$$k_{t+1} = (1+\bar{r})\varphi k_t + \left(\frac{1+\bar{r}}{\bar{r}}\varphi - \frac{1}{\bar{r}}\right)\bar{y}. \tag{A.4}$$

Note that $\Delta k_{t+1} = 0$ requires $k_t = -\bar{y}/\bar{r}$. In fact, from Eq. (A.4) we find that setting $\Delta k_{t+1} = 0$ yields:

$$(1-(1+\bar{r})\varphi)k_t = ((1+\bar{r})\varphi - 1)\frac{\bar{y}}{\bar{r}}.$$

Note also that $k_{t+1} < k_t$ when

$$(1-(1+\bar{r})\varphi)k_t > ((1+\bar{r})\varphi - 1)\frac{\bar{y}}{\bar{r}},$$

so that an amount of asset larger than $-\bar{y}/\bar{r}$ decreases over time when $(1-(1+\bar{r})\varphi) > 0$, which requires $1 > (\beta(1+\bar{r}))^{\frac{1}{\gamma}}$ or $\beta(1+\bar{r}) < 1$. In words, in this case the capital yield is low enough that our agent does not save; in fact, she prefers to deplete her assets and to go into debt up to the point where her liabilities equal the present discounted value of her labor incomes.

We now check that the consumption function (A.3) does satisfy the transversality condition:

$$\lim_{T\to\infty} \beta^T c_T^{-\gamma} k_{T+1} = 0.$$

As for capital, from Eq. (A.4), we have that (by iterated substitution):

$$k_{T+1} = ((1+\bar{r})\varphi)^{T+1}\left(k_0 + \frac{\bar{y}}{\bar{r}}\right) - \frac{\bar{y}}{\bar{r}}.$$

Therefore, taking advantage of the consumption function (A.3), and assuming that the limits on the right-hand side exist (as we will verify), we have:

$$\lim_{T\to\infty}\beta^T c_T^{-\gamma}k_{T+1}=\lim_{T\to\infty}\beta^T\left[(1-\varphi)\,\varphi^T(1+\bar{r})^{T+1}\left(k_0+\frac{\bar{y}}{\bar{r}}\right)\right]^{-\gamma}\times$$
$$\times\lim_{T\to\infty}\left[((1+\bar{r})\,\varphi)^{T+1}\left(k_0+\frac{\bar{y}}{\bar{r}}\right)-\frac{\bar{y}}{\bar{r}}\right],$$

which can be reformulated as:

$$\lim_{T\to\infty}\beta^T\varphi^{(1-\gamma)T+1}(1+\bar{r})^{(1-\gamma)T}\left[(1-\varphi)^{-\gamma}(1+\bar{r})^{(1-\gamma)}\left(k_0+\frac{\bar{y}}{\bar{r}}\right)^{1-\gamma}\right]+$$
$$-\lim_{T\to\infty}\beta^T\varphi^{-\gamma T}(1+\bar{r})^{-\gamma T}\left[(1-\varphi)(1+\bar{r})\left(k_0+\frac{\bar{y}}{\bar{r}}\right)\right]^{-\gamma}\frac{\bar{y}}{\bar{r}}.$$

Recalling the definition of φ, we can simplify the last equation to:

$$\lim_{T\to\infty}\varphi^{T+1}\left[(1-\varphi)^{-\gamma}(1+\bar{r})^{(1-\gamma)}\left(k_0+\frac{\bar{y}}{\bar{r}}\right)^{1-\gamma}\right]+$$
$$-\lim_{T\to\infty}(1+\bar{r})^{-T}\left[(1-\varphi)(1+\bar{r})\left(k_0+\frac{\bar{y}}{\bar{r}}\right)\right]^{-\gamma}\frac{\bar{y}}{\bar{r}}.$$

This makes it apparent that both terms converge to 0 as $T\to\infty$, thus the transversality condition is satisfied.

Exercise 5 The firm's problem is set up by means of the following "present-value" Lagrangian:

$$\begin{aligned}\mathcal{L}_t &= \left(1+\frac{b}{2}x_t\right)y_t-\frac{c}{2}y_t^2+\\ &+\beta\left(\left(1+\frac{b}{2}x_{t+1}\right)y_{t+1}-\frac{c}{2}y_{t+1}^2\right)+\\ &+...+\beta^\tau\left(\left(1+\frac{b}{2}x_{t+\tau}\right)y_{t+\tau}-\frac{c}{2}y_{t+\tau}^2\right)+...+\\ &-\lambda_t(x_{t+1}-y_t)-...+\\ &-\beta^\tau\lambda_{t+\tau}(x_{t+\tau+1}-y_{t+\tau})-...\end{aligned}$$

The tvc is:

$$\lim_{T\to\infty}\beta^T\lambda_{t+T}x_{t+T+1}.$$

Differentiating the Lagrangian with respect to $y_{t+\tau}$, $x_{t+\tau+1}$, and $\lambda_{t+\tau}$ for $\tau = 0, 1, ...$ yields the following first-order conditions:

$$\left(1 + \frac{b}{2}x_{t+\tau}\right) - cy_{t+\tau} + \lambda_{t+\tau} = 0, \ \forall\ \tau,$$

$$\frac{\beta b}{2}y_{t+\tau+1} = \lambda_{t+\tau}, \ \forall\ \tau,$$

and, of course:

$$x_{t+\tau+1} = y_{t+\tau}, \ \forall\ \tau.$$

In this setup, the transversality condition readily becomes:

$$\lim_{T\to\infty} \beta^T \frac{\beta b}{2} y_{t+T+1} x_{t+T+1} = 0.$$

From the first-order conditions, we obtain for the generic period τ:

$$1 + \frac{b}{2}y_{t+\tau-1} - cy_{t+\tau} + \frac{\beta b}{2}y_{t+\tau+1} = 0, \tag{A.5}$$

which is a difference equation for the firm's output; its solution takes the form:

$$y_{t+\tau} = a_0 + a_1\varepsilon_+^\tau + a_2\varepsilon_-^\tau; \tag{A.6}$$

in which:

$$\varepsilon_+ = \frac{1}{\beta b}\left(c + \left(c^2 - \beta b^2\right)^{1/2}\right), \quad \varepsilon_- = \frac{1}{\beta b}\left(c - \left(c^2 - \beta b^2\right)^{1/2}\right).$$

The assumptions $b < \bar{b} \equiv 2c/(1+\beta)$, $\beta < 1$ are sufficient (though not necessary) to guarantee that the two roots, ε_+ and ε_-, are real; note also that they are both positive. It is easy to verify that $\varepsilon_+ > 1$, while $\varepsilon_- < 1$ when $b < \bar{b}$. The fact that $\varepsilon_+ > 1$ implies that the transversality condition cannot be satisfied if $a_1 \neq 0$. Accordingly, we set $a_1 = 0$, and the solution (A.6) becomes:

$$y_{t+\tau} = a_0 + a_2\varepsilon_-^\tau.$$

From Eq. (A.5) we see that $a_0 = 2/(2c - b(1+\beta))$, since it is determined by:

$$1 + \frac{b}{2}a_0 - ca_0 + \frac{\beta b}{2}a_0 = 0.$$

Note that $b < \bar{b}$ implies that $a_0 > 0$, so the "long-run" level for output is positive. The restriction on parameter b has an economic meaning: as intuition suggests, it cannot be "too large" because a very strong learning-by-doing effect would induce the firm to ever increase its production, which is not consistent with a competitive setup. One can also show that the restriction $b < \bar{b}$ allows for a (non trivial) steady state for x_t. Finally, coefficient a_2 is pinned down by the initial condition (recall that $x_t = y_{t-1}$ is given).

Exercise 6 Assume that the maximum value function takes the form $V(k_t) = e + f \ln k_t$, thus the recursive formulation is:

$$e + f \ln k_t = \max_{c_t, l_t} \{\ln(c_t) + \gamma \ln(1 - l_t) + \beta(e + f \ln k_{t+1})\}.$$

Since there are two controls, we need to consider two first-order conditions, which–by exploiting our guess–rapidly give:

$$c_t = \frac{k_{t+1}}{\beta f} \tag{A.7}$$

and

$$\frac{\gamma}{1 - l_t} = \frac{\beta f}{k_{t+1}} (1 - \alpha) A k_t^{\alpha} l_t{}^{-\alpha}. \tag{A.8}$$

By taking advantage of the dynamic constraint and the first-order condition (A.7), we obtain a (familiar) relationship between the next-period capital and the current output, which is:

$$k_{t+1} = \frac{\beta f}{1 + \beta f} A k_t^{\alpha} l_t^{1-\alpha}.$$

Hence, the first-order condition (A.8) can be written as:

$$\frac{\gamma}{1 - l_t} = \frac{(1 + \beta f)(1 - \alpha)}{l_t},$$

which implies that the optimal labor supply is independent of the capital stock (and the productivity level). Thus, assuming that f takes its optimal value, we can write:

$$l_t^* = l^* = \frac{(1 + \beta f)(1 - \alpha)}{\gamma + (1 + \beta f)(1 - \alpha)}.$$

With $\gamma > 0$, a positive value for f is sufficient to conclude that $l^* \in (0, 1)$. In our case, $f > 0$ holds, implying that a higher capital stock benefits our agent.

We now follow a well-known path: we substitute the tentative solution into the Bellman equation:

$$e + f \ln k_t = \ln\left(\frac{1}{1+\beta f}\right) + \ln A + \alpha \ln k_t + (1-\alpha)\ln l^* + \gamma \ln(1-l^*) + \\ + \beta e + \beta f \left(\ln \frac{\beta f}{1+\beta f} + \ln A + \alpha \ln k_t + (1-\alpha)\ln l^*\right),$$

where use has been made of the fact that $c_t = 1/(1+\beta f)\, A k_t^{\alpha} l^{*(1-\alpha)}$.

Matching the coefficients for $\ln k_t$ we immediately obtain:

$$f = \frac{\alpha}{1-\alpha\beta} > 0,$$

while the constant is:

$$e = \frac{1}{1-\beta}\left(\frac{\alpha\beta}{1-\alpha\beta}\ln(\alpha\beta) + \ln(1-\alpha\beta) + \frac{1}{1-\alpha\beta}\ln A + \\ + \frac{1-\alpha}{1-\alpha\beta}\ln l^* + \gamma \ln(1-l^*)\right).$$

When $\gamma = 0$ (so that the constraint $l^* \leq 1$ binds) it can be verified that e corresponds to (3.7) (use de l'Hôpital's rule).

Exercise 7 From the perspective of period t, past consumption, being predetermined, is a state of the system. Let $c_{t-1} = x_t$, and note that this equation can be interpreted as a transition equation for x_t.

The arguments of the maximum value function are the state variables; accordingly our tentative functional form is: $V(k_t, x_t) = e + f \ln k_t + g \ln x_t$. Thus, the recursive formulation becomes:

$$e + f \ln k_t + g \ln x_t = \max_{c_t}\left\{\ln c_t - \gamma \ln x_t + \beta(e + f \ln k_{t+1} + g \ln x_{t+1})\right\}.$$

The first-order condition with respect to current consumption is:

$$\frac{1}{c_t} + \beta\left(\frac{f}{k_{t+1}}\frac{\partial k_{t+1}}{\partial c_t} + \frac{g}{x_{t+1}}\frac{\partial x_{t+1}}{\partial c_t}\right) = 0, \tag{A.9}$$

and hence, using the dynamic constraints:

$$\frac{1}{c_t} = \beta \left(\frac{f}{k_{t+1}} - \frac{g}{c_t} \right),$$

so that we readily obtain $c_t = (1 + \beta g)\, k_{t+1}/\beta f$. The fact that $k_{t+1} = Ak_t^{\alpha} - c_t$ implies:

$$k_{t+1} = \frac{\beta f}{1 + \beta g + \beta f} A k_t^{\alpha} \text{ and } c_t = \frac{1 + \beta g}{1 + \beta g + \beta f} A k_t^{\alpha}.$$

Substituting these results into the Bellman equation, we obtain:

$$\begin{aligned} e + f \ln k_t + g \ln x_t = \ln \frac{1 + \beta g}{1 + \beta g + \beta f} + \ln A + \alpha \ln k_t - \gamma \ln x_t + \\ + \beta \left(e + f \ln \frac{\beta f}{1 + \beta g + \beta f} + f \ln A + \alpha f \ln k_t + \right. \\ \left. + g \ln \frac{1 + \beta g}{1 + \beta g + \beta f} + g \ln A + \alpha g \ln k_t \right). \end{aligned}$$

Note that–in the last line of the previous expression–we have again used the fact that $x_{t+1} = c_t$.

Matching the coefficients for $\ln x_t$ we obtain that $g = -\gamma$; by exploiting the terms involving $\ln k_t$ we then obtain that $f = \alpha(1 - \beta\gamma)/\left(1 - \alpha\beta\right)$. This allows us to get the policy function, which is:

$$c_t^* = (1 - \alpha\beta)\, A k_t^{\alpha}.$$

The constant term can then be obtained by exploiting our knowledge of f and g in the following expression:

$$\begin{aligned} (1 - \beta)\, e &= \ln \frac{1 + \beta g}{1 + \beta g + \beta f} + \ln A + \beta \left(f \ln \frac{\beta f}{1 + \beta g + \beta f} + f \ln A + \right. \\ &\quad \left. + g \ln \frac{1 + \beta g}{1 + \beta g + \beta f} + g \ln A \right). \end{aligned}$$

When $\gamma = 0$, it can be easily verified that e corresponds to (3.7).

The return function used for this exercise implies that an increase in present consumption not only lowers (as usual) the marginal utility of current consumption but also reduces the next-period utility. In other words, the more the consumer eats today, the hungrier she wakes up tomorrow. In this sense, these preferences capture the notion of habit formation, where past consumption represents the consumer's "stock of habits." More precisely, our exercise concerns habits of the so-called "internal" type, because the (representative) consumer's current consumption influences *her own* future utility. A popular variant of the habit formation model considers them as "external" to the consumer. In this case, our consumer wishes to keep up with her neighbor ("the Joneses"), thus it is the *aggregate* past consumption that affects current utility. (This would imply a modification of the first-order condition (A.9) from the perspective of any individual agent: the second term in the big round parenthesis would disappear).

Exercise 8 The practice of proposing a tentative solution that has the same functional form as the return function has a long history in dynamic programming. This idea was already used in Section 3.1.

Thus, assume that the maximum value function takes the form $V(k_t) = e + fk_t^{1-\gamma}/(1-\gamma)$.

Note that, following the practice mentioned above, it would also be sensible–after all any tentative function is legitimate, as we are *guessing*–to start with a generic exponential function, i.e. $V(k_t) = e + fk_t^g$. We will briefly explore this possibility at the end of the discussion for this exercise.

For now, we consider:

$$e + f\frac{k_t^{1-\gamma}}{1-\gamma} = \max_{c_t}\left\{\frac{c_t^{1-\gamma}}{1-\gamma} + \beta\left(e + f\frac{k_{t+1}^{1-\gamma}}{1-\gamma}\right)\right\}.$$

The first-order condition for consumption gives:

$$c_t^{-\gamma} = \beta f k_{t+1}^{-\gamma}.$$

Exploiting the dynamic constraint as usual, we obtain:

$$c_t = \frac{(\beta f)^{-1/\gamma}}{1+(\beta f)^{-1/\gamma}}Ak_t, \text{ and } k_{t+1} = \frac{1}{1+(\beta f)^{-1/\gamma}}Ak_t.$$

Substituting these results into the Bellman equation gives:

$$e + f\frac{k_t^{1-\gamma}}{1-\gamma} = \frac{(\beta f)^{(\gamma-1)/\gamma}}{\left(1+(\beta f)^{-1/\gamma}\right)^{1-\gamma}}\frac{A^{1-\gamma}k_t^{1-\gamma}}{1-\gamma} + \\ +\beta\left(e + f\frac{1}{\left(1+(\beta f)^{-1/\gamma}\right)^{1-\gamma}}\frac{A^{1-\gamma}k_t^{1-\gamma}}{1-\gamma}\right),$$

which implies that $e = 0$. Furthermore, some obvious simplifications yield:

$$f = \frac{(\beta f)^{(\gamma-1)/\gamma}}{\left(1+(\beta f)^{-1/\gamma}\right)^{1-\gamma}}A^{1-\gamma} + \beta f\frac{1}{\left(1+(\beta f)^{-1/\gamma}\right)^{1-\gamma}}A^{1-\gamma}.$$

Note that the equation above allows us to conclude that f is independent of the capital stock, and thus that our guess is correct. Some further manipulations allow us to obtain:

$$f\left(1+(\beta f)^{-1/\gamma}\right)^{1-\gamma} = \left((\beta f)^{-1/\gamma}+1\right)\beta f A^{1-\gamma},$$

or

$$1+(\beta f)^{-\frac{1}{\gamma}} = \beta^{-\frac{1}{\gamma}}A^{\frac{\gamma-1}{\gamma}},$$

so that:

$$f = \frac{1}{\beta}\left(\beta^{-\frac{1}{\gamma}}A^{\frac{\gamma-1}{\gamma}} - 1\right)^{-\gamma}. \tag{A.10}$$

We now assume that $\beta A^{1-\gamma} < 1$. This restriction guarantees that $f > 0$, which means the marginal productivity of capital is high enough that a larger stock of capital benefits the representative consumer. Indeed, in an economy in which the marginal productivity of capital is constant, a case in which a larger stock of capital is welfare-reducing is too sad to be of interest. (Why?)

From our expression for c_t, we find that the policy function is:

$$c_t^* = \frac{\beta^{-\frac{1}{\gamma}}A^{\frac{\gamma-1}{\gamma}} - 1}{\beta^{-\frac{1}{\gamma}}A^{\frac{\gamma-1}{\gamma}}}Ak_t.$$

Hence, the proposed restriction also guarantees that the optimal consumption is a positive function of the capital stock (a reassuring implication).

Finally, note that the production function exhibits constant returns to the accumulable productive factor. Thus, the incentive to save–and hence to create new capital–does not fade away as the productive resources grow. As a result, this production function provides a basis for endogenous growth, which makes this structure quite popular.

We now propose an alternative "guess" for the maximum value function, and explore its implications. We assume that our tentative solution takes the form $V(k_t) = e + fk_t^g$, where e, f, and g are unknown parameters. Therefore, the recursive formulation is:

$$e + fk_t^g = \max_{c_t} \left\{ \frac{c_t^{1-\gamma}}{1-\gamma} + \beta \left(e + fk_{t+1}^g \right) \right\}. \tag{A.11}$$

The first-order condition for consumption gives:

$$c_t^{-\gamma} = \beta f g k_{t+1}^{g-1},$$

so that:

$$c_t = (\beta f g)^{-\frac{1}{\gamma}} k_{t+1}^{\frac{1-g}{\gamma}}. \tag{A.12}$$

Applying the envelope theorem to (A.11) (refer to Eq. (2.9)), we readily obtain:

$$k_t = (\beta A)^{\frac{1}{g-1}} k_{t+1}.$$

Exploiting the latter and Eq. (A.12) into the Bellman equation (A.11) gives:

$$e + fk_t^g = \frac{1}{1-\gamma} (fg)^{\frac{\gamma-1}{\gamma}} A^{\frac{1-\gamma}{\gamma}} k_t^{(1-g)\left(\frac{1-\gamma}{\gamma}\right)} + \beta \left(e + f (\beta A)^{\frac{g}{1-g}} k_t^g \right),$$

from which it is apparent that $e = 0$ and that $g = 1 - \gamma$. Moreover, it must be true that:

$$f = \frac{1}{1-\gamma} (f(1-\gamma))^{\frac{\gamma-1}{\gamma}} A^{\frac{1-\gamma}{\gamma}} + \beta f (\beta A)^{\frac{1-\gamma}{\gamma}},$$

so that:

$$f = \frac{A^{1-\gamma}}{1-\gamma} \left(1 - \beta^{\frac{1}{\gamma}} A^{\frac{1-\gamma}{\gamma}} \right)^{-\gamma} = \left(\frac{1}{1-\gamma} \right) \frac{1}{\beta} \left(A^{\frac{\gamma-1}{\gamma}} \beta^{-\frac{1}{\gamma}} - 1 \right)^{-\gamma}.$$

This corresponds to (A.10).

Exercise 9 In this setting, we have $U(c_t) = c_t^{1-\gamma}/(1-\gamma)$, and $k_{t+1} = Ak_t - c_t$. The path characterized by the fastest possible growth for capital is obtained with zero consumption in each period. Choosing this path, we have that:

$$k_t = A^t k_0.$$

The highest one-period utility is obtained by consuming the entire output that the representative agent can produce in that period:

$$U(c_t) = \frac{(Ak_t)^{1-\gamma}}{1-\gamma}.$$

Therefore, if we follow the policy prescribing to save everything up to period $t-1$ and then to consume the entire output in period t, we obtain:

$$U(c_t) = A^{(1-\gamma)(t+1)} \frac{k_0^{1-\gamma}}{1-\gamma}.$$

Imagine hypothetically, as in Subsection 3.1.1, that the above policy can be followed in every period. In this case, the lifetime utility for the representative agent would be:

$$\sum_{t=0}^{\infty} \beta^t \frac{A^{(1-\gamma)(t+1)} k_0^{1-\gamma}}{1-\gamma} = \sum_{t=0}^{\infty} \left(\beta A^{1-\gamma}\right)^t \frac{A^{1-\gamma} k_0^{1-\gamma}}{1-\gamma}.$$

For the above series to converge, we need to assume $\beta A^{1-\gamma} < 1$. When the restriction is fulfilled, the above expression yields:

$$\frac{A^{1-\gamma} k_0^{1-\gamma}}{1-\gamma} \frac{1}{1-\beta A^{1-\gamma}}.$$

Hence, when $\beta A^{1-\gamma} < 1$ there is a finite upper bound for the maximum value function, thus Theorem 2 applies, and the maximum value function is unique. Note that the condition we have just obtained is the same one we have found reasonable when discussing the results in Exercise 8. From the restriction $\beta A^{1-\gamma} < 1$ we obtain the required condition on γ, which is:

$$\gamma > 1 + \ln\beta/\ln A \text{ if } A > 1, \;\; \gamma < 1 + \ln\beta/\ln A \text{ if } A < 1.$$

Exercise 10 The solution must satisfy the first-order condition with respect to consumption, which is:

$$U'(c_t^*) + \beta V'(k_{t+1}^*)\frac{\partial k_{t+1}}{\partial c_t} = 0.$$

Also, the envelope theorem prescribes that, along an optimal path:

$$V'(k_t^*) = \beta V'(k_{t+1}^*)\frac{\partial k_{t+1}}{\partial k_t}.$$

In our case, given the tentative solution $V(k_t) = e + f \ln k_t$, these two conditions become, respectively:

$$\frac{1}{c_t^*} + \frac{\beta f}{k_{t+1}^*}(-1) = 0$$

and:

$$\frac{f}{k_t^*} = \frac{\beta f}{k_{t+1}^*}\alpha A k_t^{*(\alpha-1)}.$$

Exploiting the transition function, one easily obtains $f = \frac{\alpha}{1-\alpha\beta}$.

Exercise 11 From Subsection 2.2.3 we know that in the Ramsey model it holds that:

$$V_k(k_t) = U_c\left(f(k_t) - s_t^*\right) f_k(k_t).$$

The assumptions concerning utility and production functions introduced in Section 1.1 allow us to immediately conclude that $V_k(k_t) > 0$.

Consider then:

$$V_{kk}(k_t) = U_{cc}\left(f(k_t) - s_t^*\right)\left(f_k(k_t) - \frac{ds_t^*}{dk_t}\right) f_k(k_t) + U_c\left(f(k_t) - s_t^*\right) f_{kk}(k_t).$$

From the assumptions in Section 1.1, we note that $dc_t^*/dk_t > 0$ is sufficient to conclude that $V_{kk}(k_t) < 0$.

Exercise 12 Define the control variable $w_t = f(k_t) + (1-\delta)k_t - c_t$. This definition implies that the next-period state is equal to the current control

$(k_{t+1} = w_t)$. The Bellman problem is formulated as follows:

$$V(k_t) = \max_{w_t} \{U(f(k_t) + (1-\delta)k_t - w_t) + \beta V(k_{t+1})\},$$
$$s.t.\ k_{t+1} = w_t,$$
$$k_0 \text{ given.}$$

The first-order condition is: $U_c(f(k_t) + (1-\delta)k_t - w_t) = \beta V_k(k_{t+1})$.

Considering the *total* differential of the Bellman equation along the optimal path, we obtain:

$$V_k(k_t)dk_t = U_c(f(k_t) + (1-\delta)k_t - w_t)(df(k_t) + (1-\delta)dk_t - dw_t) + \\ + \beta V_k(k_{t+1})dk_{t+1}.$$

Using the first-order condition yields:

$$V_k(k_t)dk_t = U_c(f(k_t) + (1-\delta)k_t - w_t)(df(k_t) + (1-\delta)dk_t - dw_t) + \\ + U_c(f(k_t) + (1-\delta)k_t - w_t)dk_{t+1}.$$

Given that $dk_{t+1}/dw_t = 1$, we then obtain:

$$V_k(k_t) = U_c(f(k_t) + (1-\delta)k_t - w_t)(f_k(k_t) + 1 - \delta).$$

Exercise 13 To solve this problem, we closely refer to Section 3.2.

First, we obtain the formulations for k_{t+1} and c_t. Taking into account the tentative solution (3.11) the first-order condition (refer to 3.10) yields:

$$\gamma - \eta[(1+r)k_t - k_{t+1}] = \beta(h + mk_{t+1}).$$

The two coefficients of the maximum value function, h and m, are given by (3.16) and (3.15), respectively, thus the equation above readily gives:

$$k_{t+1} = \frac{\gamma}{\eta r}\left(1 - \frac{1}{\beta(1+r)}\right) + \frac{1}{\beta(1+r)}k_t. \tag{A.13}$$

Eq. (A.13) is a difference equation for the capital stock. Its solution is:

$$k_t = \frac{\gamma}{\eta r} + \left(\frac{1}{\beta(1+r)}\right)^t \left(k_0 - \frac{\gamma}{\eta r}\right). \tag{A.14}$$

Note that the root for the dynamic equation governing capital (A.13) is $(\beta(1+r))^{-1}$. When $\beta(1+r) > 1$, capital is bound to converge to its steady-state level (which is $\gamma/(\eta r)$), and so is consumption. When instead $\beta(1+r) < 1$, the capital stock is either ever increasing or ever decreasing, depending on the initial condition for capital. In the knife-edge case where $\beta(1+r) = 1$, the capital stock remains stationary.

Consumption is given by $c_t = (1+r)k_t - k_{t+1}$ (as implied by 3.9), thus using (A.13) we have:

$$c_t = \frac{\gamma}{\eta r}\left(\frac{1}{\beta(1+r)} - 1\right) + \frac{\beta(1+r)^2 - 1}{\beta(1+r)} k_t. \tag{A.15}$$

Exploiting Eq. (A.15), we see that the marginal utility of consumption is:

$$U'(c_t) = \gamma - \eta c_t = \left(\frac{\beta(1+r)^2 - 1}{\beta(1+r)}\right)\left(\frac{\gamma}{r} - \eta k_t\right). \tag{A.16}$$

From Eq. (1.22), the tvc is:

$$\lim_{T\to\infty} \beta^T U'(c_T) k_{T+1} = 0.$$

From Eq. (A.16) and (A.14) it is immediate to obtain:

$$\begin{aligned}
&\lim_{T\to\infty} \beta^T U'(c_T) k_{T+1} = \\
&\qquad = \lim_{T\to\infty} \beta^T \left(\frac{\beta(1+r)^2 - 1}{\beta(1+r)}\right)\left(\frac{\gamma}{r} - \eta k_T\right) k_{T+1} = \\
&= \lim_{T\to\infty} \beta^T \left(\frac{\beta(1+r)^2 - 1}{\beta(1+r)}\right)\left(\frac{\gamma}{r} - \eta\left[\frac{\gamma}{\eta r} + \left(\frac{1}{\beta(1+r)}\right)^T \left(k_0 - \frac{\gamma}{\eta r}\right)\right]\right) \times \\
&\qquad \times \left[\frac{\gamma}{\eta r} + \left(\frac{1}{\beta(1+r)}\right)^{T+1} \left(k_0 - \frac{\gamma}{\eta r}\right)\right].
\end{aligned}$$

The limit above converges to 0 if (and only if):

$$\begin{cases} \lim_{T\to\infty} \left(\frac{\beta}{\beta(1+r)}\right)^T = \lim_{T\to\infty} \left(\frac{1}{1+r}\right)^T = 0 \\ \lim_{T\to\infty} \left(\frac{1}{1+r}\right)^T \left(\frac{1}{\beta(1+r)}\right)^{T+1} = 0. \end{cases}$$

The first condition requires $r > 0$, while the second involves the additional constraint $\beta(1+r)^2 > 1$.

Hence, when $\beta(1+r)^2 > 1$, the tvc is satisfied. However–as remarked above–capital approaches its steady-state value, which is $\frac{\gamma}{\eta r}$, only when $\beta(1+r) > 1$ (the discussion of the consumption dynamics is left to the reader). When $\beta(1+r) < 1$ and the initial stock of capital is below its steady state level, capital collapses to 0 in finite time and then it diverges. These paths are not feasible, since they do not satisfy the constraint $k_t \geq 0$. Note that this behavior is not surprising, since $\beta(1+r) < 1$ implies that the return on saving does not match compensate for the agent's subjective discount of the future.

Exercise 14 The state variable is productivity. Hence, the tentative solution is:

$$V(x_t) = F + Gx_t + \frac{H}{2}x_t^2.$$

Our problem becomes:

$$F+Gx_t+\frac{H}{2}x_t^2 = \max_{y_t} \left\{ \left(1 + \frac{b}{2}x_t\right) y_t - \frac{c}{2}y_t^2 + \beta \left(F + Gx_{t+1} + \frac{H}{2}x_{t+1}^2\right) \right\}. \tag{A.17}$$

The first-order condition gives:

$$1 + \frac{b}{2}x_t - cy_t + \beta\left(G + Hy_t\right) = 0,$$

in which we have already made use of $x_{t+1} = y_t$. With $H \neq c/\beta$, we obtain:

$$y_t = \frac{2 + bx_t + 2\beta G}{2\left(c - \beta H\right)}. \tag{A.18}$$

Substituting this into Eq. (A.17) yields:

$$F+Gx_t+\frac{H}{2}x_t^2=\left(1+\frac{b}{2}x_t\right)\left(\frac{2+bx_t+2\beta G}{2(c-\beta H)}\right)-\frac{c}{2}\left(\frac{2+bx_t+2\beta G}{2(c-\beta H)}\right)^2+$$
$$+\beta\left(F+G\left(\frac{2+bx_t+2\beta G}{2(c-\beta H)}\right)+\frac{H}{2}\left(\frac{2+bx_t+2\beta G}{2(c-\beta H)}\right)^2\right).$$

We now pin down the coefficients, which also allows us to verify that our guess is correct.

Matching the coefficients for x_t^2 gives:

$$\frac{H}{2}=\frac{b^2}{4(c-\beta H)}-\frac{cb^2}{8(c-\beta H)^2}+\frac{\beta H b^2}{8(c-\beta H)^2},$$

which rapidly reduces to:

$$4\beta H^2-4cH+b^2=0.$$

The solutions for our quadratic equation are:

$$H^{(+)}=\frac{1}{2\beta}\left(c+\left(c^2-\beta b^2\right)^{1/2}\right),\quad H^{(-)}=\frac{1}{2\beta}\left(c-\left(c^2-\beta b^2\right)^{1/2}\right).$$

Note that both the roots are real since $c^2-\beta b^2>0$, given that, by assumption, $b<\bar{b}\equiv 2c/(1+\beta)$ (refer to Exercise 5). To obtain the (unique) maximum value function, we need to select the "correct" value for H. This is done by exploiting the relationship between y_t and x_t from Eq. (A.18). Note that, if $b/(2(c-\beta H))>1$, productivity and output are bound to ever increase over time. We can then observe that:

$$\frac{b}{2\left(c-\beta H^{(+)}\right)}=\frac{b}{c-(c^2-\beta b^2)^{1/2}},$$

which exceeds 1 when $b<\bar{b}$, a condition satisfied by assumption. Finally, note that:

$$\frac{b}{2\left(c-\beta H^{(-)}\right)}=\frac{b}{c+(c^2-\beta b^2)^{1/2}},$$

which exceeds 1 only if $b>\bar{b}$, a condition never satisfied given the restriction on b. Hence, we select $H^{(-)}$; note that the transversality condition is satisfied by the solution we have chosen (refer to Exercise 5).

It is now trivial to obtain the values for G and F. The first-degree terms give:

$$G = \frac{b}{2}\left(\frac{2+\beta G}{c-\beta H}\right) - \frac{b\,c\,(1+\beta G)}{2\,(c-\beta H)^2} + \frac{b}{2}\frac{\beta G}{(c-\beta H)} + \frac{b}{2}\frac{\beta H\,(1+\beta G)}{(c-\beta H)^2}.$$

This quickly reduces to:

$$G = \frac{b}{2}\left(\frac{1+\beta G}{c-\beta H}\right),$$

which pins down G. As for the constant, we have:

$$F = \frac{1+\beta G}{c-\beta H} - \frac{c}{2}\left(\frac{1+\beta G}{c-\beta H}\right)^2 + \beta\left(F + G\left(\frac{1+\beta G}{c-\beta H}\right) + \frac{H}{2}\left(\frac{1+\beta G}{c-\beta H}\right)^2\right),$$

which simplifies to:

$$F = \frac{(1+\beta G)^2}{2\,(1-\beta)\,(c-\beta H)}.$$

Because F, G and H are independent of the state variable, our tentative solution for the maximum value function is correct.

As for the restriction on the parameter b, our economic intuition is that it cannot be "too large:" a very strong learning-by-doing effect induces the firm to ever increase its production, which is inconsistent with a competitive setup.

Exercise 15 From our calculations in Section 3.1, we already know that:

$$V(k) =$$
$$= \frac{1}{1-\beta}\left(\frac{\alpha\beta}{1-\alpha\beta}\ln(\alpha\beta) + \ln(1-\alpha\beta) + \frac{1}{1-\alpha\beta}\ln A\right) + \frac{\alpha}{1-\alpha\beta}\ln k.$$

Substituting the values for the coefficients, for productivity, and for k proposed in the main text it is trivial to check the correspondence with the results in Table 2.

Exercise 16 One can verify, by setting up the constrained maximization problem, that $k_4 = 0$, an obvious result, given that our consumer lives for four periods. Accordingly, period 3 consumption is, for each state i:

$$c_3^{i*} = A^i k_3^{\alpha}. \tag{A.19}$$

We have omitted the time subscript because productivity is time-independent.

From the Lagrangian, it is easy to obtain that, from the perspective of period 2, it must hold:

$$\frac{1}{c_2^i} = \alpha\beta\left(p^H A^H \frac{1}{c_3^H} + p^L A^L \frac{1}{c_3^L}\right) k_3^{\alpha-1}.$$

Exploiting Eq. (A.19), we obtain:

$$\frac{1}{c_2^i} = \alpha\beta\left(\frac{p^H + p^L}{k_3}\right).$$

Hence, we have that $k_3 = \alpha\beta c_2^i$ (for $i = L, H$). Moreover, the intertemporal budget constraint guarantees that $k_3 = A^i k_2^{\alpha} - c_2^i$. Accordingly, we obtain the period-2 policy function for $i = L, H$:

$$c_2^{i*} = \frac{1}{1+\alpha\beta} A^i k_2^{\alpha}. \tag{A.20}$$

We then consider the Euler equation from the perspective of period 1, which implies:

$$\frac{1}{c_1^i} = \alpha\beta\left(p^H A^H \frac{1}{c_2^H} + p^L A^L \frac{1}{c_2^L}\right) k_2^{\alpha-1}.$$

Exploiting Eq. (A.20) we obtain:

$$\frac{1}{c_1^i} = \alpha\beta(1+\alpha\beta)\left(\frac{p^H + p^L}{k_2}\right).$$

Hence, we have that $k_2 = \alpha\beta(1+\alpha\beta)c_1^{i*}$ (for $i = L, H$); from the intertemporal budget constraint we have, as usual, that $k_2 = A^i {k_1}^{\alpha} - c_1^{i*}$. So, we can conclude that $c_1^{i*} = 1/\left(1 + \alpha\beta + (\alpha\beta)^2\right) A^i k_1^{\alpha}$ for $i = L, H$.

Following the steps outlined above, the reader can show that the initial period policy function is: $c_0^{i*} = 1/\left(1 + \alpha\beta + (\alpha\beta)^2 + (\alpha\beta)^3\right) A^i k_0^{\alpha}$ for $i = L, H$.

Note that, as we move farther and farther away from the final period, the policy function gets closer and closer (and actually, converges) to the one prescribed for the infinite horizon case. In fact, we have that

$$\lim_{n\to\infty}\sum_{i=0}^{n}(\alpha\beta)^i=\lim_{n\to\infty}\frac{1-(\alpha\beta)^{n+1}}{1-\alpha\beta}=\frac{1}{1-\alpha\beta}.$$

Exercise 17 The fact that the probability distribution for productivity at time $t+1$ depends on its time t realization implies that the Euler equation (obtained from the Lagrangian) is influenced by the period t realization for productivity. Hence, in period 0, when productivity is A_0^H, we have:

$$\frac{1}{c_0^H}=\alpha\beta\left(pA_1^H\frac{1}{c_1^H}+(1-p)A_1^L\frac{1}{c_1^L}\right)k_1^{\alpha-1}. \tag{A.21}$$

When instead period 0 productivity is A_0^L, we have:

$$\frac{1}{c_0^L}=\alpha\beta\left((1-p)\,A_1^H\frac{1}{c_1^H}+pA_1^L\frac{1}{c_1^L}\right)k_1^{\alpha-1}. \tag{A.22}$$

We now guess that the policy function takes the form:

$$c_0^i=\chi A_0^i k_0^\alpha \tag{A.23}$$

where χ is a coefficient to be determined. We are assuming that the propensity to consume is state-independent, as it was in the version of the model discussed in Chapter 6.

By taking advantage of the guess for the policy function, we substitute the consumption levels in the Euler equation (A.21), to obtain:

$$\frac{1}{\chi A_0^H k_0^\alpha}=\alpha\beta\left(pA_1^H\frac{1}{\chi A_1^H k_1^\alpha}+(1-p)A_1^L\frac{1}{\chi A_1^L k_1^\alpha}\right)k_1^{\alpha-1}.$$

This equation rapidly reduces to: $k_1=\alpha\beta A_0^H k_0^\alpha$.

When productivity is high in period 0, our guess (A.23) implies, for $i=H$, that $k_1=(1-\chi)\,A_0^H k_0^\alpha$. Thus, we have that $\chi=1-\alpha\beta$. To complete the solution, one should check that the consumption function (A.23) also applies when the initial productivity level is low. This can be done by starting from the Euler equation (A.22).

Hence, the probability structure considered in this exercise does not affect the consumption function. This, however, does not imply that such a probability structure is completely devoid of consequences. On this, please refer to Exercise 21.

Exercise 18 The Euler equation (which can, as always, be obtained from the Lagrangian) is:

$$\frac{1}{c_t^i} = \alpha\beta\left(p^H \frac{1}{c_{t+1}^H} A_{t+1}^H + p^L \frac{1}{c_{t+1}^L} A_{t+1}^L\right) k_{t+1}^{\alpha-1}.$$

Exploiting the guess $c_t^i = \Psi(A_t^i)k_t^\alpha$ in the equation above, we obtain:

$$\frac{1}{\Psi(A_t^i)k_t^\alpha} = \alpha\beta\left(p^H \frac{A_{t+1}^H}{\Psi(A_{t+1}^H)k_{t+1}^\alpha} + p^L \frac{A_{t+1}^L}{\Psi(A_{t+1}^L)k_{t+1}^\alpha}\right) k_{t+1}^{\alpha-1}. \quad \text{(A.24)}$$

Note that our tentative solution implies $k_{t+1} = (A_t^i - \Psi(A_t^i))k_t^\alpha$, thus, after some simplifications, Eq. (A.24) becomes:

$$\frac{1}{\Psi(A_t^i)} = \alpha\beta\left(p^H \frac{A_{t+1}^H}{\Psi(A_{t+1}^H)} + p^L \frac{A_{t+1}^L}{\Psi(A_{t+1}^L)}\right) \frac{1}{A_t^i - \Psi(A_t^i)}. \quad \text{(A.25)}$$

Since Equation (A.25) must be valid for $i = L, H$, we have:

$$\frac{A_t^H - \Psi(A_t^H)}{\Psi(A_t^H)} = \alpha\beta\left(p^H \frac{A_{t+1}^H}{\Psi(A_{t+1}^H)} + p^L \frac{A_{t+1}^L}{\Psi(A_{t+1}^L)}\right) = \frac{A_t^L - \Psi(A_t^L)}{\Psi(A_t^L)}.$$

This leads to:

$$\frac{A_t^H}{\Psi(A_t^H)} = \frac{A_t^L}{\Psi(A_t^L)},$$

which implies $\Psi(A_t^i) = \psi A_t^i$ (so that the ratio $A_t^i/\Psi(A_t^i)$ is constant).

Exercise 19 With the proposed utility function, the Euler equation takes the form:

$$c_0^{i(-\gamma)} = \beta\left[p^H c_1^{H(-\gamma)} A_1^H + p^L c_1^{L(-\gamma)} A_1^L\right].$$

Assume that the consumption function is:

$$c_0^i = \chi A_0^i k_0, \quad \text{(A.26)}$$

where χ is an undetermined coefficient. We can exploit this guess to obtain the following from the Euler equation:

$$\left(\chi A_0^i k_0\right)^{-\gamma} = \beta\left[p^H\left(\chi A_1^H k_1\right)^{-\gamma} A_1^H + p^L\left(\chi A_1^L k_1\right)^{-\gamma} A_1^L\right].$$

Note that Eq. (A.26) implies $k_1 = (1-\chi)A_0^i k_0$. After some simplifications, the equation above becomes:

$$\left(A_0^i k_0\right)^{-\gamma} = \beta\left[p^H\left(A_1^H\right)^{1-\gamma} + p^L\left(A_1^L\right)^{1-\gamma}\right]\left((1-\chi)A_0^i k_0\right)^{-\gamma}.$$

This allows us to solve for $(1-\chi)$:

$$1-\chi = \left(\beta\left[p^H\left(A_1^H\right)^{1-\gamma} + p^L\left(A_1^L\right)^{1-\gamma}\right]\right)^{\frac{1}{\gamma}}.$$

The coefficient χ can be rewritten more compactly as:

$$\chi = 1 - \left(\beta E\left[\tilde{A}_1^{1-\gamma}\right]\right)^{\frac{1}{\gamma}}.$$

This formulation reveals that, whenever $\gamma > 1$, a mean-preserving increase in the variance of $\tilde{A}$ reduces consumption, which implies the presence of precautionary saving. The parameter γ can, in fact, be interpreted as a measure of the representative agent's (relative) risk aversion.

Exercise 20 The maximum value function depends upon the two state variables, capital and productivity. Accordingly, our tentative functional form is: $V(k_t, A_t^i) = F + G\ln k_t + H\ln A_t^i$, for $i = \{L, H\}$. The recursive formulation is:

$$F + G\ln k_t + H\ln A_t^i = \max_{c_t}\left\{\ln c_t + \beta E_t\left[F + G\ln k_{t+1} + H\ln \tilde{A}_{t+1}\right]\right\},$$

in which $\tilde{A}_{t+1}$ is stochastic.

The first-order condition with respect to (current) consumption is:

$$\frac{1}{c_t^i} = \beta\frac{G}{k_{t+1}}.$$

The expectation operator $E_t\left[.\right]$ "disappears" because the capital stock at time $t+1$ is known when consumption is decided upon.

Exploiting the transition function we readily obtain:

$$k_{t+1} = \frac{\beta G}{1+\beta G} A_t^i k_t^\alpha,$$

and therefore:

$$c_t^i = \frac{1}{1+\beta G} A_t^i k_t^\alpha.$$

We now take advantage of the Bellman equation, obtaining:

$$F + G \ln k_t + H \ln A_t^i = \ln \frac{1}{1+\beta G} + \ln A_t^i + \alpha \ln k_t +$$
$$+ \beta E_t \left[F + G \ln \frac{\beta G}{1+\beta G} + G \ln A_t^i + G\alpha \ln k_t + H \ln \tilde{A}_{t+1} \right].$$

By matching the coefficients for $\ln k_t$ we get that $G = \alpha / (1-\alpha\beta)$. This allows us to obtain the policy function, which is identical to the one for the non-stochastic case (our standard "disappointing" result):

$$c_t^{i,*} = (1-\alpha\beta) A_t^i k_t^\alpha.$$

Considering the coefficients for $\ln A_t$, we then obtain that $H = 1/(1-\alpha\beta)$; finally, we match the constant terms, which incorporate $E_t \left[\ln \tilde{A}_{t+1} \right]$. Thus:

$$F = \ln \frac{1}{1+\beta G} + \beta \left(F + G \ln \frac{\beta G}{1+\beta G} + H E_t \left[\ln \tilde{A}_{t+1} \right] \right).$$

Exploiting the expressions for G and H, we readily get:

$$F = \frac{1}{1-\beta} \left(\ln (1-\alpha\beta) + \frac{\alpha\beta}{1-\alpha\beta} \ln (\alpha\beta) + \frac{\beta}{1-\alpha\beta} E_t \left[\ln \tilde{A}_{t+1} \right] \right).$$

Compare the expression for F with expression (3.7) and note that, although the variability of productivity does not affect the consumption decision, it does affect welfare.

A mean preserving spread in A reduces $E_t \left[\ln \tilde{A}_{t+1} \right]$, and therefore the overall utility of the representative consumer.

Exercise 21 In this application, the current productivity level influences the future one. Note, in particular, that if p is close to 1, the current productivity will influence production for a long time in the future. Intuitively, this should have relevant consequences for the overall utility of the representative agent. Nonetheless, we stick to our standard tentative solution:

$$V(k_t, A_t^i) = F + G\ln k_t + H\ln A_t^i, \text{ for } i = L, H. \tag{A.27}$$

The Bellman formulation is, for the generic realization i:

$$F + G\ln k_t + H\ln A_t^i = \\ = \max_{c_t^i}\left\{\ln c_t^i + \beta E_t\left[F + G\ln k_{t+1} + H\ln \tilde{A}_{t+1}\middle| A_t = A^i\right]\right\}. \tag{A.28}$$

The first-order condition with respect to current consumption is:

$$\frac{1}{c_t^i} = \beta\frac{G}{k_{t+1}}.$$

The expectation operator $E_t[.]$ "disappears" because the capital stock at time $t+1$ is known when consumption is decided upon.

Exploiting the transition function we readily obtain:

$$k_{t+1} = \frac{\beta G}{1+\beta G}A_t^i k_t^\alpha, \text{ and } c_t^i = \frac{1}{1+\beta G}A_t^i k_t^\alpha.$$

Inspecting Equation (A.28) one might be tempted to conclude that the guess is not verified, since $E_t\left[\ln\tilde{A}\middle| A = A^i\right] = p\ln A^i + (1-p)\ln A^j$, thus the right hand side of the equation also depends on the state A^j. (Note in passing that we have omitted the time subscript since this is not confusing.) However, this conclusion would be wrong. Note, in fact, that the conditional expectation $E_t\left[\ln\tilde{A}\middle| A = A^i\right]$ can be expressed as a function of the *unconditional* expectation $E\left[\ln\tilde{A}\right]$, which is a constant, and of the (log)state $\ln A^i$. In fact:

$$E_t\left[\ln\tilde{A}\middle| A = A^i\right] \equiv p\ln A^i + (1-p)\ln A^j = \\ = 2(1-p)\left(\frac{\ln A^i + \ln A^j}{2}\right) + (2p-1)\ln A^i = \\ = 2(1-p)E\left[\ln\tilde{A}\right] + (2p-1)\ln A^i.$$

This decomposition is important to verify the correctness of our guess (A.27): in fact the term $E_t\left[\ln\tilde{A}\middle| A = A^i\right]$ that appears in the Bellman problem resolves into two terms (a constant and a linear function of $\ln A^i$) which fit the guess (A.27). Indeed, exploiting the equation above and our result for k_{t+1} in Eq. (A.28) we obtain:

$$
\begin{aligned}
F + G \ln k_t + H \ln A^i = \\
&= \ln \frac{1}{1+\beta G} + \ln A^i + \alpha \ln k_t + \beta F + \beta G \ln \frac{\beta G}{1+\beta G} + \\
&+ \beta G \ln A^i + \beta G \alpha \ln k_t + \beta H \left(2 (1-p) E \left[\ln \tilde{A} \right] + (2p-1) \ln A^i \right).
\end{aligned}
$$

Matching the coefficients for $\ln k_t$ yields:

$$
G = \frac{\alpha}{1-\alpha\beta},
$$

which allows us to get the policy function. Note that the latter is not affected by the persistence probability p:

$$
c_t^{i*} = (1-\alpha\beta) A^i k_t^{\alpha}.
$$

We then consider the coefficients for $\ln A^i$, obtaining $H = 1 + \beta G + \beta H (2p-1)$, and hence:

$$
H = \frac{1}{(1-\alpha\beta)(1+\beta(1-2p))}.
$$

Finally, we determine F. Matching the left- and the right-hand side of the Bellman equation we obtain, upon substitution of G and H:

$$
F = \frac{1}{1-\beta} \left(\ln (1-\alpha\beta) + \frac{\alpha\beta}{1-\alpha\beta} \ln (\alpha\beta) + \frac{2\beta (1-p) E \left[\ln \tilde{A} \right]}{(1-\alpha\beta)(1+\beta(1-2p))} \right).
$$

Note that–using our formulation for H–F can be expressed as:

$$
F = \frac{1}{1-\beta} \left(F_0 + 2\beta (1-p) H E \left[\ln \tilde{A} \right] \right),
$$

where F_0 is a constant independent of $\tilde{A}$.

Making use of our formulation for F and adding and subtracting $HE\left[\ln\tilde{A}\right]$ to (A.27), the maximum value (conditional on A_t^i) becomes:

$$V(k_t, A_t^i) =$$
$$= \frac{1}{1-\beta}F_0 + G\ln k_t + \left(\frac{2\beta(1-p)}{1-\beta}+1\right)HE\left[\ln\tilde{A}\right] + H\left(\ln A_t^i - E\left[\ln\tilde{A}\right]\right),$$

or, by using H:

$$V(k_t, A_t^i) =$$
$$= \frac{1}{1-\beta}F_0 + G\ln k_t + \frac{1}{(1-\alpha\beta)(1-\beta)}E\left[\ln\tilde{A}\right] + H\left(\ln A_t^i - E\left[\ln\tilde{A}\right]\right).$$

This shows that persistence does not affect the ex-ante unconditional expected utility of the representative agent (why?); this fact is (once again) a consequence of choosing a log-utility function. Note however that a higher persistence strengthens the effect of the initial condition, since

$$\frac{\partial H}{\partial p} = \frac{2H\beta}{(1+\beta(1-2p))} > 0.$$

Note also that, when $p = 1$ (so that the problem becomes deterministic), the maximum value function becomes:

$$V(k_t, A^i) = \frac{1}{1-\beta}\left(\ln(1-\alpha\beta) + \frac{\alpha\beta}{1-\alpha\beta}\ln(\alpha\beta) + \frac{\ln A^i}{1-\alpha\beta}\right) + \frac{\alpha}{1-\alpha\beta}\ln k_t,$$

which matches what has been obtained in Section 3.1 (interpreting A^i as the deterministic level for productivity).

Finally, note that, when $p = 1/2$, there is no persistence, In this case, the maximum value function can be verified to correspond to that obtained in Exercise (20).

Exercise 22 As in the previous examples, the maximum value function depends on the two state variables, capital and productivity. The tentative maximum value function we choose is:

$$V(k_t, A_t^i) = F + G\frac{\left(A_t^i k_t\right)^{1-\gamma}}{1-\gamma},$$

so that the Bellman formulation is:

$$F + G\frac{\left(A_t^i k_t\right)^{1-\gamma}}{1-\gamma} = \max_{c_{i,t}} \left\{ \frac{c_{i,t}^{1-\gamma}}{1-\gamma} + \beta E_t \left[F + G\frac{\left(\tilde{A}_{t+1} k_{t+1}\right)^{1-\gamma}}{1-\gamma} \right] \right\}.$$

The first-order condition with respect to current consumption is:

$$c_{i,t}^{-\gamma} = \beta G E_t \left[\tilde{A}_{t+1}^{1-\gamma}\right] k_{t+1}^{-\gamma},$$

so that:

$$c_{i,t} = (\beta G)^{-\frac{1}{\gamma}} E_t \left[\tilde{A}_{t+1}^{1-\gamma}\right]^{-\frac{1}{\gamma}} k_{t+1},$$

Exploiting the intertemporal constraint, we readily obtain:

$$k_{t+1} = \frac{1}{1 + (\beta G)^{-\frac{1}{\gamma}} E_t \left[\tilde{A}_{t+1}^{1-\gamma}\right]^{-\frac{1}{\gamma}}} A_t^i k_t,$$

and hence:

$$c_{i,t} = \frac{(\beta G)^{-\frac{1}{\gamma}} E_t \left[\tilde{A}_{t+1}^{1-\gamma}\right]^{-\frac{1}{\gamma}}}{1 + (\beta G)^{-\frac{1}{\gamma}} E_t \left[\tilde{A}_{t+1}^{1-\gamma}\right]^{-\frac{1}{\gamma}}} A_t^i k_t.$$

The Bellman equation is now used to pin down the coefficients. Our starting point is:

$$F + G\frac{\left(A_t^i k_t\right)^{1-\gamma}}{1-\gamma} = \frac{1}{1-\gamma} \frac{(\beta G)^{\frac{\gamma-1}{\gamma}} E_t \left[\tilde{A}_{t+1}^{1-\gamma}\right]^{\frac{\gamma-1}{\gamma}}}{\left(1 + (\beta G)^{-\frac{1}{\gamma}} E_t \left[\tilde{A}_{t+1}^{1-\gamma}\right]^{-\frac{1}{\gamma}}\right)^{1-\gamma}} \left(A_t^i k_t\right)^{1-\gamma} +$$

$$+ \beta E_t \left[F + G\frac{\tilde{A}_{t+1}^{1-\gamma}}{1-\gamma} \frac{1}{\left(1 + (\beta G)^{-\frac{1}{\gamma}} E_t \left[\tilde{A}_{t+1}^{1-\gamma}\right]^{-\frac{1}{\gamma}}\right)^{1-\gamma}} \left(A_t^i k_t\right)^{1-\gamma} \right],$$

from which it is immediate to see that $F = 0$, and that G is determined by:

$$G =$$

$$= \frac{(\beta G)^{\frac{\gamma-1}{\gamma}} E_t \left[\tilde{A}_{t+1}^{1-\gamma}\right]^{\frac{\gamma-1}{\gamma}}}{\left(1+(\beta G)^{-\frac{1}{\gamma}} E_t \left[\tilde{A}_{t+1}^{1-\gamma}\right]^{-\frac{1}{\gamma}}\right)^{1-\gamma}} + \beta G \frac{E_t \left[\tilde{A}_{t+1}^{1-\gamma}\right]}{\left(1+(\beta G)^{-\frac{1}{\gamma}} E_t \left[\tilde{A}_{t+1}^{1-\gamma}\right]^{-\frac{1}{\gamma}}\right)^{1-\gamma}}.$$

The above expression–as scary as it may be–guarantees that our guess is correct. In fact, it is apparent that the coefficient G does not depend on either capital or on productivity. Indeed, by assumption, $\tilde{A}_{t+1}$ is time- and state-independent.

Moreover note that, grouping terms, it is easy to obtain:

$$G = \beta G E_t \left[\tilde{A}_{t+1}^{1-\gamma}\right] \frac{1+(\beta G)^{-\frac{1}{\gamma}} E_t \left[\tilde{A}_{t+1}^{1-\gamma}\right]^{-\frac{1}{\gamma}}}{\left(1+(\beta G)^{-\frac{1}{\gamma}} E_t \left[\tilde{A}_{t+1}^{1-\gamma}\right]^{-\frac{1}{\gamma}}\right)^{1-\gamma}},$$

and hence:

$$1 = \beta E_t \left[\tilde{A}_{t+1}^{1-\gamma}\right] \frac{1}{\left(1+(\beta G)^{-\frac{1}{\gamma}} E_t \left[\tilde{A}_{t+1}^{1-\gamma}\right]^{-\frac{1}{\gamma}}\right)^{-\gamma}},$$

so that:

$$G = \left(1 - \beta^{\frac{1}{\gamma}} E_t \left[\tilde{A}_{t+1}^{1-\gamma}\right]^{\frac{1}{\gamma}}\right)^{-\gamma}.$$

Exercise 23 In this example, there are two states and two controls. We assume that the maximum value function takes the form $V(k_t, A_t) = F + G \ln k_t + H \ln A_t$, thus the recursive formulation is:

$$\begin{aligned} F + G\ln k_t + H \ln A_t &= \max_{c_t, l_t} \{\ln(c_t) + \gamma \ln(1-l_t) + \\ &\quad + \beta E_t \left[F + G \ln k_{t+1} + H \ln \tilde{A}_{t+1}\right]\Big\}. \end{aligned}$$

The two first-order conditions quickly lead to:

$$c_t = \frac{k_{t+1}}{\beta G} \tag{A.29}$$

and to:

$$\frac{\gamma}{1-l_t} = \frac{\beta G}{k_{t+1}} (1-\alpha) A_t k_t^{\alpha} l_t^{(-\alpha)}. \tag{A.30}$$

Exploiting the dynamic constraint and the first-order condition (A.29) we obtain the (familiar) relation between future capital and current output:

$$k_{t+1} = \frac{\beta G}{1+\beta G} A_t k_t^{\alpha} l_t^{1-\alpha},$$

so that the first-order condition (A.30) can be written as:

$$\frac{\gamma}{1-l_t} = \frac{(1+\beta G)(1-\alpha)}{l_t},$$

which implies that the optimal labor supply is independent of the capital stock and the productivity level:

$$l_t = \bar{l} = \frac{(1+\beta G)(1-\alpha)}{\gamma + (1+\beta G)(1-\alpha)}.$$

Note that, when $G > 0$, then $\bar{l} \in (0,1)$.

We now follow our usual procedure: we use the tentative solution and the first-order conditions into the Bellman equation, which gives:

$$\begin{aligned} F + G \ln k_t + H \ln A_t = \\ = \ln\left(\frac{1}{1+\beta G}\right) + \ln A_t + \alpha \ln k_t + (1-\alpha)\ln \bar{l} + \gamma \ln\left(1-\bar{l}\right) + \\ + \beta F + \beta G\left(\ln \frac{\beta G}{1+\beta G} + \ln A_t + \alpha \ln k_t + (1-\alpha)\ln \bar{l}\right) + \beta H \rho \ln A_t, \end{aligned}$$

where use has been made of the fact that the evolution for productivity is described by (7.3).

Matching the coefficients for $\ln k_t$ and for $\ln A_t$ we obtain, respectively:

$$G = \frac{\alpha}{1-\alpha\beta},$$

$$H = \frac{1}{(1-\rho\beta)(1-\alpha\beta)}.$$

It is now trivial to compute F and $\bar{l}$.

The disappointment we expressed in the main text (Subsection 7.2.1) extends to the version of the model with endogenous labor supply: with logarithmic preferences, the role for productivity shocks (even when they are persistent!) appears to be limited.

Exercise 24 As in the previous exercise, we assume that the maximum value function takes the form $V(k_t, A_t) = F + G \ln k_t + H \ln A_t$, so that the recursive formulation is:

$$\begin{aligned} F + G \ln k_t + H \ln A_t &= \max_{c_t, l_t} \left\{ \ln \left(c_t - \phi l_t^{\psi} \right) + \right. \\ &\quad \left. + \beta E_t \left[F + G \ln k_{t+1} + H \ln \tilde{A}_{t+1} \right] \right\}, \end{aligned}$$

with the two first-order conditions:

$$\frac{1}{c_t - \phi l_t^{\psi}} = \frac{\beta G}{k_{t+1}}, \tag{A.31}$$

and:

$$\frac{\psi \phi l_t^{\psi - 1}}{c_t - \phi l_t^{\psi}} = \frac{\beta G}{k_{t+1}} (1 - \alpha) A_t k_t^{\alpha} l_t^{-\alpha}.$$

The ratio between the two first-order conditions gives:

$$l_t = \left(\frac{1 - \alpha}{\psi \phi} A_t k_t^{\alpha} \right)^{\frac{1}{\psi + \alpha - 1}}. \tag{A.32}$$

Eq. (A.31) and the intertemporal constraint allow us to obtain:

$$k_{t+1} = \beta G \left(c_t - \phi l_t^{\psi} \right) = A_t k_t^{\alpha} l_t^{1-\alpha} - c_t,$$

so that:

$$(\beta G + 1) c_t = A_t k_t^{\alpha} l_t^{1-\alpha} + \beta G \phi l_t^{\psi}.$$

Using Eq. (A.32), the equation above reduces to:

$$c_t = \frac{1}{1 + \beta G} \left(1 + \frac{\beta (1 - \alpha)}{\psi} G \right) \left(\frac{1 - \alpha}{\psi \phi} \right)^{\frac{1 - \alpha}{\psi + \alpha - 1}} k_t^{\frac{\alpha \psi}{\psi + \alpha - 1}} A_t^{\frac{\psi}{\psi + \alpha - 1}}.$$

The latter equation, together with Eq. (A.32), allows us to obtain from the intertemporal constraint:

$$k_{t+1} = \frac{\beta G}{1 + \beta G} \left(\frac{\psi + \alpha - 1}{\psi} \right) \left(\frac{1 - \alpha}{\psi \phi} \right)^{\frac{1 - \alpha}{\psi + \alpha - 1}} A_t^{\frac{\psi}{\psi + \alpha - 1}} k_t^{\frac{\alpha \psi}{\psi + \alpha - 1}}.$$

Let $\omega \equiv \psi / (\psi + \alpha - 1)$ and note that Eq. (A.31) can be written as:

$$c_t - \phi l_t^{\psi} = \frac{k_{t+1}}{\beta G} = \frac{1}{(1+\beta G)\,\omega} \left(\frac{1-\alpha}{\psi\phi}\right)^{\omega-1} A_t^{\omega} k_t^{\alpha\omega}.$$

Using the above results, we reformulate the Bellman equation as:

$$F + G\ln k_t + H\ln A_t = \ln\left(\frac{1}{(1+\beta G)\,\omega}\left(\frac{1-\alpha}{\psi\phi}\right)^{\omega-1} A_t^{\omega} k_t^{\alpha\omega}\right) +$$

$$+ \beta E_t\left[F + G\ln\left(\frac{\beta G}{(1+\beta G)\,\omega}\left(\frac{1-\alpha}{\psi\phi}\right)^{\omega-1} A_t^{\omega} k_t^{\alpha\omega}\right) + H\ln\tilde{A}_{t+1}\right],$$

which simplifies to:

$$F + G\ln k_t + H\ln A_t = -\ln(1+\beta G) - \ln\omega + (\omega-1)\ln\left(\frac{1-\alpha}{\psi\phi}\right) +$$

$$+\omega\ln A_t + \alpha\omega\ln k_t + \beta F + \beta G\ln\left(\frac{\beta G}{1+\beta G}\right) - \beta G\ln\omega +$$

$$+\beta G(\omega-1)\ln\left(\frac{1-\alpha}{\psi\phi}\right) + \beta G\omega\ln A_t + \beta G\alpha\omega\ln k_t + \rho\beta H\ln A_t.$$

Matching the coefficients for $\ln k_t$ and for $\ln A_t$ we obtain, respectively:

$$\begin{aligned} G &= \alpha\omega + \beta G\alpha\omega, \\ H &= \omega + \beta G\omega + \rho\beta H. \end{aligned}$$

Hence we conclude that:

$$G = \frac{\alpha\omega}{1-\alpha\beta\omega}, \text{ and } H = \frac{\omega}{(1-\rho\beta)(1-\alpha\beta\omega)}.$$

It is now trivial to compute F.

The preferences used in this exercise belong to the class proposed by Greenwood *et al.* (1988). For an agent characterized by this utility function, the amount of time she works affects the level of utility she receives from consumption as the cross-derivative of utility with respect to consumption and labor is non-zero. These preferences are very convenient to work with because the labor choice depends solely on its marginal productivity (which corresponds to the real wage in many frameworks). This dependence is in closed form as shown in (A.32). Moreover, as the marginal rate of substitution is independent of consumption and depends only on the real wage (check), there is no wealth effect on the labor supply.

Exercise 25 The maximum value function depends on two state variables: the remaining part of the cake (y_t) and the taste shock (z_t). Our guess for the value function is : $V(y_t, z_t) = F + G \ln y_t + H \ln z_t$, thus the recursive formulation is:

$$F + G \ln y_t + H \ln z_t = \max_{c_t} \left\{ \ln (z_t c_t) + \beta E_t \left[F + G \ln y_{t+1} + H \ln \tilde{z}_{t+1} \right] \right\}.$$

The first-order condition with respect to current consumption becomes:

$$\frac{1}{c_t} = \beta \frac{G}{y_{t+1}}.$$

The expectation operator $E_t\left[.\right]$ disappears because the time $t+1$ size of the cake is known when current consumption is decided upon.

Exploiting the transition function, we readily obtain:

$$y_{t+1} = \frac{\beta G}{1+\beta G} y_t, \text{ and } c_t = \frac{1}{1+\beta G} y_t.$$

We now substitute the above results into the Bellman equation, which gives:

$$F + G \ln y_t + H \ln z_t = \ln z_t + \ln \frac{1}{1+\beta G} + \ln y_t +$$
$$+ \beta E_t \left[F + G \ln \left(\frac{\beta G}{1+\beta G} \right) + G \ln y_t + H \ln \tilde{z}_{t+1} \right].$$

Matching the coefficients for $\ln z_t$ we immediately obtain that $H = 1$, while the coefficient for $\ln y_t$ turns out to be $G = 1/\left(1-\beta\right)$. Accordingly, the consumption function is $c_t^* = \left(1-\beta\right) y_t$. Note that the higher β is, the more patient the consumer is and hence the smaller the slice of the cake she decides to consume today.

Finally, one can verify that:

$$F = \frac{1}{1-\beta} \left(\ln \left(1-\beta\right) + \frac{\beta}{1-\beta} \ln \beta + \beta E_t \left[\ln \tilde{z}_{t+1} \right] \right).$$

Exercise 26 Since capital is the only input in production, the firm's return function is $p\varepsilon_t k_t - ci_t^2/2$; the recursive formulation for our problem is then:

$$V(k_t, \varepsilon_t) = \max_{i_t} \left\{ p\varepsilon_t k_t - \frac{c}{2} i_t^2 + \beta E\left[V(k_{t+1}, \tilde{\varepsilon}_{t+1})\right] \right\},$$
$$s.t.\ k_{t+1} = (1-\delta) k_t + i_t,$$
$$k_t \text{ given.}$$

Because the state variables are k_t and ε_t, our tentative solution is:

$$V(k_t, \varepsilon_t) = F + Gk_t + Hk_t^2 + I\varepsilon_t + L\varepsilon_t^2 + Mk_t\varepsilon_t.$$

The first-order condition gives:

$$-ci_t + \beta\left(G + 2Hk_{t+1} + ME\left[\tilde{\varepsilon}_{t+1}\right]\right) = 0,$$

so that:

$$i_t = \frac{\beta}{c}\left(G + 2Hk_{t+1} + M\mu\right).$$

The intertemporal constraint becomes:

$$k_{t+1} = \frac{c(1-\delta) k_t + \beta (G + M\mu)}{c - 2\beta H}, \tag{A.33}$$

from which we obtain:

$$i_t = \frac{\beta}{c - 2\beta H}\left(G + M\mu + 2H(1-\delta) k_t\right).$$

We now pin down the coefficients, exploiting our "guess" and the policy function:

$$\begin{aligned} F + Gk_t + Hk_t^2 + I\varepsilon_t + L\varepsilon_t^2 + Mk_t\varepsilon_t = \\ = p\varepsilon_t k_t - \frac{c}{2}\frac{\beta^2 \left(G + M\mu + 2H(1-\delta) k_t\right)^2}{(c - 2\beta H)^2} + \\ +\beta \left[F + G\frac{c(1-\delta) k_t + \beta (G + M\mu)}{c - 2\beta H} + H\left(\frac{c(1-\delta) k_t + \beta (G + M\mu)}{c - 2\beta H}\right)^2 + \right. \\ \left. + I\mu + L\left(\sigma^2 + \mu^2\right) + M\mu\frac{c(1-\delta) k_t + \beta (G + M\mu)}{c - 2\beta H}\right]. \end{aligned} \tag{A.34}$$

It is immediate to see that $M = p$, $I = 0$, and $L = 0$. Then, we focus on the k_t^2 terms, which give:

$$H = -\frac{c}{2}\frac{\beta^2 \left(2H\left(1-\delta\right)\right)^2}{\left(c-2\beta H\right)^2} + \beta H \left(\frac{c\left(1-\delta\right)}{c-2\beta H}\right)^2.$$

Accordingly, either $H = 0$, or:

$$1 = -\frac{2c\beta^2 H\left(1-\delta\right)^2}{\left(c-2\beta H\right)^2} + \beta\left(\frac{c\left(1-\delta\right)}{c-2\beta H}\right)^2,$$

which gives:

$$H = \frac{c\left(1-\beta\left(1-\delta\right)^2\right)}{2\beta}.$$

Note that the above solution for H implies:

$$\frac{c\left(1-\delta\right)}{c-2\beta H} = \frac{1}{\beta\left(1-\delta\right)} > 1,$$

which precludes the attainment of a steady state for k_t (consider the transition function A.33). Using the Lagrange method, one can show that this solution does not fulfill the transversality condition, and hence cannot be optimal. Thus, we select $H = 0$.

The first-degree terms in k_t give (from Eq. A.34):

$$G = \beta G\left(1-\delta\right) + \beta M\mu\left(1-\delta\right),$$

so that:

$$G = \frac{\beta\mu M\left(1-\delta\right)}{1-\beta\left(1-\delta\right)} = \frac{\beta\left(1-\delta\right)}{1-\beta\left(1-\delta\right)}\mu p.$$

As for the constant, from Eq. (A.34) we obtain:

$$F = -\frac{c}{2}\frac{\beta^2\left(G+M\mu\right)^2}{c^2} + \beta F + G\frac{\beta^2\left(G+M\mu\right)}{c} + M\mu\frac{\beta^2\left(G+M\mu\right)}{c},$$

which yields:

$$F = \frac{\beta^2\left(G+M\mu\right)^2}{2\left(1-\beta\right)c} = \frac{\left(\beta\mu p\right)^2}{2\left(1-\beta\right)c\left(1-\beta\left(1-\delta\right)\right)^2}.$$

Note that the policy function, being:

$$i_t = \frac{\beta}{c\left(1-\beta\left(1-\delta\right)\right)}\mu p,$$

prescribes, in each period, an investment level which is independent of both the state variables. (Explain why.)

Exercise 27 In this old-fashioned economy, past inflation is a state variable, as is the shock. Since the target function is quadratic, our tentative solution is a second order polynomial in π_{t-1} and ϵ_t:

$$V(\pi_{t-1}, \epsilon_t) = F + G\pi_{t-1} + H\pi_{t-1}^2 + I\epsilon_t + L\epsilon_t^2 + M\pi_{t-1}\epsilon_t.$$

We assume, with no loss of generality, that $E_{t-1}\left[\tilde{\epsilon}_t\right] = 0$, $Var\left[\tilde{\epsilon}_t \middle| I_{t-1}\right] = \sigma^2$, and we present the recursive formulation:

$$F + G\pi_{t-1} + H\pi_{t-1}^2 + I\epsilon_t + L\epsilon_t^2 + M\pi_{t-1}\epsilon_t = \max_{y_t}\Big\{-\left(y_t^2 + \delta\pi_t^2\right) + \\ + \beta E_t\left[F + G\pi_t + H\pi_t^2 + I\tilde{\epsilon}_{t+1} + L\tilde{\epsilon}_{t+1}^2 + M\pi_t\tilde{\epsilon}_{t+1}\right]\Big\}.$$

The first-order condition with respect to current output is:

$$-2y_t - 2\delta\pi_t\frac{\partial\pi_t}{\partial y_t} + \beta E_t\left[\left(G + 2H\pi_t + M\tilde{\epsilon}_{t+1}\right)\frac{\partial\pi_t}{\partial y_t}\right] = 0,$$

which gives:

$$2y_t = \beta G\gamma + 2\left(\beta H - \delta\right)\left(\pi_{t-1} + \gamma y_t + \epsilon_t\right)\gamma.$$

Accordingly, the optimal decision for a policy maker who decides the output level having observed the realization for the shock is:

$$y_t = \frac{\gamma\beta G}{2\left(1-\gamma^2\left(\beta H - \delta\right)\right)} + \frac{\gamma\left(\beta H - \delta\right)}{1-\gamma^2\left(\beta H - \delta\right)}\left(\pi_{t-1} + \epsilon_t\right), \tag{A.35}$$

so that the transition equation becomes:

$$\pi_t = \frac{\gamma^2\beta G}{2\left(1-\gamma^2\left(\beta H - \delta\right)\right)} + \frac{1}{1-\gamma^2\left(\beta H - \delta\right)}\left(\pi_{t-1} + \epsilon_t\right). \tag{A.36}$$

Exploiting Equations (A.35) and (A.36), and our assumptions about ϵ_t into the Bellman equation, we obtain:

$$F + G\pi_{t-1} + H\pi_{t-1}^2 + I\epsilon_t + L\epsilon_t^2 + M\pi_{t-1}\epsilon_t =$$

$$= -\left(\frac{\gamma\beta G}{2\left(1-\gamma^2\left(\beta H-\delta\right)\right)} + \frac{\gamma\left(\beta H-\delta\right)}{1-\gamma^2\left(\beta H-\delta\right)}\left(\pi_{t-1}+\epsilon_t\right)\right)^2 +$$

$$+ \left(\beta H-\delta\right)\left(\frac{\gamma^2\beta G}{2\left(1-\gamma^2\left(\beta H-\delta\right)\right)} + \frac{1}{1-\gamma^2\left(\beta H-\delta\right)}\left(\pi_{t-1}+\epsilon_t\right)\right)^2 +$$

$$+ \beta F + \frac{\left(\beta\gamma G\right)^2}{2\left(1-\gamma^2\left(\beta H-\delta\right)\right)} + \frac{\beta G}{1-\gamma^2\left(\beta H-\delta\right)}\left(\pi_{t-1}+\epsilon_t\right) + \beta L\sigma^2.$$

From the above expression, it is apparent that our guess is correct; it is also clear that–at this stage–the most sensible thing to do is to feed our software with values for β, δ, γ, and σ^2, and let it solve for the coefficients.

Exercise 28 The problem is analogous to the one in Exercise (20). Hence, the maximum value function is:

$$V\left(k_t, A_t\right) = \frac{1}{1-\beta}\left(\ln\left(1-\alpha\beta\right) + \frac{\alpha\beta}{1-\alpha\beta}\ln\left(\alpha\beta\right) + \frac{\beta}{1-\alpha\beta}E_t\left[\ln A_{t+1}\right]\right) +$$

$$+ \frac{\alpha}{1-\alpha\beta}\ln k_t + \frac{1}{1-\alpha\beta}\ln A_t,$$

so that the (unconditional) expected value function is:

$$E\left[V\left(k_t, \tilde{A}\right)\right] =$$

$$= \frac{1}{1-\beta}\left(\ln\left(1-\alpha\beta\right) + \frac{\alpha\beta}{1-\alpha\beta}\ln\left(\alpha\beta\right) + \frac{1}{1-\alpha\beta}E\left[\ln\tilde{A}\right]\right) + \frac{\alpha}{1-\alpha\beta}\ln k_t.$$

Substituting the values for the coefficients and the value for k_t, and using the productivity levels and their probabilities to compute the expected value, it is trivial to verify the claim.

References

Adjemian, S., M. Juillard, F. Karamé, W. Mutschler, J. Pfeifer, M. Ratto, N. Rion, and S. Villemot (2024), "Dynare: Reference Manual, Version 6," *Dynare Working Papers*, 80, CEPREMAP.

Aruoba, S.B., J. Fernández-Villaverde, and J.F. Rubio-Ramirez, (2006), Comparing Solution Methods for Dynamic Equilibrium Economies, *Journal of Economic Dynamics and Control*, 30, pp. 2477–2508.

Barillas, F. and J. Fernández-Villaverde, (2007), A generalization of the endogenous grid method, *Journal of Economic Dynamics and Control,* 31, pp. 2698–2712.

Beavis, B. and I. Dobbs, (1990), *Optimization and stability theory for economic analysis,* Cambridge University Press, Cambridge and New York.

Bellman, R., (1957), *Dynamic Programming*, Princeton University Press, Princeton.

Benveniste, L. and J. Scheinkman, (1979), On the differentiability of the value function in dynamic models of economics. *Econometrica,* 47, pp. 727–732.

Brock, W. and L. Mirman, (1972), Optimal economic growth and uncertainty: the discounted case. *Journal of Economic Theory* 4, pp. 479–513.

Caldara, D., J. Fernández-Villaverde, J.F. Rubio-Ramirez, and W. Yao, (2012), Computing DSGE Models with Recursive Preferences and Stochastic Volatility, *Review of Economic Dynamics,* 15, pp. 188–206.

Carroll, C.D., (2006), The method of endogenous gridpoints for solving dynamic stochastic optimization problems. *Economics Letters,* 91, pp. 312–320.

Chow, G.C., (1997), *Dynamic Economics. Optimization by the Lagrange Method*, Oxford University Press, New York and London.

Christiano, L.J., and J.D.M. Fisher, (2000), Algorithms for solving dynamic models with occasionally binding constraints, *Journal of Economic Dynamics and Control,* 24, pp. 1179–1232.

Collard, F. and M. Juillard, (2001), Accuracy of stochastic perturbation methods: The case of asset pricing models. *Journal of Economic Dynamics and Control,* 25, pp. 979–999.

de la Fuente, A., (2000), *Mathematical Methods and Models for Economists,* Cambridge University Press, Cambridge.

Den Haan, W.J. and A. Marcet, (1994), Accuracy in simulations, *Review of Economic Studies,* 61, pp. 3–17.

Dixit, A., (1990), *Optimization in Economic Theory*, Oxford University Press, Oxford and New York.

Farmer, L.E. and A.A. Toda, (2017), Discretizing nonlinear, non-Gaussian Markov processes with exact conditional moments, *Quantitative Economics,* 8, pp. 651–683.

Fella, G., G. Gallipoli, and J. Pan, (2019), Markov-Chain Approximations for Life-Cycle Models, *Review of Economic Dynamics,* 34, pp. 183–201.

Fernández-Villaverde, J., J.F. Rubio-Ramírez, and F. Schorfheide, (2016), Solution and Estimation Methods for DSGE Models, Ch. 9 in *Handbook of Macroeconomics,* Vol. 2.

Flodén, M., (2008), A note on the accuracy of Markov-chain approximations to highly persistent AR(1) processes, *Economics Letters,* 99, pp. 516–520.

Greenwood, J., Hercowitz, Z., and G.W. Huffman, (1988), Investment, capacity utilization, and the real business cycle. *American Economic Review,* 78, pp. 402–417.

Guerrieri, L. and M. Iacoviello, (2015), OccBin: A toolkit for solving dynamic models with occasionally binding constraints easily, *Journal of Monetary Economics*, 70, pp. 22–38.

Heer, B. and A. Maussner, (2009), *Dynamic General Equilibrium Modeling. Computational Methods and Applications* (2nd edition), Springer Verlag, Berlin and Heidelberg.

Iskhakov, F., T.H. Jørgensen, Rust, J., and B. Schjerning, (2017), The endogenous grid method for discrete-continuous dynamic choice models with (or without) taste shocks, *Quantitative Economics,* 8, pp. 317–365.

Judd, K.L., (1998), *Numerical Methods in Economics*, The MIT Press, Cambridge and London.

Judd, K.L., (2003), *Perturbation Methods with Non-Linear Changes of Variables*, mimeo, Hoover Institution.

Kopecky, K. and R. Suen, (2010), Finite State Markov-chain Approximations to Highly Persistent Processes, *Review of Economic Dynamics,* 13, pp. 701–14.

Levintal, O., (2017), Fifth-order perturbation solution to DSGE models, *Journal of Economic Dynamics and Control,* 80, pp. 1–16.

Ljungqvist, L. and T.J. Sargent, (2018), *Recursive Macroeconomic Theory,* (3rd edition), The MIT Press, Cambridge Mass. and London.

Maliar, L. and S. Maliar, (2003), Parameterized expectations algorithm and the moving bounds. *Journal of Business and Economic Statistics*, 21, pp. 88–92.

Marcet, A. and G. Lorenzoni, (1999), Parameterized Expectations Approach: Some practical issues, Ch. 7 in *Computational methods for the study of dynamic economies*, ed. by R. Marimon, and A. Scott, Oxford University Press, Oxford and New York.

McGrattan, E.R., (1999), Application of Weighted Residual Methods to Dynamic Economic Models, Ch. 6 in *Computational methods for the study of dynamic economies*, ed. by R. Marimon, and A. Scott, Oxford University Press, Oxford and New York.

Miao, J., (2014), *Economic Dynamics in Discrete Time*, The MIT Press, Cambridge Mass. and London.

Miranda, M. and P. Fackler, (2002), *Applied Computational Economics and Finance*, The MIT Press, Cambridge Mass. and London.

Rouwenhorst, K.G., (1995), Asset pricing implications in equilibrium business cycle models, in T.F. Cooley, (Ed.), *Frontiers of Business Cycle Research*, Princeton University Press, Princeton, pp. 294–330.

Sargent, T.J., (1987), *Dynamic Macroeconomic Theory*, Harvard University Press, Cambridge and London.

Schmitt-Grohe, S. and M. Uribe, (2004), Solving dynamic general equilibrium models using a second-order approximation to the policy function, *Journal of Economic Dynamics and Control,* 28, pp. 755–775.

Stachurski, J. (2009), Economic Dynamics Theory and Computation, The MIT Press, Cambridge Mass. and London.

Stokey, N.L., R.E. Lucas, and E.C. Prescott, (1989), *Recursive Methods in Economic Dynamics,* Harvard University Press, Cambridge and London.

Tauchen, G., (1986), Finite State Markov-chain Approximations to Univariate and Vector Autoregressions, *Economics Letters,* 20, pp. 177–181.

Tauchen, G., and R. Hussey, (1991), Quadrature-Based Methods for Obtaining Approximate Solutions to Nonlinear Asset Pricing Models, *Econometrica,* 59, pp. 371–396.

Thompson, P., (2004), *Lecture Notes on Dynamic Modeling*, mimeo, Florida International University.

White, M.N., (2015), The method of endogenous gridpoints in theory and practice, *Journal of Economic Dynamics and Control,* 60, pp. 26–41.

Index

For Product Safety Concerns and Information please contact our EU
representative GPSR@taylorandfrancis.com
Taylor & Francis Verlag GmbH, Kaufingerstraße 24, 80331 München, Germany

www.ingramcontent.com/pod-product-compliance
Ingram Content Group UK Ltd.
Pitfield, Milton Keynes, MK11 3LW, UK
UKHW020148200926
475702UK00016B/2613
9781041303398